Applied Cyber Security and the Smart Grid

Applied Cyber Security and the Smart Grid

Implementing Security Controls into the Modern Power Infrastructure

Eric D. Knapp

Raj Samani

Joel Langill, Technical Editor

AMSTERDAM • BOSTON • HEIDELBERG • LONDON
NEW YORK • OXFORD • PARIS • SAN DIEGO
SAN FRANCISCO • SINGAPORE • SYDNEY • TOKYO

Syngress is an Imprint of Elsevier

Acquiring Editor: *Chris Katsaropoulos*
Editorial Project Manager: *Benjamin Rearick*
Project Manager: *Punithavathy Govindaradjane*
Designer: *Matthew Limbert*

Syngress is an imprint of Elsevier
225 Wyman Street, Waltham, MA 02451, USA

Library of Congress Cataloging-in-Publication Data
Application submitted

British Library Cataloguing-in-Publication Data
A catalogue record for this book is available from the British Library

ISBN: 978-1-59749-998-9

For information on all Syngress publications, visit our website at *www.syngress.com*

Contents

Acknowledgments

We would like to acknowledge those who helped us make *Applied Cyber Security and the Smart Grid* a reality. Foremost, our families, who put up with us during the extensive months of research and writing, late-night and early-morning phone calls across the ocean, and provided much-needed moral support along the way. Next come Ben Rearick, Chris Katsaropoulos, and the rest of the team at Syngress publishing for letting us write *another* book on Smart Grid cyber security; technical editor Joel Langill who went above and beyond the call of duty to keep us honest and technically accurate; and to Jennifer Byrne, who supported this effort above all else and provided valuable insight to the content.

We would also like to acknowledge and thank the SANS Institute, who were promoting SCADA and ICS security before it became popular; the ICSJWG for their continued efforts to educate the industry and improve industrial control system security; both NIST and the EU Smart Grids Coordination Group for helping to make sense of the spaghetti-mess that is the Smart Grid; and the various organizations who have made similar efforts to document best practices for Smart Grid cyber security and implement relevant standards—we owe a lot to all of the hard work that came before us, and we offer our utmost appreciation and respect in return.

About the Authors

Eric D. Knapp is a globally recognized expert in industrial control systems cyber security, and continues to drive the adoption of new security technology in order to promote safer and more reliable automation infrastructures. He first specialized in industrial control cyber security while at Nitrosecurity, where he focused on the collection and correlation of SCADA and ICS data for the detection of advanced threats against these environments. He was later responsible for the development and implementation of end-to-end ICS cyber security solutions for McAfee, Inc. in his role as Global Director for Critical Infrastructure Markets. He is currently the Director of Strategic Alliances for Wurldtech Security Technologies, where he continues to promote the advancement of embedded security technology in order to better protect SCADA, ICS and other connected, real-time devices.

He is a long-time advocate of improved industrial control system cyber security and participates in many Critical Infrastructure industry groups, where he brings a wealth of technology expertise. He has over 20 years of experience in Information Technology, specializing in industrial automation technologies, infrastructure security, and applied Ethernet protocols as well as the design and implementation of Intrusion Prevention Systems and Security Information and Event Management systems in both enterprise and industrial networks. In addition to his work in information security, he is an award-winning author of fiction. He studied at the University of New Hampshire and the University of London.

He can be found on Twitter @ericdknapp

Raj Samani is an active member of the Information Security industry, through involvement with numerous initiatives to improve the awareness and application of security in business and society. He is currently working as the VP, Chief Technical Officer for McAfee EMEA, having previously worked as the Chief Information Security Officer for a large public sector organization in the UK and was recently inducted into the Infosecurity Europe Hall of Fame (2012).

He previously worked across numerous public sector organizations, in many cyber security and research orientated working groups across Europe. Examples include the MiData Interoperability Board, as well as representing DIGITALEUROPE on the Smart Grids Reference Group established by the European Commission in support of the Smart Grid Mandate.

In addition, he is currently the Cloud Security Alliance's Strategic Advisor for EMEA having previously served as the Vice President for Communications in the ISSA UK Chapter, where he presided over the award of Chapter Communications Programme of the Year 2008 and 2009, having previously established the UK mentoring programme. He is also on the advisory council for the Infosecurity Europe show, *Infosecurity Magazine,* and expert on both searchsecurity.co.uk, Infosec portal, and regular columnist on *Computer Weekly*. He has had numerous security papers published, and appeared on television (ITV and More4) commenting on computer security issues. He has also provided assistance in the 2006 RSA Wireless Security Survey and was part of the consultation committee for the RIPA Bill (Part 3).

Next to his work he has also obtained:

CESG Listed Advisor Scheme (CLAS), Certified Information Systems Security Professional (CISSP), Certified Ethical Hacker (CEH), Microsoft Certified Systems Engineer (MCSE – in NT4, Win2k, Win2003), Check Point Certified Security Administrator (CCSA in NG and 4.1), Check Point Certified Security Expert (CCSE - NG), Citrix Certified Administrator (CCA), QualysGuard Certified, RSA

Certified Systems Engineer (SecurID), Cisco Certified Network Administrator (CCNA), as well as a BA (Hons), and a MSc.

He can be found on Twitter @Raj_Samani.

About the Technical Editor

Joel Langill has worked for 30 years exclusively in the industrial automation and control industry. His experience was developed through in-depth, comprehensive architecture design, product development, implementation, and system migration in a variety of roles having exposure to most industry sectors. Having worked on both greenfield and brownfield projects around the world, he has rare and insightful insight into the risks and mitigation of cyber threats in industrial control systems as they have been designed, deployed, and maintained.

He is currently an independent consultant focusing on assisting clients in assessing and defending their automation systems from the risk of cyber threats that may originate both inside and outside the enterprise. He founded and maintains the popular security website SCADAhacker.com which offers visitors extensive resources in understanding, evaluating, and securing control systems. He also developed a specialized training curriculum that focuses on understanding and securing control systems from cyber threats based on a combination of awareness, standards-based practices, industry-leading technologies, and customized methodologies focusing entirely on control system architectures.

His unique experience and proven capabilities have fostered business relationships with several large industry firms, including Gartner, Kaspersky Labs, McAfee, Siemens, Tofino Security, and Waterfall Security Solutions. He devotes time to independent research relating to control system security, and regularly blogs on the evaluation and security of control systems.

He is a voting member of the ISA99 committee on industrial security for control systems, and was a lead contributor to the ISA99 technical report on the Stuxnet malware. He is also the Director of Critical Infrastructure and SCADA representative for the Cyber Security Forum Initiative. His certifications include: Certified Ethical Hacker (CEH), Certified Penetration Tester (CPT), Certified SCADA Security Architect (CSSA), and TÜV Functional Safety Engineer (FSEng). Joel has also obtained extensive training through the US Dept. of Homeland Security FEMA Emergency Management Institute, having completed ICS-400 on incident command and crisis management. He is a graduate of the University of Illinois–Champaign with a BS (Bronze Tablet) in Electrical Engineering.

He can be found on Twitter @SCADAhacker

Foreword by Troels Oerting

It is a pleasure for me, as the head of the newly established European Cybercrime Centre (EC3), to introduce this important book. During my seat in the Board of the International Cyber Security Protection Alliance I have met Raj Samani together with many other important and influential Cyber Protection and Security experts and stakeholders. Raj has a long track record of documented results in influencing the debate and work in the cyber security environment, and he is a forward-looking professional with an impressive insight in this complex topic.

Cyber protection is being hyped these years, for good and bad reasons. And that is also why it is important not to lose focus and get distracted. The development in our shared cyberspace will lead to huge achievements for humanity: more growth, transparency, sharing, innovation, development, and prosperity. Not just for a selected part of the world but eventually for the whole world. But as always, there is no such thing as only good things. The flip-side of the medal is the dark side of humanity: the criminals, the terrorists, the dictators. And they have already exploited the weaker spots in this developing new cyber world. Just like in the real off-line world we need to have rules, regulations, guidelines, and enforcement in the on-line world.

And with the rapid development of cybercrime and the speed of the development of new threats, we need to share good, solid, and well-documented knowledge and best practice. Mr. Samani and Eric Knapp, his co-writer, know what they are writing on. They are truly professionals in this challenging field.

It is easy for me to recommend this well-written and forward-looking book, and I am really looking forward to see more outcomes from the hands of these two excellent professionals—which indirectly help me in assisting EU Member States in maintaining a safe, free, open, and transparent Internet!

Troels Oerting,
Head of European Cybercrime Centre (EC3)

Foreword by Robert P. Lockhart

"Utility cyber security is in a state of near chaos."

Those words, published in November 2011, earned me 15 min of fame that I would rather not have had. Picked up by news agencies worldwide, translated into several languages, and regularly misquoted as, "Utilities are in a state of chaos"—those 10 words were somehow far more alarming in Google results than they had looked on my laptop. But they were accurate.

If anything, the situation has deteriorated since then. Experts tell me during interviews that they see little innovation in cyber security. One vendor, perhaps in a moment of confession, said, "At every Smart Grid security conference for the past three years, I have seen the same vendors giving the same presentations." A few innovative start-ups buck the trend, with novel approaches based upon operational knowledge. But the majority of Smart Grid cyber security offerings are recycled financial or health care security offerings with new glossy brochures.

Meanwhile, Smart Grid security standards progress slowly, when they progress at all. One insider described standards-building meetings as poisonous. Once the domain of a few cyber security experts, standards working groups now count membership in the hundreds. Vendors attend to protect their turf. Utilities send lawyers to limit the scope of their commitments. The outcome is no shock: NERC CIP v4, which does nothing more than add 16 clauses to the definition of critical cyber asset, will end up taking nearly 5 years from conception until it is enforceable. Standards are the whipping boy of the industry but they are important nonetheless. Vendors tell me that without standards, they are not sure what products they should build. Likewise, absent standards, utilities are not sure what to buy. But many utilities define their security program as bare minimum compliance with enforceable regulations, which is far removed from actual protection.

To summarize, innovation is on sabbatical while standards advance glacially. Those who would attack our grids must barely be able to believe their luck. While we argue about scope and vote on terminology, attackers—subject to neither standards nor laws—sail full steam ahead. NERC CIP v5, aimed at current threats, will most likely become enforceable 7 years after Stuxnet was created. Waiting for standards is not a plausible strategy to protect Smart Grids.

But there is hope. Despite all the doom-saying, a majority of my research contacts agree that today we have sufficient security capabilities to protect a Smart Grid. The barrier is not a lack of products but a lack of approach. Security budgets remain elusive, often because there is no clear path from investment to protection. I have never met a utility that is against security, but I have met quite a few utilities that do not understand how to get there. Decision makers may not know what goes into a security architecture but can sense something missing in many proposals for security programs.

The missing link is how to apply what we have today to create a secure Smart Grid. Part of my research analyst job is to attend industry conferences—lots of industry conferences. As a rule, vendor-sponsored conferences are the most interesting, because the discussions are nearly all "applied"—real-world problems to solve. The steady diet of theory at general industry conferences is of little interest to those at the coal face. A real-world problem requires application of real-world capabilities. In glossy brochures—like any other fantasy—everything and everyone is perfect. In the real world, often the best choice is actually the "least worst" choice. And that is the heart of applied cyber security, and the hope for securing our electric grids—not theory, but application of real-world security to real-world problems.

The first order of business is to focus on what matters. For all the huffing and puffing about smart meters—their vulnerability to attack, their capture of personal information, their perceived (and disproven) health threats—they have not been the target of major attacks. The most worrisome attacks have been aimed at the control systems that manage transmission and distribution of energy. Hostile nation-states and organized crime consistently target energy supply, not energy demand. There are many possible reasons why attackers have energy supply in their crosshairs and understanding why it is of little value. It is less important to understand the attackers' psyche than to know with confidence where the next attacks will be aimed.

Despite the record of attacks, smart meters remain the most often discussed topic in Smart Grid security. This may be because smart meters are easy to understand and easy to talk about. They are by definition modern IT-enabled devices, with well-known computing and networking capabilities. By contrast, control networks usually include thousands of devices that we charitably call legacy but are in fact just plain old—with a long service life remaining. How to secure a control network with a mix of ancient and modern devices—that is a real-world application of Smart Grid cyber security.

All things considered, utilities are on their own. In this book, Raj and Eric write directly to the audience that will secure our power grids. In the trenches, cyber security is one of the least glamorous professions imaginable. The day-to-day existence is a nonstop battle for funding, straining mightily against daunting technical challenges, and planning implementations to a degree of detail that is beyond anyone's ability to imagine. All this for a solution that will be no better than tolerable. There is no such thing as absolute security; the real world of security is an endless sequence of choosing the most palatable option in the absence of a desirable option. It is hard work and success is usually achieved anonymously. But it is enormously important.

Who controls the grid, controls the economy. Each utility has a role to keep that control in the right hands. The time to act is now.

Robert P. Lockhart
Senior Research Analyst, Navigant Research

Introduction

Book overview and key learning points

Cyber security is big business today. Smart Grid is big business today. Therefore let's put the two together and write a book? Well, surely there will be some individuals that may make that assumption as to the motivation behind the publication of this book. The real motivation behind the development of this book is because this is a very real issue, and the failure to address the cyber security risk within the Grid may have serious repercussions for every single one of us.

Our intention of course is not to use FUD (Fear, Uncertainty, Doubt) as the business case for implementing cyber security measures to protect the Grid. However, there are potentially some very alarming ramifications should such measures fail to be implemented. This was highlighted with recent reports of stranded passengers on trains, traffic lights no longer working, and electric crematoriums shutting down with half-burnt bodies—only a small subset of the implications following recent power outages experienced at the end of July 2012 for almost 700 million Indian citizens.[1] This is of course refers to one of the world's worst power blackouts, which affected 20 of the 28 Indian states. Almost three weeks after the failure of three of country's five electricity grids, the government provided a report to investigate the cause of the failure.

Included in the report was a section that focused on cyber security, which stated that "Grid disturbance could not have been caused by a cyber attack." It does however acknowledge that the Grid could be impacted by cyber attacks in the future. The recognition of such an impact being caused by a cyber attack was also discussed in the United States, where at the same time the U.S. Cybersecurity Act was being debated:

"All one needs to do is look at what is going on in India today. There are no cyber problems there that I am aware of, but one-half of the country of India is without electricity today[2]"
Senator Harry Reid, the Senate Majority Leader, said.

All of which leads us to the evolution to the modern grid, a world in which devices that are owned by end customers, Grid operators, and a multitude of other third parties are interconnected. Such devices have the potential of impacting the integrity and availability of the broader Grid unless appropriate controls are in place. Equally, the grid will process an unprecedented wealth of personal data, and so when we consider the potential security considerations of the Smart Grid, we must not lose sight of the privacy risks. To be clear, this is not an either or discussion. In other words, it is not a question of security or privacy, but the development of a Grid that considers both the security and privacy issues and implements controls to mitigate any risks.

Before the Smart Grid becomes ubiquitous, we have an opportunity to address these concerns by building controls into the design of such implementations. Unlike the world of cloud computing that is inundated with a plethora of standards resulting in confusion among customers and providers, operators have the opportunity to come out of recent disasters and provide confidence to their customers in their ability to provide a safe and secure service.

Book audience

As with the previous book, *Industrial Network Security: Securing Critical Infrastructure Networks for Smart Grid, SCADA, and Other Industrial Control Systems,* by one of this book's authors, the goal here is to educate on concepts with just the right level of detail—enough to satisfy the more technical reader while keeping things simple enough to ensure that the important general concepts and ideas are not lost to those who are new to cyber security, the Grid, or both.

This was done because, like the Smart Grid itself, those interested in Smart Grid security are diverse and varied. Electrical engineers, line technicians, cyber security professionals, IT administrators, utility operators, service providers, and many other professionals will have an interest in the cyber security concerns of the Smart Grid. Therefore, every effort was made to accommodate a very wide range of knowledge and skills. If there's anything that's too simple or too complicated for you as the reader, the authors are readily available on twitter using the handles @CyberGridBook, @ericdknapp, and @Raj_Samani and are eager to answer questions, address concerns, and extinguish flames.

Diagrams and Figures

The network diagrams used throughout this book have also been intentionally simplified and have been designed to be as generic as possibly while adequately representing the systems that interconnect to form what we think of as the Smart Grid. While this means that some diagrams lack specific detail, it was felt that this was necessary in order to prevent confusion and distraction. The Smart Grid is simply too complex, broad, and diverse in both scale and scope to treat otherwise. Unfortunately, as a result, the diagrams will undoubtedly differ from "real" Smart Grid network designs and may exclude details specific to one particular implementation while including details that are specific to another.

What's in the Book

The book is divided into eight chapters, with the intention to provide the information in a particular flow. Starting with a high-level discussion of what the Smart Grid is followed by a more detailed architectural discussion of how it is built, specific vulnerabilities and exploits of the Grid, and how to protect both the Grid and the supply chain used to build it. The book ends with some predictions of the future that may or may not be correct, but which will hopefully inspire some thought about where we're headed. Of course, there is no prerequisite to follow our approach, but many of the later chapters do reference information presented earlier in the book. Where possible, we call out these references to make easier to follow a particular topic independent of the chapters, which are as follows:

Chapter 1: The Smart Grid Defined

The purpose of this chapter is to describe the Smart Grid and outline its key components. This is important, as it sets the foundation for the proceeding chapters, and will begin to introduce some of the many acronyms that are typical with the Smart Grid.

Chapter 2: Architectural Details

Following the description of the Smart Grid, this chapter is intended to technically describe the network architecture behind generation, transmission, and distribution. It also considers some of the protocols in use within the Smart Grid.

Chapter 3: Attack Vectors

The purpose of Chapter 3 is to introduce the cyber security risks that are likely to affect the various components of the Smart Grid. In particular, it looks to consider the various components and describes the threats specific to each component.

Chapter 4: Privacy Concerns

Although the book is entitled cyber security, there are some considerable privacy related risks associated with the Smart Grid. This chapter intends to present some of the threats to user privacy that exist within the Smart Grid, as well as some recent research activities that may affect user confidentiality.

Chapter 5: Security Models for SCADA, ICS, and Smart Grid

There exist distinct technical zones within a Grid operator, typically such zones have led isolated lives with their own architecture and staff to run and manage assets within these zones. This chapter considers the composition of these zones, and how in today's world threats pay no heed to this air-gapped model.

Chapter 6: Securing the Smart Grid

After considering the threat landscape, and the various risks to the Smart Grid from a security perspective, this chapter asks what controls should be deployed, and how should they be configured? Once security controls are in place, how do you manage those controls deployed through a system as complex as a Smart Grid? This chapter looks at the concept of security controls and countermeasures, as well as how to leverage these and other tools to obtain situational awareness to ensure that everything in the Smart Grid is working as expected.

Chapter 7: Securing the Supply Chain

There is a very old adage that security is only as strong as its weakest link. This is never more true when we consider the number of potential suppliers to the Grid, not only in terms of providing hardware and software but also organizations providing services. This chapter will consider the key third parties that will work within the Grid, and some of the mechanisms used within industry to manage potential risks from the supply chain.

Chapter 8: The Future of Smart Grid Cyber Security

This chapter really is our opportunity to get out our crystal balls (no pun intended!) and propose how we see the Grid in the future, as well as some of the cyber security and privacy considerations that we have to implement to ensure that all of us have a secure, and fully available energy network in the future.

Appendices: Reference Architectures and Recommended Reading

Some of the security models, diagrams, and architectures referenced throughout the book, as well as recommendations for further reading, have been included in the Appendices for your convenience.

What's NOT in the book

The thing with the cyber threat is that it constantly evolves. Consider that just over 10 years ago the most sophisticated piece of malware attempted to trick people into opening an e-mail with the promise of a picture of tennis star Anna Kournikova, and less than 10 years later malware was apparently (and allegedly) targeting the nuclear facilities in Iran and with success. Incidentally, just to set the record straight there is no intention to discuss this particular threat, which for the sake of clarity, we will name here: Stuxnet. Henceforth within this book, the term will be avoided or, if unavoidable, censored. This of course may sound a little strange, but it has been covered so much, and quite frankly any serious discussions about protecting the Grid are railroaded by endless conversations and speculations about this one attack, and who was behind it. Who cares? We are not Sidney Poirot, but security professionals aiming to provide some real-world advice on how to implement cyber security controls to protect against threats that have come out in the most current timeframe, while also helping you be prepared for threats in the future. Therefore, we'll treat the term like a bad word and will avoid its use at the risk of punishment: if you ever hear either of us (the authors) mention the word St****t from this point on, then you have the authority to remind us of this paragraph and demand five dollars or pounds, depending on who you bump into!

Despite the rumors, conjecture about attribution, media hype, and general oversaturation in the news, we do need to consider the technical advancement of these types of threats. Specific threats are a proof point, but what this means is that the overall threat is constantly evolving, and in this constant cat-and-mouse game between the good guys and bad guys (okay a very general over-simplification), these eight chapters should provide a starting point for a process that implements security and privacy controls throughout the Smart Grid.

References

1. Huffingtonpost.com. *India power outage: 620 million people affected by one of the world's biggest blackouts*; July 2012. <http://www.huffingtonpost.com/2012/07/31/india-power-outage_n_1722356.html> [cited October 2012].
2. The Economic Times. *Hackers can cripple India's power grids*; August 2012. <http://articles.economictimes.indiatimes.com/2012-08-02/news/33001456_1_cyberattack-power-grids-blackout> [cited October 2012].

What is the Smart Grid?

INFORMATION IN THIS CHAPTER:

- Energy demands
- Grid resilience
- Environmental performance
- Operational efficiencies
- Common components of the Smart Grid
- Pitfalls of the Smart Grid

Understanding how the Smart Grid works first requires an understanding of how industrial networks operate, which in turn requires a basic understanding of the underlying communications protocols that are used, where they are used, and why. There are many systems that comprise the larger system of the "Smart Grid," which utilize both common and open protocols as well as many highly specialized protocols used for industrial automation and control, most of which are designed for efficiency and reliability to support the economic and operational requirements of large distributed control systems. Similarly, industrial protocols are designed for real-time operation requiring deterministic results with continuous availability. Combined together, this blend of open and proprietary networks enables the much larger network of measurements, controls, metering, and automation that is the Smart Grid. This amalgam of disparate systems and networks is also a major factor in the cyber security concerns facing the Smart Grid today.

Consider the plug socket in your home today. Regardless of whether there are two or three pins the net result is that it provides us with the foundation on which our modern society is built upon. Although this may sound somewhat farfetched, just consider the inconvenience we experience when there is a power outage. Although an inconvenience for us as consumers, the impact for a business can be considerably significant. We have come to expect that when we plug something into the socket, that electricity will be supplied. A recent paper by Schneider Electric entitled "How Unreliable Power Affects the Business Value of a Hospital" cited the following example:

> *"The financial impact of power disruption was demonstrated during the August 2003 blackout, which affected 45 million people in eight US states and 10 million*

people in parts of Canada. Healthcare facilities experienced hundreds of millions of dollars in lost revenue from canceled services, legal liability, and damaged reputations. Six hospitals were in bankruptcy 1 year later.[1]"

To address this and other issues with our current energy network, a dramatic transformation is underway to develop the concept of the Smart Grid. Much like every other industry, technology is acting as a catalyst to provide efficiencies that we could only previously dream about. The need for transformation is of the upmost priority, with demand for energy over the next 20 years anticipated to grow exponentially. More importantly, our desire for reliable and clean energy is fast becoming an imperative to our modern society.

Energy demands

According to the United Nations, the world population is anticipated to reach 10.1 billion within the next 90 years, reaching 9.3 billion by 2050. Combining the population growth with the forecasted income growth and the demands for more energy becomes clear. According to the BP Energy Outlook, "Since 1900 the population has more than quadrupled, real income has grown by a factor of 25, and primary energy consumption by a factor of 22.5." In a world today when according to the International Atomic Energy Agency, one in four people still do not have electricity, and many in the Western world have to live through numerous blackouts the need for a greater energy becomes clearer. Consider the cost of these blackouts; which according to the US Department of Energy is $150 billion in the US alone, roughly the equivalent of $500 per US citizen.

The answer? Well there is considerable focus on the modernization of the energy network with the provision of greater automation of the electricity grid, as well as the development of a communication infrastructure. There are of course many definitions of the Smart Grid, which itself appears to be the newest buzzword (obviously overtaking the "cloud"). The following are a list of definitions from established sources:

- "A Smart Grid is a modern electricity system. It uses sensors, monitoring, communications, automation, and computers to improve the flexibility, security, reliability, efficiency, and safety of the electricity system."[2]
- "Smart Grid generally refers to a class of technology people are using to bring utility electricity delivery systems into the 21st century, using computer-based remote control and automation. These systems are made possible by two-way communication technology and computer processing that has been used for decades in other industries. They are beginning to be used on electricity networks, from the power plants and wind farms all the way to the consumers of electricity in homes and businesses. They offer many benefits to utilities and consumers—mostly seen in big improvements in energy efficiency on the electricity grid and in the energy users' homes and offices."[3]

Despite the number of various definitions, there are some key objectives expected from the Smart Grid, according to the Canadian Electricity Association these are to increase grid resilience, improve environmental performance, or deliver operational efficiencies.

Grid resilience

In 2004, the House of Commons Trade and Industry Committee published their report into the Resilience of the National Electricity Network.[4] The report was written in response to power cuts in the United Kingdom only 1 year earlier, and focused on addressing concerns about the resilience of the electricity network. Although the report highlighted the relative reliability of the UK network as opposed to other nations, clearly identified a number of risks: for example, like the energy networks of other countries found that "UK's electricity transmission and distribution network was built in two main periods of activity, in the late 1950s and the mid 1960s–early 1970s. The design life of the assets used in the network was about 40 years." In light of the aging equipment, there were some concerns raised about their maintenance. In particular, The Institution of Civil Engineers raised concerns that the operators were reducing the skill levels of the maintenance staff, and witnesses to the enquiry questioned the logic of decreasing the technical knowledge of engineering staff when the need to maintain equipment is only likely to increase. In order to prevent the need for such enquiries in the future, a smarter grid is absolutely necessary, a grid capable of reacting to unforeseen events and maintaining the availability of energy to its customers, otherwise known as resilience. The term resilience refers to the capability of a given entity to withstand from unexpected actions, and recover very quickly thereafter. The development of these predictive maintenance technologies help offset reduction in both skill level and numbers of support staff—effectively improving maintenance efficiencies. Clearly in the case of the electricity network, a Smart Grid should be able to withstand such environmental threats (both intentional or unintentional), and recover in a timely fashion.

To illustrate the requirements for greater resilience for the modern electricity network, we can use the case study presented by Smart Grid Australia. The nation itself is faced much like the world with geographical growth pockets, in this case within South East Queensland and Western Sydney. This growth, when combined with the ever-increasing demands for more energy to power such devices as air conditioning, and heating to combat the fluctuating seasonal weather provide an insight into some of the reasons why the nation has recognized the need for the replacement of its aging generation assets. Moreover, there is recognition that the current electricity network is almost 50 years old and has also suffered from outages due to extreme weather events. Such events are not limited to Australia, with numerous examples of blackouts experienced globally, and consumers are warned that this is simply the tip of the iceberg. The Electric Reliability Council of Texas, for example, recently warned that the state's energy grid has almost reached capacity.[5] The council is responsible for overseeing power, rather unsurprisingly for the state of Texas. In early 2011, approximately 4400 Texans mainly from the west of the state were subjected to rolling blackouts and given the advice to conserve power particularly in the morning. With peak demands for power experienced largely in the morning, it is expected demand will reach record levels. Satisfying these peak demands can be particularly costly, generally there exist three levels of satisfying electricity demands, and these are as follows:

- *Baseload generating units:* Such units are intended to satisfy the base level of electricity demand. Meeting such demand has low operating costs and is able to meet fluctuating demands (to a degree) by increasing power generation, or decrease based on demands.
- *Intermediate units:* To address greater fluctuations in energy demands are intermediate units. Although they often have higher operating costs than baseload units, there ability to quickly adapt to demand fluctuations make them more appropriate to meeting higher energy demands.
- *Peaking units:* To meet the peak, demands are peaking units. These units typically have the highest operating costs but are able to quickly provide a full load within a short period, as well as able to shutdown again within minutes. Due to the nature of their operations and obvious cost, the peaking units only operate for a number of days per year.

Of course, there are significant risks regarding the availability of electricity because the equipment in the grid is very old as was highlighted in the House of Commons report, and susceptible to environmental pressures. Take the case in Texas, for example, apparently the almost 5000 citizens from the west of Texas were left without power, apparently due to frozen pipes at two power plants. Another significant risk is that any targeted intentional action aimed to disrupt the electricity network can equally have significant ramifications. The grid today is very much centralized, which means that a malicious event will only need to attack specific strategic points within the grid in order to impact thousands (and perhaps more) consumers and subsequently impact a key component of our critical infrastructure.

The psychological impact of being in a power outage in today's world may lead to a feeling of sheer terror. For many, if the lights do go out, or people are stuck in lifts, the question of whether this is caused by terrorist action. A New York citizen who experienced recent blackouts immediately assumed the incidents were due to terrorist actions, "It's almost like 9/11," she said. "Everybody panicked, wondering what happened. Anything could happen when the dark comes down."[6] Of course, the impact of such fear should not be underestimated; however, there are other impacts of such actions. More recently, many citizens in both India and the United States experienced a world without power. Consider not only the impact of the storm, or outage itself but also the secondary effects. For example, the loss of communications that were felt (e.g. something as simple as not being able to charge a cell phone). To emphasize the impact on energy supply disruption, a simulation exercise was conducted by the Heritage Foundation in June 2010. Its intention was "to assess the strategic and economic impact of a major energy supply disruption caused by coordinated terrorist attacks on key nodes in the global energy infrastructure," and although it focused on the broader impact of a disruption of the energy sector, the findings did identify the financial implications are severe resulting from deliberate actions, and the failure to develop a resilient energy network[7]:

- Petroleum prices jump from $75 per barrel to $250 per barrel and eventually fall back to $125 per barrel after 2 years;
- Gasoline prices jump to $8 per gallon and remain above $4 per gallon throughout the first year;
- Gross domestic product (GDP) losses exceed $300 billion per year for both years of the crisis;
- Employment drops by more than 1.3 million the first year and drops an additional 1.1 million in the second year for a total two-year drop of 2.4 million.

These figures are certainly very sobering and really emphasize the importance on developing an energy network that is capable of dealing with external threats and maintaining the availability of energy to everybody that demands it.

Environmental performance

The overwhelming edict of all governments and policymakers worldwide is to reduce CO_2 emissions, and it is perceived that the Smart Grid has the capability of reducing such emissions. One such example of the potential impact is a research study that predicts by "improving the efficiency of the [US] national electricity grid by 5% would be the equivalent of eliminating the fuel use and carbon emissions of 53 million cars."[8]

Reducing emissions through the benefits provided by the Smart Grid, these include the following: Greater Efficiency; Integration of Renewable Technologies; Reduction in the need for new power plants; Support for Electric Vehicles; and Smarter Appliances.

Greater efficiency

According to the Electric Power Research Institute (EPRI), the provision of demand response within Smart Grids provides the opportunity to reduce overall energy consumption. When combined with efficiency improvements, EPRI predicts that the annual growth in electricity consumption will be approximately 0.7% between 2008 and 2035.

The concept of demand response is defined by the Federal Energy Regulatory Commission (FERC) as "changes in electric usage by end-use customers from their normal consumption patterns in response to changes in the price of electricity over time, or to incentive payments designed to induce lower electricity use at times of high wholesale market prices or when system reliability is jeopardized."

Integration of renewable technologies

The source of electricity today is largely composed of traditional fossil fuels (see Figure 1.1). Based on the US Energy Information Association, renewable energy provides less than 15% of energy today. The integration of renewable sources into the energy network at levels higher than this 20% does require more advanced management solutions, according to the European Wind Energy Association (EWEA).

Clearly, supporting the greater proliferation of renewable generation sources will clearly have considerable environmental benefits. Renewable generation sources have clear advantages in reducing environmental impacts to modern society. Not only in terms of the reduction of emissions, but there is also the benefit of supporting smaller installations of renewable technologies. For example, consider the solar

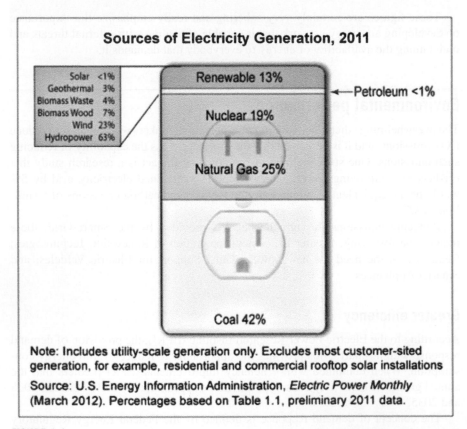

FIGURE 1.1

Sources of electricity generation.

panels on a domestic roof, this reduces the expenditure of transmitting energy, and of course, the associated loss in energy transmission. The Smart Grid will allow the integration of a high number of decentralized generation technologies. The potential impact according to EPRI is that the greater integration of renewable technologies could reduce emissions by 58% against a baseline taken in 2005.

Using renewable sources for energy is critical toward achieving environmental benefits, the use of wind as "20% of the US power supply would save 4 trillion gallons of water typically used in electricity generation between now and 2030."[9]

Reduction in the need for new power plants

In April 2012, the New York Times published an article discussing the overwhelming need India has for new power plants.[10] Its strategy was to build new plants to meet the burgeoning demands for more power, had began to run into problems due to the lack of fuel, namely coal. Such is the need for new power that interviewees would complain about losing power every evening, and all day on Wednesdays and Saturdays. However, this is nothing new, we have already discussed the need for greater power, but what is interesting is that the strategy of building more power plants appears to only address short-term needs. Furthermore, if a country the size of India is forced to cancel two-dozen large projects because there is not enough coal to fuel them, it does represent the need to support more renewable generation sources. Of course the net result of this greener approach does represent huge environmental benefits. Firstly, consider the costs of building a new power plant; a recent BBC article[11] discussed the financial costs of nuclear versus traditional plants with nuclear costing upward of 2 billion pounds, and gas and coal fired approximately half of that amount.

Of course these costs have an enormous financial impact, but there are also environmental considerations related to the materials and construction costs in the building of new power plants. For a new nuclear power station, for example, there is a considerable amount of raw materials required. Based on the Department of Energy report entitled "DOE NP2010 Nuclear Power Plant Construction Infrastructure

---

NOTE

How much does it cost to build a nuclear power station?

There are few recent examples to draw on, but a new plant being built in Finland gives some indications.

The Olkiluoto project is Western Europe's first new reactor in a decade and is expected to cost about £2.25 billion ($4.5 billion), but there have been serious delays there.

Other analysts put the cost of a plant at £1.5 billion.

How does that compare with other types of power station?

Gas and coal-fired power stations are much cheaper to build.

RWE Npower is planning a gas-fired power station in the UK for £800m.

The controversial scheme for a coal-fired power station in Kent is expected to cost about £1 billion.

Source: BBC—The costs of nuclear energy.

Assessment,"[12] the following bulk materials are estimated for a single US Generation III+ (GEN III+) nuclear power plant:

- Concrete—460,000 cubic yards (not including concrete for site preparation). Reinforcing Steel and Embedded Parts—46,000 tons.
- Structural Steel, Miscellaneous Steel, and Decking—25,000 tons.
- Large Bore Pipe (>21/2 in.)—260,000 ft.
- Small Bore Pipe—430,000 ft.
- Cable Tray—220,000 ft.
- Conduit—1,200,000 ft.
- Power Cable—1,400,000 ft.
- Control Wire—5,400,000 ft.
- Process and Instrument Tubing—740,000 ft.

Ignoring the resource and heavy equipment requirements, just considering the raw materials alone would provide an indication of the benefits Smart Grids may have to the environment and its ability to integrate multiple decentralized renewable generation sources. For example, one of the major components of concrete is cement which is one of the largest producers of carbon dioxide, outputting 5% of the worlds CO_2 emissions, more than the entire aviation industry. The development process of standard cement, for example, releases 0.8 tonnes of CO_2 per tonne of cement. With concrete comprising of approximately 10–15% cement, the CO_2 impacts the case for finding a new approach to energy becomes clear.

Support for electric vehicles

This of course becomes very obvious, but the Smart Grid is considered as an imperative to support the rise in the adoption of electric vehicles. This is though the provision of a charging infrastructure, which is intelligent in nature by, for example, charging during off-peak hours and mitigating the load constraints of the grid. Of course at present, this is not a major issue because the proliferation of electric vehicles remains low. Based on the US 2009 census, there were only 57,185 electric vehicles registered in the United States, accounting 0.02% of the 246,283,000 vehicles registered nationwide.[13] There is of course fierce debate about whether the electric car can reduce emissions; in particular, many of the naysayers focus on the electricity generation being comprised of fossil fueled power plants. As we have already discussed, the newer and smarter grid is intended to decrease our dependence on these sources and utilize more renewable methods. If we focus purely on the tailpipe emissions, and consider that electricity generation dependence on fossil fuels will decrease, then electric cars can have a positive impact on our environment BUT they cannot do it alone.

Smarter appliances

It does seem that every single paragraph in this chapter has used the word smart, and this paragraph is no different, largely because the grid will allow the integration of smarter appliances that are capable of detecting power fluctuations and reduce their power consumption to prevent any major emergencies. Some of the other benefits of this to the consumer are that these appliances can run at low-price periods (e.g. off-peak) meaning that they should reduce the cost of the energy bill for the consumer. Some of the additional functionality will be the connected capability that allows these devices to be connected via mobile devices. For example, consider connecting to your refrigerator to determine whether you need to pick up some milk, or connecting to your washing machine via a wireless network to check its status.

Of course, these features are NOT dependent on the grid, and perhaps more importantly dependent on when this book is read it may not be as revolutionary as it seems today. However, this does represent a significant shift in the manner in which we operate our daily lives. More importantly as we discuss the security implications, and in particular privacy (as it relates to you and I), all of our lives are potentially available to malicious actors. We will discuss this later, but when we discuss malicious actors, we don't necessarily mean hackers. Consider that our personal data, data about our energy consumption, and even what we eat are valuable to companies trying to sell us more of their products or services. This shift toward consumer-based pricing will allow merchants to know what the consumer needs and adjust their pricing accordingly. With the adoption of smarter appliances, while may be able to reduce, our energy bills WILL collect data about us and our family's living habits, and these data will be sought by a variety of sources. Of course, this will be discussed in detail later in the book.

A caveat about the earlier statement is that the additional features of smarter appliances are not dependent on the grid. Although accurate, their wide-scale adoption is likely to be. This is because the additional price premiums may be acceptable to some, the ability to achieve cost savings with energy efficiency, and off-peak utilization will allow the general public to recognize the value in such appliances, and of course "pay off" the devices through cheaper energy bills.

Operational efficiencies

Consider your current energy bill. According to the Energy Retailers Association of Australia, almost half of your bill is comprised of costs associated with the transmission and network distribution, and rising costs are passed onto each of us, the consumer. If as expected cost of maintaining an aging infrastructure will only increase, the future for each of us will be higher bills. Staying in Australia to demonstrate the example, the Independent Pricing and Regulatory Tribunal (IPART) confirmed that price rises for retail customers in New South Wales over the next 3 years will be up to 42%.

Of course, the above example only cites the short-term cost implications of not adopting a Smart Grid infrastructure, and in particular the consumer impacts. There exist numerous analyses, which attempt to predict the benefit to us as a society. One such example is the work undertaken by Endeavor Energy that calculates the overall benefit to society will be $2 billion over 15 years with well over half of that figure being a benefit to the consumer. Much of these consumer benefits do include the objectives cited in this chapter, such as greater reliability, minimizing the infrastructure costs increases as well as customer enablement opportunities. The customer enablement opportunities refer to the provision of greater consumer choice and control over their use of electricity. For example, providing the consumer with lower prices during off-peak times allows households to run non-urgent appliances during these hours. The ability to make these informed choices does not exist today, but with the provision of a Smart Grid, it will be possible for consumers to remotely monitor and control usage even down to an individual appliance. This would then allow the consumer to schedule the washing machine to run at 3 am, for example, when the lowest price tariff exists. This clearly provides an immediate short-term cost benefit to the consumer, but also the grid operator can begin to move away from the current "peaky" energy demands.

It is these "peaky" demand cycles that cause significant operational inefficiencies in today's electricity network. Consider the scenario for South Australia, where it has to deal with demand for electricity on certain days that may be doubled that in an average day. This peak demand invariably occurs on hot days, and where the demand outstrips supply may lead to a power outage. To prevent such outages, large quantities of energy must be produced for short periods, which invariably results in significantly higher costs for both generation and the transmission. Today, according to the US Energy Information Administration, the industrial and transportation sectors consume the most energy, but then with the residential market. However, all sectors have forecasted growth in energy between 2010 and 2035. Therefore, the need to manage such demands becomes imperative.

Of course, managing peak demand is simply one example of a Smart Grid creating greater operational efficiencies. Some of the other areas of improvement include as follows:

- *Line loss reduction:* During the transmission and distribution of electricity, there will likely be some loss. What this really means is that there is a difference between the amount of energy actually produced by the power plants, and the amount sold to the end customer. There are many estimates as to the exact amount lost, but in general the figure is about 7% for United States. In terms of the amount of power actually lost. It is estimated that the United States loses approximately "300 billion kWh of power from transmission and distribution (T&D) line loss. Improvements in T&D technologies and efficiency would mean utilities could generate less power and lower their carbon emissions as a result."[14]
- *Asset management:* There are many devices within the electricity network, probably more devices than any other industry network. With so many devices in the network, is it possible to manage the many assets (or devices) in the network in a better way? By doing so, it would be possible to increase the life of the asset, and also its performance. This of course provides greater efficiency and has the potential to reduce costs for all stakeholders.

So we should really be left in no doubt that the "Smart Grid" can provide significant benefits to not only the energy companies, or its consumers, but also to our environment. However, what exactly is it beyond the definition? And what does it physically look like?

Common components of the Smart Grid

Beyond the descriptions, and of course its objectives, what exactly is the Smart Grid? And more importantly why should I care? There will be many explanations, with entire books dedicated to the subject. However, there are some key technical components of the grid: Substation Automation; Synchronized Phasor Measurement; and the Advanced Metering Infrastructure.

Substation automation

In order to improve reliability, there is a growing trend to automate the operations within substations. Such systems facilitate a real-time automated system that reports on the conditions within the substation.

With the benefits that result from greater management within substations, it is predicted that the market for automation solutions will grow significantly.

Pike Research stated that this new trend will lead to faster growth in the global substation automation market, which will expand from $2.7 billion in 2012 to $4.3 billion in 2020.

"Even as individual equipment costs and per-substation spending are declining due to technology advances and a shift towards retrofits, we expect that the overall market will continue to grow," said chief research director Bob Gohn. "The Smart Grid trends driving automation deeper into the distribution network, combined with continued growth in Asia, will sustain steady growth in the overall substation automation sector."[17]

Phasor measurement units

When you mention the term Smart Grid, the first device may think of is the meter. Of course, perhaps this is what we did by mentioning the Advanced Meter Infrastructure first. However, one of the first devices that are often considered is the Phasor Measurement Unit (PMU), alternatively known as synchrophasor. The intention of the PMU is to measure specific parameters; invariably, these parameters include voltage and current and are placed across various locations across the grid. By providing details of voltage and current magnitude and phase at specific locations, and at very short intervals (every few seconds), it is possible to get a very accurate status of the grid. True synchronization is possible through precise time sources made available with Global Positioning Satellites (GPS). When combining this information with other PMU's across the grid, the operator is able to get a very clear view across the network and understand and react quickly. For example, should there be unprecedented demand for energy, and the operator could transfer the load from a plant that may be struggling to meet demand. Equally, such information is critical in the post mortem should there be an outage, and critical in reducing the likelihood of such instances occurring again. The use of PMU's can also allow operators to improve power capacity of existing transmission networks due to more accurate visibility into the network's parameters.

Advanced Metering Infrastructure

An Advanced Metering Infrastructure (AMI) refers to the use of systems that are able to provide the transmission of relevant information to appropriate stakeholders. Typically speaking, this involves a device at the customer home, and this device uses some form of communication networks to transmit information such as the amount of the service used to the appropriate operator.

There exist a variety of meters, for example, it is possible to have a meter dedicated to provide measurement information for the use of electricity, water, or gas. Such devices are typically installed at the customer home and will be connected to a communications network. This network is used for two-way communications between the meter (and customer) and the operator. There are of course no hard and fast rules about the exact nature of the communications network. In the recent report by Internet security company McAfee, it was reported that based on the participants in its survey that "More than half (56%) of the executives whose companies are planning new Smart Grid systems also plan to connect to the consumer over the Internet."[15]

By allowing for a communication mechanism to exist between the device at the customer home and the operator, this allows the operator to reduce the need for meter readings. Simply put, the meter readings can be submitted in real time without the added burden of requiring someone to physically attend the customer premises in the hope that someone may be at home. Furthermore, the readings will be considerably more accurate; the current model uses estimated readings to determine the bill whether a physical reading is not taken. This level of accuracy is beneficial to the customer as well, but equally by allowing the operator, the opportunity to communicate with the meter in real time (or near) any potential issues can be quickly detected and subsequently corrected.

Pitfalls of the Smart Grid

It is worthwhile considering some of the pitfalls about the Smart Grid concept, not in terms of the security and privacy risks because that will of course be discussed later in the book, but in particular, the potential exclusion of certain communities. In particular, certain communities may not have the opportunity to leverage its advantages, and this may lead to a concept known as energy poverty. For example, many communities could well be based at home all day and subsequently unable to take advantage of the prices promoted during off-peak hours. Moreover, there become other challenges with those individuals unable to grasp the information overload that will be presented to them and subsequently be unable to understand how to take advantage of the multitude of new offers.

All of this of course is largely theoretical, but there are some elements that we will clearly be aware of. For example, market economics of new smarter appliances point to the fact that smarter appliances (e.g. those able to communicate with the grid and automatically take advantage of lower pricing periods) will invariably be charged at a higher premium than non-smart appliances. Of course, the adoption curve for any new technologies does invariably leave a long tail (e.g. look at the adoption of flat screen televisions); however, in the case of Smart Grid benefits, it will likely mean the most vulnerable being left with higher bills due to the inability for large capital expenditure of new appliances, and/or the inability to take control and understand the plethora of information sources made available to them.

Also, there could be an issue related to those consumers that rent their properties. There does not remain an incentive for landlords to invest in smarter devices that could reduce utility bills, largely because the benefit is felt by the tenant whereas invariably the outlay is the responsibility of the landlord. Of course, the market should create a scenario where proposed tenants will begin to demand for a smarter home, but again this will take time, and a long tail for adoption will ensue.

A clear engagement strategy is required to reduce the long tail of adoption, and this of course will be different based on the different consumer groups. The Smart Grid Australia report[16] presents four distinct groups illustrated in Figure 1.2. (*Note:* Based on research and trials performed by various utilities, research organizations and technology vendors, including Essential Energy, Endeavor Energy, CSIRO, Charles Sturt University, Accenture, IBM, Honeywell.)

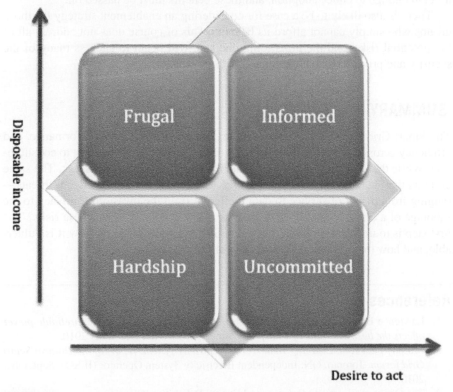

FIGURE 1.2

Smart Grid adopters.

These groups are as follows:

Uncommitted: Unconcerned by their energy consumption and its cost to themselves or the environment. Research suggests this group represents 25% of consumers, but consume approximately 50% more electricity than other groups.
Informed: Dedicated to reducing their consumption of energy, not only from a personal financial perspective, but also its impact on the environment.
Frugal: This group focuses on price and service and will be driven by the opportunity to personally save money.
Hardship: A group that may suffer form health issues, low incomes, or may have communication difficulties. Effectively unable to adjust their consumption or realize the Smart Grid benefits.

Certainly one thing becomes apparent is that while the Smart Grid represents remarkable benefits to its participants. There are some significant challenges in allowing all participants to realize its benefits. While the business case is very apparent, an effective engagement strategy is required so all consumer groups can realize its benefits. More importantly, the value proposition from the operator must be significant enough to entice adoption, and these benefits must be passed on.

There is also likely to be a case for considering an enablement strategy for those groups who simply cannot afford its benefits. This of course does not address all of the potential risks, and the proceeding chapters will begin to address many of the security and privacy risks of the Smart Grid.

SUMMARY

The Smart Grid represents a new technological era of resilience, performance, and efficiency across the entire power industry, from generation all the way to consumption. While the benefits are numerous, the Smart Grid also represents risk. The same systems that increase the value of the grid also expose the grid to digital threats—ranging from denial of service to data theft, and from the invasion of privacy to the sabotage of a critical national infrastructure. How can you address these risks? The first step is to understand what "the Smart Grid" is, how it is built, how it is vulnerable, and how those vulnerabilities can be minimized and mitigated.

References

1. Lawrence Bernie, Hancock Martin, Stieva Ginni. *White Paper: How unreliable power affects the business value of a hospital*? Schneider Electric; December 2010.
2. Murphy Paul et al. Enabling *Tomorrow's electricity system: report of the Ontario Smart Grid forum*. Toronto, ON: Independent Electricity System Operator (IESO); September 2010.
3. The Office of Electricity Delivery and Energy Reliability (OE).
4. Resilience of the National Electricity Network. *House of commons*. London, UK: Trade and Industry Committee; March 2004.

5. Vega Cynthia. *ERCOT warns of more rolling blackouts* [document on the Internet]; February 2011. <http://abcnews.go.com/US/story?id=90244&page=1#.T_sWDWh1RhN> [cited July 2012].

6. Sealey Geraldine. *Power outage brought terror worries*. New York: ABC News [document from the Internet]; August 2011. <http://www.wfaa.com/news/local/ERCOT-warns-of-more-rolling-blackouts-115709399.html> [cited July 2012].

7. *Coordinated terrorist attacks on global energy infrastructure*. Washington, DC: The Heritage Foundation; March 2011.

8. Ford Matt, CNN. *Can a 'Smart Grid' turn us on to energy efficiency?* [document on the Internet]; March 2009. <http://articles.cnn.com/2009-03-01/tech/eco.smartgrid_1_smart-grid-energy-efficiency-national-electricity-grid?_s=PM:TECH> [cited July 2012].

9. Litos Strategic Communication. *How the Smart Grid promotes a greener future* [document on the Internet]. <http://energy.gov/sites/prod/files/oeprod/DocumentsandMedia/Environmentalgroups.pdf> [cited July 2012].

10. Bajaj Vikas. *India struggles to deliver enough power*. New York Times [document from the Internet]; April 2012. <http://www.nytimes.com/2012/04/20/business/global/india-struggles-to-deliver-enough-electricity-for-growth.html?pagewanted=all> [cited July 2012].

11. BBC News. *The costs of nuclear energy* [document on the Internet]. <http://news.bbc.co.uk/1/hi/business/7180539.stm> [cited July 2012].

12. US Department of Energy. *DOE NP2010 nuclear power plant construction infrastructure assessment*. Washington, DC; October, 2005.

13. Pennington Nicole, Naassan Nicole. *Electric vehicles: fact and fiction*. Smart Grid News [document from the Internet]; November 2011. <http://www.smartgridnews.com/artman/publish/End_Use_Electric_Transportation/Electric-vehicles-Fact-and-fiction-4268.html> [cited July 2012].

14. Smart Grid News. *New effort exploring ways to reduce T&D loss and save power* [document on the Internet]; November 4, 2009. <http://www.smartgridnews.com/artman/publish/Delivery_Transmission_News/New-Effort-Looking-at-Ways-to-Reduce-T-D-Loss-and-Save-Power-1362.html> [cited July 1, 2012].

15. McAfee and the Center for Strategic and International Studies (CSIS). *In the dark: crucial industries confront cyberattacks*. Santa Clara, CA; 2011.

16. *Smart Grid Australia: maximising consumer benefits*.

17. Subnet Solutions. *Substation automation market to hit $4.3 billion by 2020* [document on the Internet]; August 2012. <http://www.subnet.com/news-events/press-releases/substation-automation-market-to-hit-4-3-billion-by-2020.aspx> [cited November 2012].

Smart Grid Network Architecture

INFORMATION IN THIS CHAPTER:

- Bulk and distributed generation architectures
- Transmission and distribution architectures
- Metering architecture
- Microgrids
- In-home systems
- System interdependencies
- Standards and protocols

Now that the term "Smart Grid" has been defined, it's important to understand how the Smart Grid is architected. Unfortunately, the "Smart Grid" is not a single easily defined system, but rather an extremely complex interconnection of multiple systems. Many of these individual systems are also complex and built upon newer, more intelligent components of generation, transmission, distribution, and metering. Understanding the individual components—and how they are interconnected and deployed—will help to understand how vulnerable or secure a Smart Grid is.

Architecturally, the Smart Grid can be thought of as a modernization of the existing generation, transmission, distribution and metering infrastructures that have delivered electricity to businesses and residences for decades. The components themselves—meters, voltage regulators, transformers, breakers, and so on—serve the functions as always. However, by becoming "smart," these components can now provide more information about their respective tasks and communicate that information to other centralized systems where it can improve efficiency and reliability through automation. There are also entirely new systems designed to enhance the grid and provide enhanced features and capabilities. These include measurement systems (such as synchronized phasor measurement systems), energy management systems, and even meteorological and environment monitoring systems—all of which provide valuable information with which to enhance or automate the production, delivery, and utilization of energy. However, it's important to remember that information on its own does not a Smart Grid make. Reliable communication of real-time information is the key. Therefore, to benefit from this new level of intelligence, it is also necessary to build interconnectivity between the various systems and services so that the data can be collected and utilized. If you think of the Smart Grid in human terms, the increased monitoring and measurement systems might equal the eyes, ears, and nose as well as the sensory receptors of the brain. The communication systems might equal the mouth, vocal chords, and the ears, as well as the communicative center of the brain. Finally, the automation systems might equal the arms, hands, and fingers, as well as the motor functions of the brain. The analogy seems trite, but serves a purpose: to highlight the common participation of the brain. This illustrates the underlying concern about Smart Grid cyber security: manipulation of the Smart Grid's brain allows manipulation of all aspects of measurement, communication and automation.

Ultimately, the brain of the Smart Grid exists to make energy delivery efficient and cost-effective. This requires upgrading the existing infrastructure—from generation through T&D to metering—to a digital anatomy of microprocessors, software, and network communication channels. The various components of the Smart Grid are evolving to provide:

- *Monitoring and Measurement:* More intelligence at each device.
- *Network Connectivity:* Communications between devices.
- *Automation:* Closed-loop process control capability within and between key systems.

Unfortunately, intelligence, communications, and automation also represent a significant cyber security challenge. The grid, through this evolution, has become accessible digitally. The manipulation of any one of these capabilities can affect the entire Grid. A manipulated reading of a synchrophasor might initiate an unnecessary load shed. The interruption of the metering network might prevent an end user from being billed (and in turn, the utility from getting paid!). The manipulation of automation systems within a substation might cause a loss of service to an entire community.

Even more unfortunate is that with this evolution of capability, there are also new, strong motives for a malicious actor or attacker to target the cyber assets of the Smart Grid. Primary motives include the theft of information and the manipulation of automated systems for purposes of disruption or sabotage.

Perhaps, one of the largest security concerns of the Smart Grid, however, supersedes the individual systems of measurement, communication, and control. It is the sheer *interconnectedness* of it all. Intelligence and communications and automation are simply the means to an end: the real "Smart Grid" is built upon many systems that leverage these mechanisms. Advanced metering leverages information from distribution management systems and distribution control (SCADA) systems. Transmission systems leverage information from generation SCADA. Systems ranging from customer management to demand-response systems and from automated dispatch servers to phasor data concentrators all interconnect, creating an unprecedented playground for a malicious actor or attacker. The attack surface is large, the attack vectors are many, and once inside the Smart Grid, an attacker can migrate to almost any system from the generator to the meter to inside the home (and into your refrigerator).

Starting at generation, and moving through transmission, distribution, and metering, each of these systems will be explored to identify how they operate, looking at the types of devices utilized by each and identifying the specific risks and vulnerabilities of those devices.

Bulk and distributed generation architectures

The first step in understanding Smart Grid architecture is a step away from what most people think of as "the grid," to discuss the architecture of energy generation. This is because energy generation is an important component of the Smart Grid. While it seems that a Smart Grid discussion should focus on the transmission and distribution infrastructure, energy generation systems are tightly integrated into T&D intelligence and automation, with many Smart Grid systems—such as demand-response systems—directly leveraging the generation infrastructure. A discussion of generation systems is also important as the T&D infrastructure evolves to support field generation and even in-home generation. Distributed generation at a micro level— inbound power from small wind and solar farms, residential batteries, electric vehicles, etc.—further integrates the complexities and risks of generation systems into the Smart Grid.

Finally, discussing generation architecture is important because of the relative maturity of the two markets: While "the grid" is evolving into something more connected and automated, electrical generation has been automated for many years. Generation architecture, therefore, provides an excellent frame of reference around any discussion of Smart Grid security.

For this reason, the architecture described herein will begin with a discussion of generation systems before we move on to transmission, distribution, and metering. Understanding generation architecture—and the cyber security risks and vulnerabilities of that architecture—is an important first step to understand cyber security for the Smart Grid, as many of the concepts here apply to the evolving grid infrastructure as well.

Types of electrical generation

Electric generation sources include several distinct mechanisms, built around the specific fuel used to create electricity—for example, a hydro-electric plant uses water, a nuclear facility uses controlled nuclear fission, fossil fuel facilitates use oil or natural gas, solar uses the power of the sun, wind farms are driven by wind turbines, etc. Each system represents its own vulnerabilities that are inherent in their designs, and therefore each represents its own unique security challenges.

A fossil fuel generation system represents several processes that aren't present in generation systems using water, wind, or sunlight as fuel. Fossil fuels must be conditioned, fed into a burner, combusted to generate steam, which then drives a

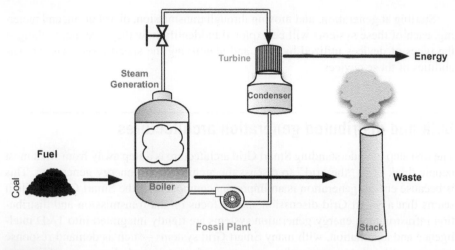

FIGURE 2.1

Electric generation system (fossil fuel).

turbine to generate electricity (Figure 2.1). Condensers are required to reclaim water to drive continued steam generation. In contrast, solar generation can convert sunlight directly to electricity. Solar cells are used to generate direct-current electricity, which is collected for conditioning (conversion from direct to alternating current) and transmission (Figure 2.2). Solar power can also be used to power boilers for steam generation, replacing the coal fuel and burners of Figure 2.1 with solar energy.

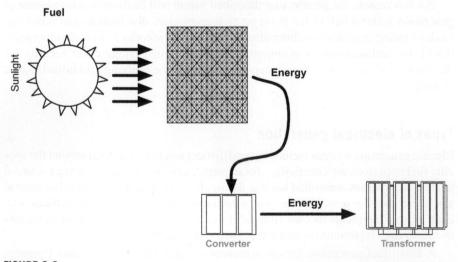

FIGURE 2.2

Electric generation system (solar).

Functionally, most electrical facilities operate in the same general process:

- Fuel is utilized to create raw "kinetic" energy.
- Raw "kinetic" energy is converted to electricity, typically using a turbine generator (or, in the case of solar, photoelectric cells).
- The electricity is collected, transformed into the correct voltages and frequencies, and either stored (in the case of direct current with batteries) or given to the T&D system.

At the same time, there are other important processes that are of concern. These include the following:

- The storage, transportation, and utilization of fuel.
- The storage, conditioning, and utilization of boiler feed water.
- The collection and removal of waste material.

For each function, industrial control components are used to automate a process loop, and together they make up the larger distributed control system that consists of many such process loops.[1] Figures 2.1–2.5 illustrate the energy generation process across industries, distinguished by fuel. In each functional system the devices, architecture and logic differ slightly.

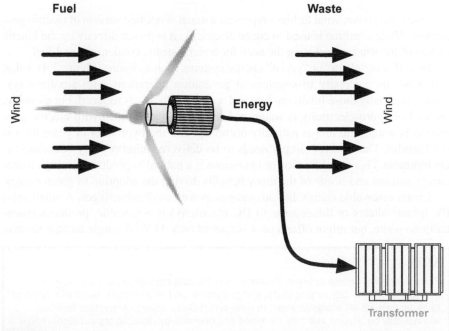

FIGURE 2.3

Electric generation system (wind).

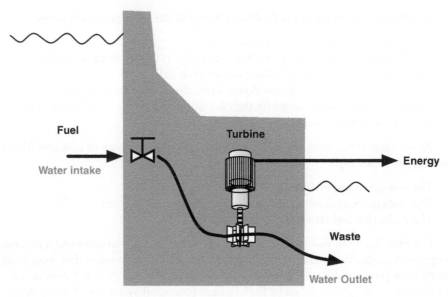

FIGURE 2.4

Electric generation system (hydro-electric).

Like solar power, wind turbines represent a much simplified version of electric generation: While a turbine is used to create electricity, it is driven directly by the kinetic energy of the wind, eliminating the need for boilers, steam, condensers, and fuel.

Note that in "clean" or "green" energy systems such as hydro (Figure 2.4), solar, and wind, the necessity to supplement generation operations with auxiliary systems—especially those involving fuel and waste handling—is reduced. For example, the fuel of hydro-electricity is water, and the waste material of hydro-electric generation is water. The fuel is naturally occurring, and the byproduct of generation is not harmful. The "waste" simply needs to be delivered appropriately back into the environment. This simplification of operations is a natural byproduct of using cleaner energy sources and is one of the many benefits driving the adoption of green energy.

Clean, renewable energy has advantages as well as disadvantages. A small solar PV (photovoltaics or direct solar to DC electricity) is renewable, produces essentially no waste, but might offer a peak output of only 3 kV.[2] A single nuclear reactor,

---

NOTE

There is ongoing debate between industries over the cost-efficiencies of each type of generation. With widely varying costs, energy outputs, and other factors, there will continue to be markets for all energy sources. In most Smart Grids, several generation facilities will typically be present and may be owned and operated by multiple organizations. Large generation facilities, small private, commercial, or military micro generation facilities, and home energy generation all converge within the transmission and distribution systems.

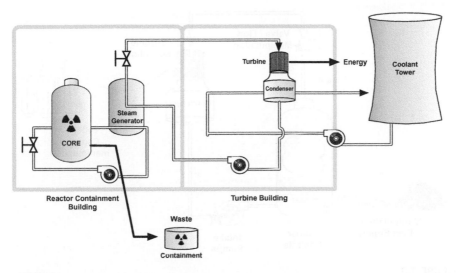

FIGURE 2.5

Electric generation system (nuclear).

though significantly more complex (Figure 2.5), will typically output in excess of 1000 MW.[3] The sheer capacity of generation, combined with the nature of the fuel, processing, and waste also leads to increased regulations. Not surprisingly, nuclear generation facilities are heavily regulated, and security (both physical and cyber) is a primary concern among plant operators.

Generation system architecture

Regardless of the type of generation facility, there are common concepts around information generation, utilization, and automation that are used heavily within the facility. By examining the specific areas that are vulnerable to potential exploitation, we can start to identify how information and automation systems might be attacked or manipulated by a malicious actor.

Some general areas of risk have been illustrated in Figure 2.6. Basically, any system that is controlled by a microprocessor or that is controlled by any device that contains a microprocessor and an operating system can be compromised. The few examples illustrated here are as follows: the mechanism(s) used to feed fuel into the burner; the mechanisms of the burner itself that control rate of combustion, regulate temperature via steam pressure, etc.; the mechanisms used to control the intake and flow of water/steam that is used to drive the turbine; the turbine generator; and the mechanisms used to transform the generated energy to the appropriate voltages and frequencies for transmission and distribution. While the accessibility to these various mechanisms will vary, the manipulation of any one mechanism can influence the generation process as a whole.

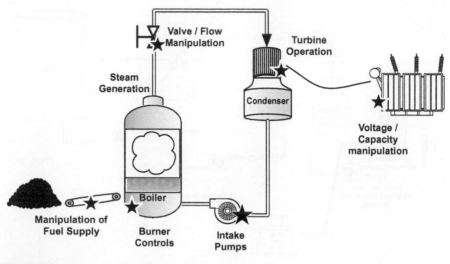

FIGURE 2.6

Potential areas of exploitation.

Figure 2.7 takes this same concept and illustrates it in greater detail, in order to further explore the ways in which a generation facility might be subject to a cyber attack. Using a coal-fired steam generator as an example, we can see that the functional mechanisms that are generalized in the Figure 2.6 map to specific designs consisting of several controllers, inputs, and outputs. For example, the fuel supply is an automated system consisting of a hopper and conveyor mechanism, while the generation itself consists of an interconnected system of burner, steam turbine, and coolant systems. There are sensors (inputs) that measure the available fuel in the hopper, as well as sensors that indicate the speed of the conveyor, the amount of fuel in the burner, the pressure in the steam system, the speed of the turbine, and many other inputs that are not illustrated here. There are also controls (outputs) that react to these inputs, such as the fuel pulverization motors, the fuel conveyor, the burner within the steam boiler, and various pumps and valves which control the pressure and rate of both the steam and coolant water.

Corresponding with this architecture, of course, is the specific controller logic used to automate each specific process loop. In this example, we look at two specific process controllers: labeled PLC 1 and PLC 2 in Figure 2.7. PLC 1 is a modular PLC consisting of I/O to the process devices, a processing module to store and execute control application, and a network interface card for Ethernet connectivity to the SCADA network, including basic control via process-specific HMIs as well as a SCADA server to manage the entire generation process. PLC 1's I/O is used for fieldbus connectivity to coal preprocessors and to the conveyors that feed the burner facility with the newly pulverized coal, and HMI 1 provides local control of coal pulverization and delivery.

PLC 2 is also a modular PLC, whose I/O connects to devices that make up the burner and energy generation processes, and with specific logic used to control

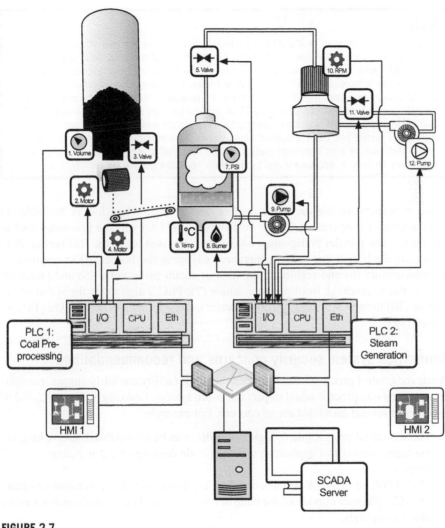

FIGURE 2.7

Electric generation system design.

those processes. Again, Ethernet is used to connect PLC 2 to the SCADA network, via which HMI 2 and the central SCADA server are connected. PLC 2's I/O is used for fieldbus connectivity to the burner, steam regulation, and turbine systems that generate electricity, and HMI 2 provides local control of these processes.

The two process loops in this example are as follows: PLC1 reads volume of the fuel supply from the hopper (1) of the coal pulverizer. When coal is available, it is fed through an opening (2) at a controlled rate through grinders (3) that pulverize the coal. The pulverizer can be set to grind to various granularities to accommodate

> **NOTE**
>
> This example is intended to illustrate the interactions of inputs and outputs within a generation facility and has been deliberately simplified and obfuscated. In a real generation facility, additional controllers would be used to operate these and other processes, which would be much more complex than represented here. There may also be other dedicated control subsystems used for specific functions like turbine control that are connected via the Ethernet network to the PLCs and SCADA server. The logic used in PLC 1 and PLC 2 is also simplified here and would be significantly more complex in a real environment. Again, the control system has been simplified here to make it more understandable to the reader who is less familiar with industrial control systems and also to remove details that could potentially be used to engineer a real cyber attack against a generation facility.

different burners: In this case, it is set to a fine powder. When fuel is available (1) and the grinder is operating (3), the feed conveyor (4) delivers the powdered coal to the burner. The powder is deposited onto a conveyor that feeds the fuel burner. PLC 2 controls the burner and steam generation: engaging the burner (8) in response to the temperature (6) and regulating the flow of steam using valve (5) and pump (9) in response to readings from pressure sensor (7). PLC 2 also reads the speed of the turbine (10) to adjust the flow of coolant water using another series of valves (11) and pumps (12).

Generation system security concerns and recommendations

While the control processes used in this generation facility are fairly simple, manipulation of any one process could impact the entire system. Looking at Figures 2.7–2.9, we can see several areas that are of concern. For example:

- The individual programmable logic controllers can be manipulated, overwriting the legitimate control application with new code designed for a malicious purpose.
- PLC, HMI, or SCADA systems could be used to establish a command and control (C2) channel outside of the control room, to enable data theft and/or further attacks remotely.
- The HMI could be accessed and used to manually control specific aspects of the control process.
- A man-in-the-middle attack inline on the Ethernet network could alter or misrepresent I/O values to the HMI (read values) and PLC (write values).

Any of these attacks would expose all aspects of the automated processes (in this case, pulverization and generation) to a hacker. The consequences of this exposure could include any or all of the following:

- Steal data about the process or about production.
- Slowing or interrupting the supply of fuel, impacting the efficiency of the burner or potentially taking the burner offline which would reduce steam flow to the turbine eventually causing it to trip and stop producing electricity.

- Increasing the supply of fuel, causing over firing of the burner or possible inter-ference with the injection of fuel into the burn chamber, potentially taking the burner offline (again resulting in a turbine trip).
- Limit the flow of steam while increasing pump pressure, causing unintended strain on the pump (as it attempts to raise pressure beyond levels allowed by mechanical relief valves or blowdown valves) and increasing the chances of a pump failure.
- Increase the flow of steam to overrun the turbine.
- Misrepresent the measurements of any of the above inputs to hide the breach from human operators.
- Misrepresent otherwise accurate measurements from non-altered inputs, to trick the human operator into mal adjusting an output.
- Crash the HMI creating a loss-of-view and effectively disabling basic control within the plant.
- Crash the PLC creating a loss-of-control situation that disables supervisory control while locking the process in its current state.

Without attacking the PLC directly, an attacker can still obtain control and manip-ulate a process, using the HMI systems.

- The communications to or from the SCADA server and the controller's I/O could be manipulated, either:
  - To alter the existing programmable logic, create and implement new logic, alter HMI interfaces, or change set points in order to maliciously affect the IS.
  - To alter or manipulate the data being reported back to the SCADA server, to trick the operator into making a change that is (unintentionally) out of spec.

- The communications to or from the controller's I/O and the field devices could be manipulated, either:

  - On the network via inline intrusion, tapping, etc. Network attacks could include man-in-the-middle exploits, network replay, or denial-of-service attacks.
  - Manipulation of the fieldbus commands given by the controller, so that the field devices operate out of spec.
  - Manipulation of the data produced by field devices, tricking the controller into operating in an unauthorized manner despite being functionally within specification.

Exploiting the controllers

The controllers (PLC 1 and PLC 2) shown in Figure 2.7 are fictional examples of modular logic controllers consisting of device I/O, network I/O, and automated con-trol logic. PLC vendors offer a wide range of products that include controllers, some of which are built using common hardware and a commercially available operat-ing system (e.g. Windows), while many utilize an embedded operating system (e.g.

> **NOTE**
>
> The ICS-CERT provides a reference for known and disclosed ICS vulnerabilities and is a valuable resource for any control system cyber security professional. Available as a specialized organization within the US-CERT, the Industrial Control Systems Cyber Emergency Response Team (ICS-CERT) provides a control system security focus in collaboration with US-CERT to[4]:
>
> - respond to and analyze control systems-related incidents,
> - conduct vulnerability and malware analysis,
> - provide onsite support for incident response and forensic analysis,
> - provide situational awareness in the form of actionable intelligence,
> - coordinate the responsible disclosure of vulnerabilities/mitigations, and
> - share and coordinate vulnerability information and threat analysis through information products and alerts.
>
> The ICS-CERT serves as a key component of the strategy for securing control systems, which outlines a long-term, common vision where effective risk management of control systems security can be realized through successful coordination efforts.[4]

embedded Windows) or a real time operating system (e.g. VxWorks). Network connectivity to SCADA servers is almost ubiquitously via Ethernet and TCP/IP, exposing the PLC to a routable network. At the same time, the device I/O is typically a fieldbus protocol (also commonly running over Ethernet, although serial bus protocols are still widely used). This makes the PLC potentially vulnerable: It has many available network interfaces and a commercial OS, and therefore, an attacker can theoretically gain access via the network and exploit a known OS vulnerability. As with any computer operating system, if new and patched appropriately, these controllers may be more secure. However, for the sake of this example, we will assume that they are running older code revisions.

Note that most of these threats involve the manipulation or alteration of the process logic. As with any logic that executes in a loop, new code could easily be inserted at any point to cause that process to stall. Furthermore, once network access has been obtained, standard engineering and configuration tools could be used to modify various ICS components. At the 2011 Applied Control Solutions Conference in Washington DC, Ralph Lagner presented a 14-byte Siemens Step 7 routine that would, at a given time, put a PLC into an endless loop, bypassing the intended ladder logic and essentially fixing the process into whatever state it was in when the 14-byte payload executed.[5] This highlights what was first exemplified by the "St****t" malware that manipulation of PLC logic is not limited to the alteration of existing logic, but can be used to introduce entirely new logic, replacing or appending legitimate code to almost any end. At a high level, logic manipulation can result in the following:

- Manipulation of the intended process. Examples might include altering set points, timing, or other variables without otherwise changing the nature of the process.
- Insertion of new process commands. Examples include the aforementioned "logic time bomb," manipulation of I/O, etc.

- Removal of process commands. Examples include process alterations to bypass or override critical steps of a process and to sabotage the process or bypass safety.
- Exfiltration of process commands. Examples include the theft of a manufacturing "blueprint"—essentially stealing the target's intellectual property.

By looking at the logic in our steam generation example, we can see exactly how these threats could materialize. The logic of PLC 1 is simple: While there is a supply of fuel and demand for fuel (based on readings from the burner), the fuel pulverizer processes coal through a manipulation of a feed valve and a grinding motor and delivers powdered coal on to a conveyor that delivers the fuel at a controlled rate (based on readings from the pulverizer and the burner) to the burner. It can be seen how manipulation of this logic could impact the fuel delivery processes:

- Manipulation of coal pulverization to introduce unsuitable fuel onto the conveyor.
- Manipulation of pulverized coal delivery to introduce too little or too much fuel to the conveyor.
- Manipulation of the conveyor to deliver fuel too quickly or too slowly to the burner.
- Misrepresentation of available fuel levels, causing the process to run without fuel, or to stop running when there is fuel.
- Combinations of the above manipulations to alter or sabotage the process.
- Introduction of malware to the process to lock the process into the manipulated state.
- Disabling of SCADA connectivity to prevent remote management or remediation of the incident.

The logic of PLC 2 is similarly based upon measurements and reactions to those measurements: The burner combusts fuel to reach optimum temperature within the boiler (determined by temperature readings within the burner), to boil water into steam. Water is pumped into the boiler as needed to produce steam. The steam is moved at a given rate (based upon pressure of the steam lines, which is controlled by valves) to drive a turbine, which generates electricity. A condenser then converts the steam back into water using a regulated cooling system, for reuse by the boiler. In this example, it can be seen how manipulation of this logic could impact the burner and steam generation processes:

- Manipulation of temperature readings to cause under or over burning.
- Manipulation of pressure readings to cause unsafe steam pressure levels.
- Manipulation of release valves to prevent safe bleeding of excess pressure.
- Manipulation of available water to the steam system, causing failures in the boiler or turbine.
- Manipulation of available water to the coolant system, preventing adequate condensation and causing overheating or other damage to the turbine.
- Manipulation of turbine sensors to prevent adequate flow of steam or coolant.

- Misrepresentations of any input or output values to HMI or SCADA, to trick human operators into making errors.
- Combinations of the above manipulations to further alter or sabotage the process.
- Exfiltration of process data to report energy production levels to a malicious actor.
- Introduction of malware to the process to lock the process into the manipulated state.
- Disabling of SCADA connectivity to prevent remote management or remediation of the incident.

Network attacks

While the controllers and other devices are likely targets for attack, industrial control environments possess many inherent network-based vulnerabilities. Fieldbus protocols, whether running over legacy serial or new Ethernet transport, represent a security risk in industrial control environments. These protocols—DNP3, Modbus, PROFIBUS/PROFINET, CIP, and others—are ultimately designed around a common paradigm of request and respond. Each protocol is designed for a "master" device such as an HMI to send commands to subordinate "slave" devices such as a PLC to retrieve data (reading inputs) or instigate control (writing to outputs). Because many of these protocols lack authentication, encryption, or other basic security measures, they are ripened for network-based attacks, allowing a malicious actor or attacker to utilize the "request and respond" system as a mechanism for "command and control" like functionality.[1] Specific security concerns common to most industrial control protocols include the following[1]:

- Network or transport errors (e.g. malformed packets or excessive latency) can cause protocol failure.
- Protocol commands may be available that are capable of forcing slave devices into inoperable states, including powering-off devices, forcing them into a "listen only" state, disabling alarming.
- Protocol commands may be available that are capable of restarting communications and otherwise interrupting processes.
- Protocol commands may be available that are capable of clearing, erasing, or resetting diagnostic information such as counters and diagnostic registers.
- Protocol commands may be available that are capable of requesting sensitive information about the controllers, their configurations, or other need-to-know information.
- Most protocols are application layer protocols transported over TCP; therefore it is easy to transport commands over non-standard ports or inject commands into authorized traffic flows.
- Protocol commands may be available that are capable of broadcasting messages to many devices at once (i.e. a potential DoS).

> **NOTE**
>
> It cannot be stressed enough that in order for these malicious events to occur, access must be granted to the network upon which the devices are connected. This makes something that otherwise appears to be a trivial attack, into one that actually requires sophisticated resources. If the network is not properly protected, however, the attacks do become trivial, which is why ICS networks should never be directly connected to public networks like the Internet.

- Protocol commands may be available to query the device network to obtain defined points and their values (i.e. a configuration scan).
- Protocol commands may be available that will list all available function codes (i.e. a function scan).

These inherent vulnerabilities make network-based attacks very feasible. Simple injection of malicious protocol commands provides control over the target process, while "bit flipping" legitimate protocol traffic can alter information about a process as well as disrupt the legitimate controls that are in place over that process. A man-in-the-middle attack could provide both control over a process and misrepresentation of data back to operator consoles.

Data manipulation

- The concept of data manipulation has recurred throughout this chapter because of important role that "data" play in the overall automation process and because the alteration of that data can either directly or indirectly manipulate that process. "Data" here represent the values of the generation facility—the specific inputs and outputs used by the logic of the control applications. It is used within the controllers such as the PLC, but also reported to HMIs and SCADA consoles, where it is consumed by a human operator. Manipulation of these values can influence all aspects of automated production, distribution, safety, and reliability.
- Showing a human operator misleading values from the plant could cause the operator to override the (legitimate) automation logic, effectively sabotaging their own process. While the operator's intentions are good, they are tricked into action through the dissemination of false data.
- Manipulating values used by other controllers could prevent supplementary systems—potentially including protection systems—from behaving properly. For example, if an alarm is supposed to trigger at a certain boiler temperature, the alteration of that set point from 400°F to 500°F could prevent the alarm from triggering at the appropriate level. At the same time, the value could be altered so that within management consoles, the set point still reads 400°F, covering the tracks of this exploitation.

Data manipulation can also impact higher-level operations and business functions including the manipulation of production data to influence energy trading,

> **NOTE**
>
> Editor's note: St****t infected both SCADA servers and PLCs, so that multiple changes could be made: first, the engineering and HMI workstations were blocked from seeing what was actually occurring in the PLC (a sort of man-in-the-middle-attack); second, PLC logic was altered; third, specific centrifuges used in the enrichment of uranium were altered to spin at widely varying frequencies; fourth, the SCADA communications were altered to report false values back to the SCADA system, fooling the human operator into complacency; and finally, the engineering and operator databases were corrupted to automatically infect any newly added devices to the ICS.

demand-response systems, and other back-end systems that utilize real-time energy production data. Because many of these information systems are integral to "Smart Grid" services, the manipulation of data within the process control systems of a generation facility can cascade throughout all areas of the Smart Grid.

Transmission and distribution architecture

Once energy is generated, it must then be transmitted to distribution points, where it can be intelligently and efficiently delivered to the end user. While transmission systems and distribution systems are architecturally similar, there are very important differences. For example, transmission occurs at high voltages (115 kV and above) to transport large amounts of electricity between primary substations, whereas distribution systems step down the voltages to deliver safe and usable electricity to homes and businesses. This means that as energy is generated, it must first be "stepped up" to the high voltages that are necessary for efficient transmission and then "stepped down" for use by the final consumer.

Transmission architecture

Understanding how generation SCADA systems work and how they may be susceptible to a cyber attack helps to understand the risks that are facing the transmission system as substation operations, line management, and protection all become more automated.

The transmission architecture begins where generation ends. Shown in Figure 2.8, transmission architecture varies from generation architecture in several key ways, however. By its nature, transmission systems are highly distributed, with power lines covering large geographic areas. Unlike generation systems, transmission systems are also physically accessible. A generation plant is typically behind closed walls with strict access controls and physical security mechanisms in place. While transmission substations are physically secured, the lines themselves are easily assessable. Also, while substations may utilize a variety of physical security controls, more remote substations still represent a physical access risk, as they can be relatively easy

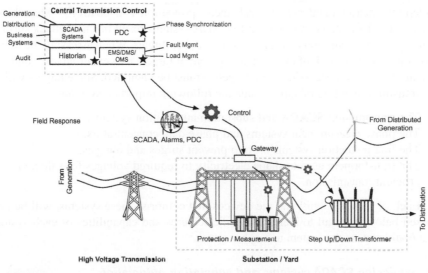

FIGURE 2.8

Transmission architecture.

targets, physically. Finally, transmission systems require wide-area communication technology to support real-time measurement of the infrastructure, and they require SCADA systems to enable the automation of real-time operations. In other words, the transmission network is just as accessible logically as it is physically.

Electricity enters the transmission system after a transformer steps up the voltage to levels that are suitable for bulk transmission to the grid. This typically occurs at generation facilities, but voltages may also be stepped up or down at substations where multiple lines converge, aggregate, or intersect. Substations or "yards" are a primary component of transmission systems. Substations also provide voltage measurement, voltage regulation, and line protection so that electricity can be transmitted as safely and efficiently as possible. Transmission lines carry electricity over either multiphase alternating current (AC) or high voltage direct current (HVDC), typically at high voltages (115–345 kV), extra high voltages (500–765 kV) and ultra-high voltages (greater than 800 kV).[6] The high-voltage energy is transmitted to distribution systems, including secondary and tertiary substations, where electricity is then stepped down to usable voltages and distributed to the end customer.

Modernization of transmission focuses on adding intelligence and automation to make energy transmission more efficient (through grid optimization such as dynamic load and condition management), more reliable (through attack-resistant and self-healing capabilities), and more flexible (supporting distributed generation).[6]

As with generation systems, modernization of the grid to accommodate smart transmission systems presents a cyber security challenge. Many components of a transmission system—substation automation, GPS/satellite timing and other wide-area measurement systems, advanced protection and control[6]—when combined with distributed controllers and SCADA systems result in a new attack surface that exposes transmission to a variety of new cyber threats. When assessing the transmission system for risk of cyber attack, potential targets of a cyber attack—and the potential vectors of accessing these targets—must be identified. Some targets within the transmission infrastructure include the following important systems:

- The transmission SCADA and substation automation systems.
- The phase measurement systems and phase data concentrators.
- The line protection systems used to prevent surges and outages.
- The transformers used to shape electricity to required voltages for safe and efficient transmission.

Each of these systems, and the devices that comprise these systems, will be discussed below in detail to identify specific features and capabilities of each system that could expose the system to a cyber attack.

Transmission SCADA systems and substation automation

Transmission SCADA systems, or T-SCADA, provide similar functions to transmission that generation SCADA or G-SCADA systems discussed at the beginning of this chapter provide to generation facilities, that is, they provide supervisory (monitoring) control (automation) and data acquisition (measurement). T-SCADA systems are typically designed to manage and control automated substation processes, in the same way that a G-SCADA system manages and controls automated generation processes.

T-SCADA systems depend very heavily on a combination of capabilities: measurement (or collection of measurements from device I/O), monitoring via a user console, and control (via automation logic or direct HMI). Many substation gateways combine T-SCADA functions with network communication capabilities, and act as a central nexus of information aggregation, translation, and communication in addition to SCADA functions. These gateways provide several key functions to the transmission system:

- They provide translation between multiple device and protocol messages from substation protection systems, controllers (remote PLCs or RTUs), intelligent electronic devices (IEDs), synchrophasors, etc. and centralized substation management systems or energy management systems (EMS).
- They provide substation control and distributed T-SCADA. The gateway, which is a computing platform (a server), executes process automation logic (such as ladder logic) much like a PLC.
- The gateway provides activity logging to the substation, where faults, events, and other data (e.g. measurements) are recorded.
- They provide communication back to the control room. Communication channels typically include communication between gateway T-SCADA and centralized T-SCADA or EMS systems (for central management) as well as communication to substation devices for remote maintenance or management of individual assets.

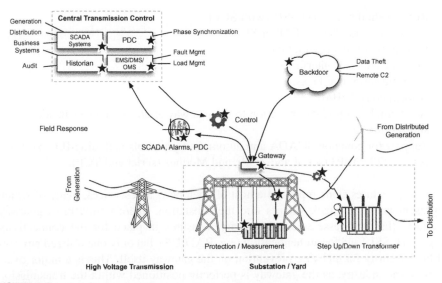

FIGURE 2.9

Targets of a substation cyber attack.

Figure 2.9 illustrates some of the systems that are accessible and/or that can be manipulated through the compromise of T-SCADA. Manipulation of transmission systems—such as phase measurement and synchronization, power conditioning, load, etc.—is obvious. Less obvious is the manipulation of G-SCADA and distribution SCADA systems, which often utilize data from T-SCADA to ensure proper loads are being generated and delivered to the distribution systems. Historians are also influenced, as falsified or manipulated data inbound from T-SCADA into a historian result in a lack of historical data integrity. Data historian systems are also being used more and more for real-time business intelligence purposes: Rather than simply archiving data for historical reference, the historian is calculating efficiency metrics, isolating trends, and otherwise adding business context to process data. Perhaps, even more significant, however, is the role that more advanced substation gateways play in transmission.

Looking at several commercially available substation gateways, a number of common features are available that raise cyber security concerns. At least one gateway (which will not be identified here) supported e-mail notifications. While ICS best practices limit SMTP to outbound messaging, and therefore prevent inbound attacks using SMTP, the use of common services such as SMTP does raise questions of risk. Can outbound messages be altered, spoofed, or otherwise manipulated? Almost all gateways offered the following:

- Time synchronization via the network time protocol (NTP) and/or IRIG-B.
- Web-based data viewing via HTTPS.
- Event logging via Syslog.

- Remote shell access via SSH (with SCP).
- Remote file transfer via FTP or SFTP.
- USB ports for data extraction.
- Multiple Ethernet interfaces.
- Multiple serial interfaces.
- A local console/HMI.
- A terminal server (for connection to the gateway and/or to devices inside the substation).
- Support for common SCADA and automation protocols including IEC 61850, IEC 60870, DNP3 (serial and TCP), and Modbus (serial and TCP).

These features alone represent a host of open ports and services, many of which represent potential attack vectors into the substation. Interestingly, most gateway products that were assessed had security measures in place for the connectivity (e.g. SSH, SSL) and for authentication (e.g. RADIUS), but only one utilized any sort of host security for malware prevention on the gateway itself. This is a major oversight in the industry, as the gateway is perfectly positioned within the transmission architecture for use by a cyber attack: It is reachable via both the wide area network (TCP/IP) and the device network (serial bus protocols), it supports both control and data acquisition aspects of SCADA, it is responsible for messaging to and from the control room, and (typically) it runs a commercially available OS. Figure 2.9 illustrates many systems that could be influenced or manipulated with root or administrative access to a substation gateway. Essentially, by compromising the gateway, an attacker would have the ability to directly manipulate all communications to and from the substation—including the command and control capability of centralized T-SCADA or EMS (see Figure 2.10).

Possible exploitation of T-SCADA, therefore, includes compromise of the substation gateway in addition to compromise of the wide-area communication infrastructure (including VPN keys, et al.) and/or the compromise of the T-SCADA/EMS servers.

⚠ Compromise of the wide–area communication infrastructure

Compromise of the WAN connections between substations and the control room is a serious concern. Luckily, at least some degree of secure connectivity was offered in most of the systems that were researched for this book. The use of SSL and/or TLS—which is specified for communication under the IEC 61850 standards—is used almost ubiquitously for wide-area connectivity, for example. However, vulnerabilities still exist—man-in-the-middle attacks can breach some SSL connections, while newer SSL exploits may be used to effectively denial of service (DoS) an SSL server, shutting off its ability to communicate on the network by causing a storm of SSL renegotiations[7] and a successful attack against an endpoint can allow a hacker to benefit from secure transmission to operate invisibly, unless a mechanism has been deployed to inspect encrypted communications. Older versions of TLS are also susceptible to toolkit-based attacks from the Browser Exploit Against SSL/TLS (BEAST).[8] In other words, defense of a substation requires a broader defensive strategy than TLS alone.

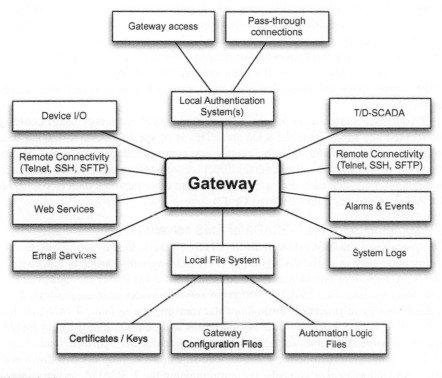

FIGURE 2.10

Distributed T-SCADA/gateway services.

Of significant concern is the continued use of e-mail and web services in these devices. Email is used primarily for sending alarms, diagnostic messages, and other notifications to administrators. While convenient, sending an e-mail requires an open port. HTTP is mostly used to access a web interface, but again requires the use of open TCP ports. These ports and services represent a clear (and unnecessary) avenue for compromise. Attacks might include man-in-the-middle attacks, manipulation of the TCP/IP communication channels between the substation gateway and the T-SCADA server(s) in the control room, creation of "covert" communication channels between a compromised substation and other substations in the network, denial of service, or data exfiltration.

Because the T-SCADA server or substation gateway controls the movement and protection of high-voltage electricity, reliability and safety can be impacted directly if the communication to and from these devices becomes compromised. The malicious injection of SCADA protocol traffic to or from the substation, for example, could directly manipulate automated protection systems to trip lines unnecessarily, causing an outage. The reliance upon Syslog for communication of activities outside of the substation (inside the substation, messaging typically occurs via GOOSE or similar protocols) simplifies misdirection to corporate IT resources by manipulating or blocking messages. In addition, centralized cyber security detection systems that rely upon logs (e.g. log management or security information and event management systems) can be misled through the malicious injection of logs from the substation to the control room, unless caution is taken to transfer logs over secure and authenticated channels.

Privacy issues are also a concern, as important data about energy usage could be intercepted and stolen from the wide area. This is of special concern whether data from the advanced metering infrastructure are communicated back to the control room via T&D communications, versus direct secure AMI communication, as metering data often include customer usage, billing, and other personal data (see Chapter 4, "Privacy Concerns with the Smart Grid").

⚠ Compromise of the T-SCADA or EMS server(s)

Compromise of the T-SCADA or EMS server(s) results in the same risks to reliability and safety as in the discussion of G-SCADA systems earlier in this chapter: The SCADA system provides ultimate command and control over the industrial process, and therefore, breaching the T-SCADA server provides ultimate command and control over those processes throughout the transmission system. T-SCADA, like G-SCADA, is responsible for monitoring inputs and outputs: Inputs might include phasor measurement, line voltages, frequency, transformer settings, load, faults, while outputs might include capacitance, load adjustments, (step-up/step-down controls), protection/breaker controls. By compromising the T-SCADA server(s), these inputs and outputs can be redefined:

- Values can be misrepresented to centralized SCADA console, to centralized data historians, and to other auxiliary systems that utilize T-SCADA data (e.g. other interconnected SCADA systems or back-office systems).
- New values/logic can be written to the controller(s)—for example, to substation automation logic in the gateway or to distributed IEDs or RTUs on lines or in secondary substations.
- Direct manipulation of secure communication channels to substation gateways and other substation assets (most secure communication channels between T-SCADA servers and substation gateways) utilizes SSL or TLS and utilizes certificate-based authority. By compromising an authorized device with appropriate certificates, the secure wide-area communications are also compromised.

⚠ Compromise of the substation gateway

Again, the substation gateway is a prime target for attack, because it provides communications between a substation and the control room, in addition to substation automation capabilities. Gateway communication capabilities typically extend to provide a central access point (via a terminal server) to substation devices that are managed via the gateway's I/O. Therefore, compromise of the gateway allows an attacker to manipulate many systems:

- Manipulation of substation devices, via direct injection of SCADA commands onto the device network.
- Manipulation of other substation devices, via pass-through access to device configuration/diagnostic interfaces.
- Manipulation of substation devices, via manipulation of automation logic controlling those devices.
- Manipulation of gateway authentication to enable unauthorized remote access (i.e. a backdoor) to substation devices.
- Indirect manipulation of substation automation logic, via false reporting to centralized T-SCADA systems, tricking the human operator into making unnecessary and potentially harmful changes to the automation logic.
- Remote manipulation of substation automation logic via remote access of the gateway's "local" HMI (i.e. "popping the HMI").

Phasor measurement units/synchrophasers/phasor data concentrator

Electricity flows from higher voltages to lower voltages and from higher phase angles to lower phase angles. Therefore, to effectively transmit electricity throughout the transmission system, it is necessary to understand the voltage and phase angle at key locations in the grid. A phasor measurement unit (PMU) is a device that measures these electrical characteristics on the grid and then communicates them back to a phasor data concentrator (PDC) and ultimately to T-SCADA systems.

> **NOTE**
>
> The accessibility of industrial control systems used in Smart Grid and other industries is often called into question, because of the traditional "air gap" separation of SCADA and ICS systems from other private and public networks. In February of 2012, the US Department of Energy's Industrial Control Systems Cyber Emergency Response Team (ICS-CERT) issued an alert in response to growing trends in both control system accessibility and the emergence of ICS exploitation tools, "that increase the risk of control systems attacks. These elements include Internet accessible ICS configurations, vulnerability and exploit tool releases for ICS devices, and increased interest and activity by hacktivist groups and others." The availability of publically released tools—targeting PLCs from General Electric, Koyo, Rockwell Automation, Schneider Electric, and Siemens, as well as well-used industrial protocols such as EtherNet/IP—put any accessible control system at risk. At the same time, "The ERIPP and SHODAN search engines can be easily used to find Internet facing ICS devices, thus identifying potential attack targets. These search engines are being actively used to identify and access control systems over the Internet. Combining these tools with easily obtainable exploitation tools, attackers can identify and access control systems with significantly less effort than ever before."[9]
>
> In the context of the Smart Grid, we now have SCADA industrial automation systems that are both digitally accessible and geographically distributed, and in many cases, physically accessible as well. The result is a "perfect storm" of accessibility and vulnerability that puts the Smart Grid's automation systems at extreme risk.

> **NOTE**
>
> The volume of phasor measurements is an important consideration when looking at PMUs from a cyber security perspective, as changes in phasor readings can indicate a disruption within the grid, which is a valuable indicator for cyber event correlation tools, which attempt to detect complex, blended, and sophisticated cyber attacks through the correlation of different events, from different devices across a system. Correlating phasor measurements with network and security events, SCADA activity, and other activities could indicate whether an outage, overage, or other fault is the result of a cyber attack. However, the high rate of phasor measurements, compounded by the large number of PMUs deployed throughout a Grid, can quickly exceed the analytical capabilities of available event correlation tools. If attempting to utilize phasor measurements in this manner, it may be necessary to deploy dedicated event correlation systems in order to accommodate the high rate of information. For more information about utilizing phasor measurements for security monitoring, see "Situational Awareness" in Chapter 6, "Securing the Smart Grid."

PMUs are often called synchrophasors because modern PMUs synchronize multiple phasor measurements from different points on the grid to a common time source (typically using IRIG-B, a GPS-based time synchronization protocol). A synchronized PMU or synchrophasor is able to accurately measure the quality of the grid, both in terms of voltage and in terms of current, at any given time across all measurement points. Understanding distributed phasor measurements allows the grid to be utilized more efficiently, by adjusting load throughout the grid to the maximum dynamic limits of the transmission system, at any given point. The result is more efficient, reliable and safe transmission, because available transmission lines are able to transmit the maximum amount of power, while surges or ebbs in load can be reduced or eliminated.

Synchrophasors consist of measurement, synchronization, and logging functions. Typical PMUs will provide multiple measurements up to 30 times per second, as specified by the IEEE Synchrophasor Standard, C37.118–2005[10] (see "Standards and Protocols," below). However, an assessment of several commercially available synchrophasors as many as 64 samples per cycle may be supported. These readings are time-stamped to the synchronized time source and collected by the PDC, which samples the data logging mechanisms of the PMU in real time. The centralized and synchronized measurements are then utilized by T-SCADA and energy management systems to adjust transmission rates, manage outages, and other functions.

Many automation devices include phasor measurement capabilities, just as many synchrophasors support remote management and control, enabling transmission quality to be automated. Unfortunately, this also exposes transmission quality to the same vulnerabilities and exploitations of other SCADA system components.

As with substation gateways, most commercially available synchrophasors researched for this book provided a variety of features that in turn equate to open ports and services—in other words, to direct attack vectors:

- Networking interfaces, including Ethernet for routable connectivity and RS485, RS232, RS422, G.703, and others device I/O.
- Multiple protocols, including IEC 61850, DNP 3.0 (serial and TCP), Modbus (serial and TCP), IEC 60870-5-104, and the Ethernet Global Data (EGD) protocol.

- Remote communication between PMUs and PDCs via IEEE C37.118 Standard for synchrophasors for power systems.
- Console or management access to phasor data at the PDC, often over open protocols such as HTTPS.

Synchrophasors, like most industrial automation systems, utilize commercial operating systems (typically Windows, especially on larger PMUs and PDCs). Combined with a variety of interfaces, ports, and services, a synchrophasor that is misconfigured by the vendor or the end user could represent a degree of vulnerability to the device itself.

⚠ Compromise of the phasor measurement infrastructure

If a synchrophasor is compromised, the damage that results could be as subtle as a loss of transmission efficiency up to the disruption of service. For example:

- Disabling a PMU or PDC could stall line condition monitoring and any automation process that depends upon it.
- EMI jamming of satellite synchronization could cause erroneous load condition reports due to improper timing.
- Manipulating a PMU or its phasor measurements could cause erroneous load condition reports that could lead to improper load management.
- Manipulating phasor measurements could result in erroneous fault indicators, resulting in unnecessary recovery actions.
- Manipulating process logic on a PMU or PDC could result in improper operations as the result of accurate phasor measurements.
- Manipulation of phasor measurements could interfere with line protection, enabling power swing, out of step conditions, or other unwanted line conditions.[11]

Line protection and monitoring systems

Line protection systems combine metering and measurement with protection mechanisms to prevent undercurrent and overcurrent conditions. Typically, line protection consists of breakers that will trip to prevent a potentially hazardous fault—much like a home circuit breaker will trip in response to a power surge, in order to prevent a fire or other hazard. More sophisticated protection systems combine line monitoring with automation logic to allow appropriate and efficient responses to a variety of line conditions, overcurrent protection, power swing protection, and recovery, including under-frequency load correction, breaker fault detection and isolation, and synchronization loss detection and recovery.[11]

Line protection systems obviously rely heavily upon line monitoring, including current, voltage, frequency, power, energy, and phasor measurement. The measurement functions of a protection system overlap with phasor measurement units, and therefore, many protection systems include PMU capabilities (according to IEEE C37.118) or integrate with external PMUs.

Line monitoring is also important for the detection of various abnormal conditions that might indicate equipment failure (or imminent equipment failure). Proactive maintenance of substation devices such as transformers and breakers can extend their life, and therefore, condition monitoring can directly influence the ROI of substation equipment. Proactive maintenance also enables failing equipment to be safely repaired or replaced prior to an incident or outage.[12]

Protection and monitoring devices once again rely heavily upon common standards and are often built atop commercial operating systems. Researching several protection systems, there is once again a common set of features including:

- Ethernet interfaces, serial interfaces, and USB interfaces.
- Protocol support including TCP/IP, IEC 61850, IEC 60870, Modbus (serial and TCP), DNP3 (serial and TCP), EGD, and IEEE C37.118.
- Support for TFTP, HTTPS, SMTP, and other common network services (SNMP, NTP, PTP, etc.).
- Support for local automation logic, used to control outputs (e.g. breakers) in response to inputs (line measurements).
- Local and remote consoles or displays for management and control of protection services.
- Event and alarming mechanisms to log measurements and activities and provide alerts in response to faults or other conditions.

Transformers

A transformer is a device that transfers electricity from one coil to another via inductive coupling, either stepping up or stepping down the current by varying the delta between the coils. Step-up-transformers are necessary for electric transmission, as they are able to increase voltages to levels where power can be transmitted efficiently over long distances. Step-down-transformers reduce voltages, ultimately to 110V/220V for consumption by the end user. Step-up transformers are therefore located at the ingress to the transmission system (from generation), while step down transformers are located at the egress of the transmission system (to distribution). "Step-up/step-down transformers" are transformers capable of either stepping up or stepping down voltages, and are useful in substation applications where voltage regulation must be controlled to support the optimized, self-healing, and reliable nature of a smart transmission system.

Transformers typically communicate to protection systems and/or substation automation systems over IEC 61850. There may be a direct communication to a centralized T-SCADA system, or an indirect communication to centralized T-SCADA via substation automation systems in PMUs, gateways, and protection systems.

Examining several commercially available transformers, these devices provide a much smaller attack surface than other components of the transmission system:

- Network communications are typically limited to IEC 61850 (ideally, protected according to IEC 62351).
- There are no inherent SCADA or controller functions; the transformers rely on external control from protection systems and T-SCADA systems.
- There are no Web-based consoles or interfaces, or other remote consoles using common protocols.

This does not exclude transformers as targets for cyber attacks, but it does limit their usefulness as an initial attack vector. The important role that transformers play in the transmission and distribution systems makes them a likely target to an attacker that gains a foothold in other systems, such as substation automation, protection, condition monitoring systems, and other systems that interact with the transformer. One reason for concern is that manipulation of a transformer could cause significant short-term or long-term damage. For example, by transforming electricity to non-optimal voltages while reporting expected measurements back to monitoring systems, equipment deterioration could be accelerated and imminent failures might go unnoticed. Likewise, voltages could be increased to levels that are unsafe due to downstream line conditions.

Distribution architecture

The "distribution" architecture begins at the termination of the transmission system, and ends at the meter—the demarcation where a home or business consumes the distributed electricity. Again, transformers are used to shape electricity, typically stepping down voltages for distribution at lower voltages and ultimately stepping voltages down to levels usable by the metering infrastructure and the end consumer. Distribution lines are numerous and typically support many end users: from city blocks, to suburbs, to neighborhoods, to counties, etc.

Like transmission systems, distribution systems also utilize substations for energy conditioning, monitoring, protection, and automation. Also like transmission systems, distribution systems communicate back to a centralized SCADA master terminal unit (MTU), distribution management systems (DMS), outage management systems (OMS), and a variety of back-office systems located in a data center or central control facility. Like transmission systems, they also rely heavily upon line measurement and protection systems to effectively manage energy usage, monitor and respond to outages, etc.

In fact, distribution systems operate similarly to transmission substations in many, though they tend to be smaller, more numerous, and operate at lower voltages than the primary and secondary substations used in the transmission system. The specific functions of a distribution system also differ slightly: where transmission systems focus more on generation control, delivery, condition management, energy storage/reserve management, interchange management; distribution focuses more on load management and modeling, two-way power flow, risk analysis and outage management, and dynamic feeder reconfiguration (DFR), islanding and other isolate, bypass or otherwise avoid outages.[6]

The distribution architecture is shown in Figure 2.11, and consists of several important systems:

- Field sensors and monitoring.
- SCADA and DMS systems.
- Field controllers and automated field devices.
- Metering and AMI.

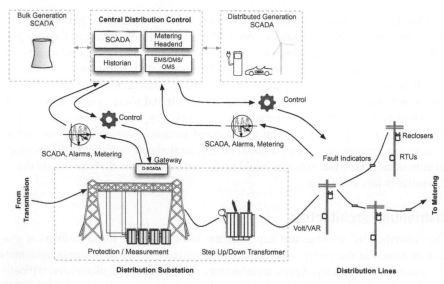

FIGURE 2.11

Distribution architecture.

Each of these systems will be discussed below in detail to identify specific features and capabilities of each system that could expose the system to a cyber attack.

Distribution SCADA/DMS

Distribution SCADA or D-SCADA systems are responsible for the control of distribution operations, including manual and automated control of load management and DFR.[6] Distribution substation automation, like transmission substation automation, is typically controlled via D-SCADA systems within the substation, often in a gateway device, while also communicating back to a larger D-SCADA system in a central control center. Remote D-SCADA servers will typically offer similar features and capabilities as those used in transmission—they are communication gateways that provide: the network communications capability to substation devices (LAN, serial) and to centralized systems (WAN); data concentration functions to collect and aggregate substation data from other systems; automation capability through programmable logic (i.e. a controller); metering functions; fault recording and alerting; and transformer monitoring and control.

Just as in transmission substations, D-SCADA systems are often feature rich and designed to accommodate many remote communication and control functions. It is therefore very typically for a distribution gateway to support:

- Time synchronization via NTP or IRIG-B.
- Management interfaces via HTTP, SSH, or terminal access.
- Terminal server capabilities for remote connectivity to other substation devices.

- Event logging via Syslog.
- File transfer via FTP or SFTP for configuration, data acquisition, and upgrades.
- Keyboard, video, mouse, and USB ports.
- Multiple Ethernet and serial interfaces.
- Local console/HMI access.
- Support for common SCADA and automation protocols.

Again, the robust nature of D-SCADA provides a broad attack surface: The many available interfaces, ports, and services combined with the use of commercial operating systems and both LAN and WAN connectivity make these systems a likely inbound attack vector, as well as prime targets for attacks. This enables both direct attacks (to impact substation automation) and staged attacks (using the gateway as a launching point for attacks against protection, conditioning, monitoring, and other systems), by exploiting weaknesses and vulnerabilities in D-SCADA.

⚠ Compromise of distribution SCADA

The problem of interconnectivity continues to present a cyber security challenge throughout the distribution system. With automation and intelligence come vulnerabilities and attack vectors, and the interdependence of these systems on each other provides a playground for cyber attackers. Figure 2.12 highlights some of the systems that can be reached and compromised in automated distribution systems.

The interdependence of disparate systems requires that communications be established. That established communication path then becomes a vector for threat propagation. Once D-SCADA is compromised, it is therefore possible to access and

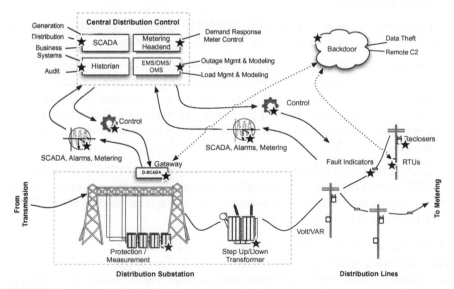

FIGURE 2.12

Targets of a distribution cyber attack.

breach outage management systems, the AMI headend, or even G-SCADA systems back at the beginning of the process in the power generation facility! As more systems become interconnected, this risk increases unless digital access controls are established between all interconnections. At the same time, as more systems become interconnected, it becomes cost prohibitive (and often logistically challenging) to implement security controls to enforce each and every interconnection.

Field controllers and automated field devices

A field controller is a remote terminal unit (RTU), IED or other distributed controller used throughout the distribution system, outside of the substation. Automated field devices include auto-reclosers, breakers, volt/VAR (voltage and VAR, or volt–ampere reactive) regulators, and capacitors.[6]

Examining commercially available RTUs, there is once again a proliferation of interfaces, protocols, ports, and services that give substation gateways such a broad attack surface:

- Ethernet and serial interfaces. Often with multiple Ethernet LAN interfaces and optional wireless capabilities including WiMax, radio, CDMA, GSM, and satellite.
- Support for IEC 61850, DNP3 (serial and TCP), and Modbus (serial and TCP).
- Support for automation either as a node in a centralized automation systems (connecting back to a centralized D-SCADA system) or as a distributed automation system using built-in controller logic.
- USB interfaces and/or removable flash-card interfaces for data extraction and firmware upgrades.

Examining commercially available volt/VAR systems, reclosers, feeders, and other field devices, there are far fewer communication vectors:

- Limited network interfaces—often limited to two-wire serial interfaces.
- Support for IEC 61850, DNP3 (mostly serial), and/or Modbus (mostly serial).
- Limited support for automation. Some auto-reclosers included local control capability, as did some capacitor controllers and some distribution feeder controllers. However, the majority of field devices examined connected only to the field RTU or IED.

Luckily, field devices tend to rely almost exclusively on 61850 or serial Modbus or DNP3 communications for automation, utilizing the upstream controller for all operator interaction. As a result, unnecessary network services such as HTTP, SMTP, SSH, FTP are rarely found in field devices.

⚠ Compromise of distribution field devices

The compromise of field controllers and/or field devices in the distribution network could result in almost any type of consequences ranging from inefficiencies in operations, to inaccuracies in reported data and to outages. For example, auto-reclosers are designed to protect against power surges and to recover once conditions are normal.

Manipulation of line conditions could cause a recloser to trip unnecessarily. The result would cascade throughout the distribution system. A truck might be dispatched to repair a fault that doesn't exist, for example. At the same time, a recloser might be compromised and taken offline while open, locking remote control and requiring a truck roll to restore power where there otherwise wouldn't have been an outage.

Complete compromise of an RTU could allow a cyber attacker to insert malicious logic into the controller. Consider a scenario where a cyber hacker breaches the power distribution of a neighborhood with certain demographics. Malware within a field RTU could cause random, intermittent failures, while normal conditions are reported back to DMS and central D-SCADA systems—effectively disrupting power distribution to a target area. This could be a nuisance attack or something more consequential. If politically motivated, the attack might be used to disrupt power to voting facilities in opposing political territories. Stronger motives could attempt to coordinate power outages in police or emergency response centers during a terrorist incident

False indications of outages could instigate a storm-level response scenario, again for relatively benign reasons or highly sinister intent. The potential for disruption gets worse when you consider the many tangential systems that are reachable via the distribution network, specifically advanced metering.

Metering and AMI

While advanced metering will be discussed in detail later in this chapter (see "Metering Infrastructure"), it's important to note that advanced metering headends are often located in distribution substations. This is because advanced metering, demand-response systems, and distribution are closely interdependent systems. A successful cyber attack on a distribution device could therefore be the first step in a staged attack against the AMI.

Advanced metering architecture

In legacy power systems, analog meters measured usage at the demarcation of the home or business. The meter lacked any advanced communication capability, requiring a human to visit and read each and every meter (many modern meters provide contact-free collection of information, but a human still must be in close proximity). While analog meters could be "hacked" by manipulating the magnetic resistance that controlled the analog meter dials, the result of such an attack was isolated to the source (and also fairly easy to detect). Smart Grids add considerable sophistication to metering, and as such they utilize new "smart meters" that not only measure energy utilization, but can also be used to remotely connect or disconnect meters. Smart meters are able to receive commands and communicate utilization to and from a centralized system, eliminating the need for a human meter reader.

This is accomplished by the advanced metering infrastructure (AMI). AMI systems are utilized by many energy, water, and gas utilities. AMI architecture consists of three primary components: smart meters, a communication network, and an AMI server or headend. [13]

The smart meter is a digital meter consisting of a few key elements:

- A solid-state meter for real-time data collection
- A microprocessor and local memory to store and transmit digital meter measurements.
- A communication network often including a home network connection for home automation and other advanced in-home services.

As with any device, the presence of a microprocessor and memory equates to some degree of risk. Depending upon the complexity of the code and the maturity of the smart meter vendor's secure coding practices, it may be possible to compromise the meter directly.

Smart metering also requires interconnectivity of smart meters, which may be deployed by the millions. As such, a highly scalable communication network is required. A variety of network technologies are used in AMI systems, including broadband over power line (BPL), power line communications (PLC), radio networks, or telecommunications (landline, cellular, paging, etc.) networks. [13]

Smart meters communicate, ultimately, to the AMI headend. A headend will typically consist of an AMI server, which is primarily responsible for collection of meter data, and a meter data management system (MDMS), which manages that data and shares it with demand response systems, historians, billing systems, and other systems. [13]

Smart meters are also closely connected to in-home systems such as home energy management systems (HEMS), interfacing with both HEMS and in home devices (IHDs) via a home area network (HAN)—primarily as a means of home power efficiencies. This can include enabling the home power consumer to purchase energy when the pricing is low and store it as a reserve against periods where rates are higher, rather than relying solely on time-of-use management and improved in-home energy monitoring. [14] In-home systems vary widely in the design, devices, and technologies, and therefore fall outside the scope of this book. However, they are discussed briefly below under "In-home Systems," because they are an interconnected system and should be considered both an attack surface and a potential vector of attack to AMI and distribution systems.

An assessment of commercially available smart meters found several common features and capabilities, mostly around network connectivity and manageability. Network interfaces, including IEC 61107 optical ports, RS232, RS485 serial ports, modems (typically GSRM or CDMA), ZigBee, and others. Diagnostic ports are often infrared or short-range wireless interfaces to enable easy connectivity to digital meter readers and diagnostics tools carried by a technician.

Remote management and configuration capability are often provided via a dedicated software system, providing meter configuration, as well as utilization and demand assessment, load profiling, disconnect capability, and other capabilities. These remote management systems are typically software based and installed on a utility-owned Windows computing platform. If installed on an unsecured server, these systems could be compromised, providing direct access to the configuration of entire smart meter fleets.

Looking at AMI headends, collection and MDMS systems are also typically software based, utilizing utility-owned Windows computing platforms. In addition, most MDMS systems utilize commercial relational database management systems (RDBMS). The use of an uncontrolled commercial operating system introduces the risk of OS vulnerabilities, especially as deployed systems age—just like with SCADA servers, gateways, controllers, and other devices throughout the Smart Grid; these systems, while relatively new at the moment, can be expected to operate over many years, and there distributed nature and real-time operation makes patching difficult. In addition, the use of commercial databases to store collected data presents the risk of a database attack. Either risk represents a vulnerability to the AMI and all underlying systems, such as demand-response and billing systems.

⚠ Compromise of the smart meter

Smart meters can be physically hacked to provide the same metering manipulation that could be had from analog meters using magnets and wire. Smart meters may be hacked by directly accessing on board memory, connecting to diagnostics ports, or via any available network interface(s). Security researcher Brian Krebs points to the use of common optical converter hardware, available for a few hundred dollars online, to access optical diagnostic ports on smart meters. Krebs also cites an FBI report that indicates this type of meter manipulation could lead to hundreds of millions of dollars of losses, as meters are altered to fraudulently under-report utilization.[15]

Smart meters could also be subject to DoS style attacks to prevent communication to the AMI (and therefore to billing and demand-response systems), also incurring losses to the utility. The nature of the DoS obviously varies by the AMI network being utilized: for cellular based systems, downloadable war-dialing tools could be used; both cellular and radio networks can be jammed; and more sophisticated standards such as ZigBee can be exploited using readily available tools such as the Metasploit Framework.

⚠ Compromise of AMI

Because most AMI headends utilize Windows-based applications, a variety of network-based OS and application layer attacks could compromise the headend. Why attack the headend? A successful Windows exploit on an MDMS server would provide unauthorized control over all aspects of AMI, including the representation of AMI data to other systems and the messaging and communication of AMI. Manipulation of the AMI communication network could manipulate AMI data in transit, introduce rogue or faulty data, or prevent the transmission of authorized data. This could be used to alter readings, prevent the remote disconnect of a rogue meter, or force a remote disconnect to a targeted meter—preventing electricity from being delivered to a specific target such as a hospital, airport, or other facility. Database exploits would allow direct manipulation of historical meter information or readings, but could also be used as a launching point to obtain additional access to AMI components or to propagate to other databases such as billing and customer management systems. These systems contain customer information ranging from usage profiles to billing information and represent a significant privacy concern.

In-home systems

In-home systems have not been included in the diagrams and are only briefly mentioned here. This book will not delve into the vulnerability and security of in-home devices, smart appliances, HEMS, electric vehicle charging stations, and other in-home devices (IHDs), focusing instead on the Grid infrastructure up to the home demarcation point (the smart meter). However, HEMS, IHDs, and the HANs that interconnect them do need to be acknowledged as a potential vulnerability to both the larger grid infrastructure and personal information (see Chapter 4, "Privacy concerns with the Smart Grid"). Here, we will simply acknowledge in-home systems and how they interconnect with the larger infrastructure:

- Home area networks (HANs) represent any in-home communication. Like a local area network (LAN), wide area network (WAN), or metro area network (MAN), a HAN defines the scope of the network itself rather than the devices it interconnects.
- Home energy management systems (HEMS) provide a system to monitor, manage, and automate in-home energy usage. HEMS interface with IHDs via the HAN, the AMI, and even distribution and utility back-office systems. HEMS may be located in-home as an end-user operated server, but are commonly managed Web interfaces or cloud-based systems.
- Smart appliances and in-home devices (IHDs) imbue residential appliances both large and small with intelligence, allowing HEMS to monitor and control in home power usage.
- Private generation, such as residential solar or wind generation, can be considered extremely small-scale instances of distributed generation. While they may be too small to justify large degrees of automation, they will still essentially follow the generation architectures discussed earlier in this chapter. Electric vehicle charging stations may also have the ability to sell power back to the grid and can be considered an in-bound energy source to the larger grid.

Microgrids

Microgrids are integrated energy systems that are typically used either in campuses and communities that are either remote or require sufficient load to justify local generation and distribution or in military or critical industries where a private and segmented and secured energy facility is required. Microgrids may operate in parallel with the public grid, or they may run in isolation. According to Pike's Research, "a Microgrid is really just a small-scale version of the traditional power grid that the vast majority of electricity consumers in the developed world rely on for power service today. Yet the smaller scale of Microgrids results in far fewer line losses, a lower demand on transmission infrastructure, and the ability to rely on more localized sources of power generation."[16] At the same time, Microgrids are often deployed for specific purposes, such as military mobile electric power initiatives, which deploy Microgrids in theaters of operation to support military activities. According to the United States Army Program Executive Office for Command, Control and Communications-Tactical (PEO C3T), "A 1-megawatt, or MW, Microgrid will replace 22 of the complex's generator sets with just four larger sets, simplifying maintenance as well as cutting fuel consumption, Bolton said. Another 180-kW, or kW, Microgrid configuration will not replace any of the remaining 74 generators, but will allow up to six of them to communicate and turn on and off in response to demand."[17] This makes Microgrids a viable solution to the issue of providing energy in the battlefield.

Even in non-mobile and civilian applications, Microgrids represent a solution to challenges of long-range transmission while increasing efficiency and reliability of energy to remote facilities. Their small scale facilitates upgrades and enhancements to the infrastructure, making it easier and more cost-effective to implement and maintain a "Smart Microgrid" than it is to deploy a full-scale public Smart Grid.

In terms of the Smart Grids in the larger sense, Microgrids represent the same technologies, systems, vulnerabilities, and cyber security challenges—although the physical location of the attacker is much more concise, these Microgrids do not have large, geographically distributed WANs as part of their architecture. In terms of Smart Grid architecture in the context of this book, Microgrids operating in parallel with the larger Grid can be considered as both independent grids—consisting of generation, transmission, distribution, and metering—as well as distributed generation facilities to the larger grid.

System interdependencies

This book, like any discussion on Smart Grid cyber security, will continuously revisit the interconnectivity and interdependency of the many systems that comprise a Smart Grid. The reason is simple: Interdependency and interconnectivity represent digital communication and data exchange, which in turn represent a vector for attack or a vector of propagation through which a successful attack can spread to other systems. The interconnectivity itself is complex—as is evident in Figure 2.13 (a reprint of NISTIR 7628 Figure 2.3). Rather than recreate these complex inter relationships here, this book will take a high degree of system-to-system communication and interdependency as a given, and will discuss specifics only as examples of attack vectors and vulnerabilities, deferring to the published reference models of NIST, the IEEE, and other groups for comprehensive mappings. However, understanding the

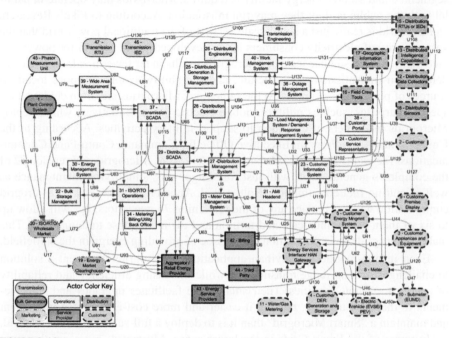

FIGURE 2.13

NIST Smart Grid logical reference model (Reprinted from NISTIR 7628 Figure 2.3 as public information.).[18]

interrelationships of the many systems within the overall Smart Grid infrastructure is necessary when planning to implement cyber security controls, and it is therefore necessary to consider these dependencies within an appropriate cyber security model (see Chapter 5, "Smart Grid Cyber Security Models"). Excerpted architectural models from NISTIR have been included in both Chapter 5 and Chapter 10, "Reference Architectures," for convenience. In addition, both NISTIR 7628 and IEEE 2030–2011 are also listed in Appendix B, "Continued Reading."

Protocols

Most industrial protocols play a part within the Smart Grid to some degree, as the Smart Grid is a system of multiple constituent systems—many of which are industrial control systems. Most protocols—including DNP3, Modbus, OPC, ICCP (TASE.2), Profibus, Profinet, EtherNet/IP, et al.—will not be addressed in-depth within this book, however, as they are well documented elsewhere and are not exclusive to a Smart Grid (see, "Industrial Network Security: Securing Critical Infrastructure Networks for Smart Grid, SCADA and Other Industrial Control Systems" by Eric

Knapp, one of the authors of this book, for more information about these protocols). While certainly not the only protocols in use within the grid, the IEEE C37.118, IEC 62351, IEC 61850, and ZigBee are of particular interest, and have special relevance to the Smart Grid.

IEEE C37.118

The Institute of Electrical and Electronics Engineers C37.118–2005 standard covers the synchronization and communication of phasor measurements, superseding the legacy IEEE 1344–1995 standard for synchronized phasor measurements. The standardization of phasor measurements is important as it allows multiple measurements to be synchronized together to obtain overall power quality assessments. Because an isolated phasor measurement has little value, the synchronization of multiple measurements, as well as the communication of multiple synchronized measurements is also defined, the real-time communications of a measurement from a PMU to a phasor data concentrator (PDC). Synchronization is accomplished by tagging each measurement with an absolute time reference, such as a GPS clock. C37.118 communication can occur over any medium, with serial and Ethernet being common implementations. The protocol requires a CRC to ensure integrity and specifies default port numbers for use over IP (4712 for TCP and 4713 for UDP) and can consist of several frame types.[19] Data frames communicate the phasor measurements along with some additional information to help manage measurements in the PDC when a large numbers of PMUs are being aggregated, but there are also configuration frames, command frames, and header frames. Configuration frames describe current PMUs, while command frames can make changes to PMU.[19] Header frames provide PMU details in a human-readable format and are analogous to the application banners used in fingerprinting, vulnerability assessment, and other penetration testing techniques.[19] C37.118 therefore represents a similar challenge to other industrial control protocols: It lacks inherent security and provides intrinsic mechanisms to obtain data or impose control. Without sufficient compensatory protection of the PMUs and PDCs, as well as their inter communications, phasor measurements can be easily intercepted or manipulated.

Phasor measurement can represent information transfer and management challenges. The measurements themselves do occupy bandwidth, although being a lightweight protocol a single PMU is unlikely to generate excessive data rates. However, the widely distributed nature of PMUs may also necessitate low-bandwidth connectivity, and so it is a factor. More challenging will be the utilization of phasor measurements within the context of security analysis: While a PDC is designed to assess large amounts of inbound data, security information and event management tools are already burdened with potentially hundred or thousands of other data sources throughout the infrastructure and adding phasor data to that could be a challenge (see Chapter 7, "Situational Awareness"). For example, "… a phasor reporting rate of 60 phasors/for a voltage, 5 currents, 5 W measurements, 5 VAR measurements, frequency, and rate of change of frequency—all reporting as floating point values—will require a bandwidth of 64,000 bps. On the other hand, data reporting rate of 12 phasors/s for 1 voltage, 5 currents, and frequency—reported in 16 bit integer format—can be accommodated over a 4800 bps channel."[20] This will also result in 60 events per second or 12 events per second of sustained messaging to a security management tool, per PMU.

IEC 62351 and IEC 61850

IEC 62351 provides security specifications for substation communications and is broken down into several parts. 62351-3 requires transport layer security (TLS) for all TCP/IP based communications, as well as node and message authentication. 62351-4 covers manufacturing message specification (MMS) and again requires authentication and TLS. 62351-6 concerns the security of 61850 messaging, which is of particular interest.[21] IEC 61850 provides data modeling, reporting, data transfer and command capability, as well as event messaging using GSE (GOOSE/GSSE) and for the storage of substation configuration data using the substation configuration language (SCL). The 61850 standard does not include security specifications of its own, deferring to IEC 62351-6. Some 61850 communications are relevant to 62351-3, requiring TLS and authentication. Some, such as GOOSE messaging, operates at layer 2 for performance reasons. Encryption is not supported because it would be impossible to maintain GOOSE's 4ms performance requirement, so VLANs (also a layer 2 capability) are used for protection, using two reserved fields within the PDU to establish a digital signed authentication value.[22] Note that this raises additional concerns, as VLANs are not a valid security control: VLAN IDs are easily spoofed, allowing an attacker to easily "hop" between VLANs, bypassing layer 3 network controls.

ZigBee

ZigBee is also a predominant standard for smart energy management, home automation and many other services, and is supported by many smart meters. ZigBee is a standards-based wireless technology managed by the ZigBee alliance and is specifically designed for low-cost, low-power wireless applications. ZigBee is designed for use across many industries and application, and as such "connects the widest variety of devices" giving "unprecedented control of the devices."[23] The ubiquitous use of ZigBee combined with readily available information about the standard and the "unprecedented control" that ZigBee provides makes it of particular interest regarding cyber security.

SUMMARY

The Smart Grid is a very complex collection of systems that are highly intelligent and communicative. The combination of prolific measurement and monitoring produces large amounts of valuable data throughout all areas of generation, transmission, distribution, and metering. In order for this data to be used by many advanced systems—including the automation of many T&D functions, as well as advanced metering capabilities such as remote disconnect, demand-response, and billing automation—new communication networks must be established between these devices. By looking at each area of the Smart Grid, and by taking a close look at the devices that comprise each system and the networks that interconnect them, the overall vulnerability of the Smart Grid is evident. Many devices pose significant cyber security risks due to unnecessary use of ports and services, and because most systems are interconnected, the exploitation of one device could allow an attacker to migrate to other more critical systems. Individual exploitations can easily be used to launch larger, more sophisticated attacks against the Smart Grid (see Chapter 3, "Hacking the Smart Grid").

References

1. Knapp Eric. *Industrial network security: securing critical infrastructure network for Smart Grid, SCADA, and other industrial control systems*. Waltham, MA: Syngress; 2011.
2. Ombello Carlo. *Nuclear vs solar: clash of the numbers* [document on the Internet]; August 2010. <http://www.opportunityenergy.org/?p=215> [cited July 2012].
3. Nuclear Energy Institute. *US nuclear power plants* [document on the Internet]; <http://www.nei.org/resourcesandstats/nuclear_statistics/usnuclearpowerplants/> [cited July 2012].
4. US CERT. *Control systems security program (CSSP), industrial control systems cyber emergency response team* [document on the Internet]; <http://www.us-cert.gov/control_systems/ics-cert> [cited July 2012].
5. Lagner Ralph. In *2011 ACS conference*, September 21, Washington DC; 2011.
6. Sorebo Gilbert N, Echols Michael C. *Smart Grid security: an end-to-end view of security in the new electrical Grid*. Boca Raton, FL: CRC Press; 2011.
7. Fisher Dennis. *Attack tool released to exploit SSL DoS issue*. Threat post [document on the Internet]; October 2001. <http://threatpost.com/en_us/blogs/attack-tool-released-exploit-ssl-dos-issue-102411> [cited July 2012].
8. Common Vulnerabilities and Exposures. *CVE-2011-3389* [document on the Internet]; <http://www.cve.mitre.org/cgi-bin/cvename.cgi?name=CVE-2011-3389> [cited July 2012].
9. United States Department of Energy. ICS-ALERT-12-046-01—Increasing threat to industrial control systems, February 2012.
10. Stenbakken Gerard., Nelson Tom. Gaithersburg, MD: National Institute of Standards and Technology; Zhou Ming., Virgilio Centeno. Virginia Polytechnic Institute and State University. Reference values for dynamic calibration of PMUs. Blacksburg, VA.
11. IEEE Power System Relaying Committee Working Group D6. *Power swing and out-of-step considerations on transmission lines*, IEEE; 2005.
12. McDonald John. *P.E. Substation automation basics—the next generation*. Electric energy online [document on the Internet]. <http://www.electricenergyonline.com/?page=show_article&mag=43&article=321> [cited July 2012].
13. EPRI. *Advanced metering infrastructure (AMI)*. Palo Alto, California; 2007.

14. HEMS Technology. *Energy efficiencies in a home energy management system (HEMS)* [document from the Internet]; August 9, 2010. <http://hemstech.com/blog/?p=66> [cited october 2, 2012].

15. Brian Krebs. *FBI: smart meter hacks likely to spread* [document on the Internet]; April 2012. <http://krebsonsecurity.com/2012/04/fbi-smart-meter-hacks-likely-to-spread/> [cited July 2012].

16. Pike Research. *Abstract of microgrids: distributed energy systems for campus, military, remote, community, and commercial & industrial power applications: market analysis and forecasts.* Navigant Consulting, Inc. 1Q, 2012 [document from the Internet]. <http://www.pikeresearch.com/research/microgrids> [cited October 3 2012].

17. Schwerin Claire Heininger. *Army deploys microgrids in Afghanistan for "smart" battlefield power.* United States Army PEO C3T. [document from the Internet]; June 28 2011. <http://www.army.mil/article/60709/> [cited October 3 2012].

18. The Smart Grid Interoperability Panel—Cyber Security Working Group. *NISTIR 7628 guidelines for Smart Grid cyber security: vol. 1, Smart Grid cyber security strategy, architecture, and high-level requirements.* US Department of Commerce, National Institute of Standards and Technologies; August 2010.

19. Martin KE, Hamai D, Adamiak MG, Anderson S, Begovic M, Benmouyal G, Brunello G, Burger J, Cai JY, Dickerson B, Gharpure V, Kennedy B, Karlsson D, Phadke AG, Salj J, Skendzic V, Sperr J, Song Y, Huntley C, Kasztenny B, Price E. Exploring the IEEE standard C37.118–2005. *IEEE Trans Power Deliv*, 2008;**23**(4).

20. Adamiak Mark, Premerlani William, Kasztenny Bogdan. *Synchrophasors: definition, measurement, and application* [document on the Internet]. <http://www.gedigitalenergy.com/multilin/products/synchrophasors/synchrophasors.pdf> [cited October 5 2012].

21. IEC Technical Specification 62351–1. *Power systems management and associated information exchange—data and communications security Part 1: communication network and system security—Introduction to security issues.* Geneva, Switzerland: International Electrotechnical Commission (IEC); 2007.

22. IEC Technical Specification 62351–6. *Power systems management and associated information exchange—data and communications security Part 6: Security for IEC 61850.* Geneva, Switzerland: International Electrotechnical Commission (IEC); 2007.

23. The ZigBee Alliance. *About ZigBee* [document from the Internet]. <http://www.zigbee.org> [cited July 2012].

Hacking the Smart Grid

INFORMATION IN THIS CHAPTER:

- Motive
- Identifying a target
- Vulnerability
- Attack tools
- Attack methods

Now that we have an understanding of Smart Grid architecture (see Chapter 2) and we can start examining Smart Grid attack methodology. Depending upon the motive of the attacker and the target of the attack, the exact methods of attack may vary.

Understanding the motives of the attacker and the inherent vulnerabilities of the systems helps to determine exactly how an attacker might approach, assess, and breach a Smart Grid. As with any cyber attack, there are well-defined steps to hacking a Smart Grid. Starting with reconnaissance and then scanning, the architecture of the grid can begin to be mapped—the aid of open-source intelligence can greatly simplify this important first step. Then—once a target system is identified—enumeration, penetration, and infection occur. Once breached, the attacker can continue to enumerate and propagate, spreading the infection among any or all interconnected systems, or use these systems to "pivot" into other isolated systems. Because some of the prime targets of a Smart Grid cyber attack include data residing in back-office or control room systems, it is often the blended attack that is of the most concern.

> **NOTE**
>
> As mentioned in the Introduction, the authors have to pay five US dollars or five British pounds every time they mention the first malware to target an industrial control system by its name (St****t). However, it's hard not to do so in a chapter on attacking the Smart Grid, so the word has been censored in consideration of the authors' personal finances.

Motive

Because a Smart Grid is so complex and diverse, cyber attacks against the Smart Grid are most easily classified by their intent. The most common motives for a cyber attack against a grid infrastructure are the theft of information for profit or reconnaissance, and denial of service, either as a means to sabotage the grid itself, or to impede the business processes of the operator, which could be part of a much larger blended attack. By looking at attacks by motive rather than attack process, a broader risk assessment can be determined. Similarly, remediation of those risks can occur at a higher level, by attempting to eliminate motive as the first step in a broader effort to protect against specific attack methodologies (see "Attack Methods" later in this chapter).

For example, if personal and financial information about consumers is accessible from the advanced metering infrastructure, threats against AMI can be disincentivized by isolating, encrypting, or otherwise disassociating this target data from the AMI infrastructure.

Theft of information

There is a lot of valuable information housed within the nebulae of a Smart Grid. Personal information about Smart Grid consumers—such as finance and billing information—is available from CRM and billing systems, for example. Similarly, information about energy consumption can be obtained from the advanced metering infrastructure and from other components of the Smart Grid and used to derive additional personal information. The privacy risk of the Smart Grid is considerable enough to justify a more in-depth discussion in Chapter 4, "Privacy."

In addition to personal information, the SCADA and automation systems within the grid also provide a blueprint to the inner workings of the grid operations. This is valuable intellectual property that could be used for malicious purposes ranging from

---

NOTE

What is "Risk?" Risk is a function of: (1) a given threat against a physical or logical asset; (2) exercising one or more vulnerabilities against a targeted asset; and (3) the consequences that could result from the successful execution of the threat against the targeted asset. Each function of risk is in itself complex. The threat is similarly complex: (1) it must be initiated by a malicious actor or attacker—who must possess capability, motive, and opportunity; (2) there must be an accessible threat vector through which the attacker can initiate the attack; and (3) there must be an identified target asset. When evaluating risk, it is important to consider both the "logical" asset and the "physical" asset. For example, the AMI may be the physical asset, but the real target might be the logical assets such as personal data about the end user, financial information. It is one of the most important and difficult challenges in Smart Grid cyber security to protect both physical and logical assets, as a vulnerability in either one can impact the safety and reliability of the other.

the influence of energy trading to the development of a targeted, weaponized attack against the grid infrastructure or against the grid operator and/or their customers.

Denial of service

One of the most basic attacks remains the denial-of-service attack. In today's networks—with high-bandwidth, high-performance end systems, and modern operating systems—a denial-of-service attack can require some orchestration. Even something as simple as oversubscribing a network interface can present scalability issues. Distributed denial-of-service attacks, where large number of infected systems are used in a coordinated attack, are necessary in many cases. When the systems are publically facing, such as a corporate web server or VoIP service, attackers can easily rise to this challenge by spreading malware as prolifically as possible through the Internet. With millions of home computers connected to dedicated broadband Internet access, the resources at an attacker's disposal are virtually limitless.

Once again, however, the Smart Grid—especially the SCADA and industrial control systems used within the Smart Grid—is different. Ideally, they are not (supposed to be) publicly accessible, which is an added obstacle to an attacker; at the same time, they are also not "modern" systems—many are running outdated and unpatched operating systems, over lower-bandwidth networks, and supporting real-time and very fragile industrial protocols.

The nature of many Smart Grid systems, therefore, makes them much more susceptible to a denial-of-service attack. All attackers need to do sufficiently influence the network—injecting traffic, performing an aggressive scan, or even something as simple as duplicating an existing IP address—and they can potentially interrupt that service. One attack, presented at the Digital Bond S4 conference in 2010 used a simple wireless jammer to cause an 802.11 discovery cascade to disrupt industrial systems.[1] The attack didn't target the ICS at all, but rather the networking infrastructure around it, knowing that the result could accomplish the same goal.

The Smart Grid complicates this scenario by combining the relative fragility of SCADA and ICS systems with an attack surface that rivals the Internet itself. However, unlike the Internet, security measures implemented to protect this network

---

NOTE

Industrial protocols in and of themselves represent a challenge to cyber security. These protocols—EtherNet/IP, DNP3, ICCP IEC 61850, IEC 60870, Modbus, OPC (classic and unified architecture), and others—are designed to operate in real time. By nature, many of these protocols are sensitive to latency, and what would be a minor IT event in a business network could cause an interruption in service in automated Smart Grid systems. Because most of these protocols provide command and control functionality to the system, an interruption could result in the failure of substation automation, dynamic load management, fault isolation, and even protection systems. For more details on other Industrial Control Protocols, refer to "Industrial Network Security: Securing Critical Infrastructure Networks for Smart Grid, SCADA, and other Industrial Control Systems."

will typically reside in the hands of the grid operator and not an experience service provider (ISP). Therefore, it is now possible to choreograph distributed attacks against these critical communications systems. This could pose particular risks to substation automation systems, where distributed denial-of-service attacks are perpetrated inbound over long-range wireless frequencies, or even through the advanced metering infrastructure. Where cellular connectivity is provided (such as is common for Smart Meters) war-dialing attacks could be used as a denial-of-service attack against the metering infrastructure. For field devices within the distribution system, cellular, satellite, and radio, vectors could be used.

Because the "service" of a Smart Grid is ultimately the delivery of energy, manipulating the systems within the Smart Grid can cause an outage—such as spoofing a GPS time source to bring a line out of phase and trip protection circuits, or faking an outage to trick an EMS into routing power around a service area—to effectively create a "denial of service" of energy. In other words, rather than a traditional DoS or DDoS, we have a manipulation of service that prevents utility service to the end user. For example, by manipulating demand load measurements, it could appear that less power is required in a given area than what is actually needed. This could cause service to be re-routed elsewhere, and potentially bring down swing units—effectively causing a brownout and general grid instability in a target area.

Manipulation of service

The difference between denial of service and manipulation of service is subtle but important. Where denial-of-service attempts to make a network or device unavailable to its operators, the goal of a manipulation of service is to preserve the availability of a service while effecting or altering its operation. Rather than preventing the service from functioning at all, it manipulates it. Examples of manipulation of service include very simple attacks, such as spoofing GPS time synchronization to de-synchronize distribution phasor readings, to very complex attacks, such as the St****t attack, which penetrated and altered the specific control instructions in both SCADA and ICS field systems—the same types of systems used in substation automation, distributed generation and other Smart Grid systems.

Because the Smart Grid is built upon a foundation of real-time measurement within and between many interconnected systems, manipulation is often as easy as the example above: a particular measurement is altered to impact whatever system(s) rely upon that data (this is covered in more detail below under "Setting Phasors to Kill"). Examples of manipulated data and the systems that the attack could impact are provided in Table 3.1.

Note that the manipulation of some data sources could be catastrophic: by manipulating the low- and high-voltage sides of a transformer (either by directly or by tricking an operator or automated program by providing false measurements), an arc condition can quickly overheat coils, boil the mineral oil used as insulation, and cause a massive explosion. Other results could be relatively benign, such as billing errors, or the dispatch of a field services crew to repair a "good" line that is being measured as "bad." In a study of transformer failures by the International Association

Table 3.1 The Impact of Smart Grid Measurements on Operations

Target Device/ Measurement	Available Measurements	Impact
Yard protection	• Feeder measurements (overcurrent, undercurrent) • Voltage/frequency • Power swing detection • Impedance/faults • Relay state/trip/close • Inter-relay communication (61850)	• Yard safety • Device condition/lifespan of transformers, relays and other systems • Load management systems • Line safety and protection systems
Transformers	• Voltage/frequency	• Yard safety • Energy management systems • Transmission/distribution voltage (step-up/step-down operations) • Load management systems • Line safety
Synchrophasors	• Phasor measurement unit/ power quality • Phasor synchronization/ GPS time	• Transformer safety • Protection systems • Load management systems
Energy management systems	• Current load • Historical load profiles	• Load management systems • Fault management systems • Advanced metering • Billing
Reclosers	• Fault/close	• Fault management systems • Field response management • End-user availability/disruption of distribution
Volt/VAR	• Voltage • VAR (volt-amp-reactive) • Capacitor state	• Available voltage • Load management systems
Advanced metering	• Consumption (energy, gas, water)	• Meter data management systems • Billing systems • Customer information systems • Demand response systems
Events and alarms	• Faults, events, alarms, and other device- or system-initiated messages	• All information, event and alarm management systems

of Engineering Insurers, research shows that nearly 15% of transformer failures in a year are attributed to overloading, improper operation, or surges[2]—all of which could occur as the result of manipulated energy system measurements.

Identifying a target

One of the first steps in a cyber attack is to identify a target. Because of the complexity of the Smart Grid and the many interconnected systems that comprise it, there are many targets to choose from, and many systems that could be targeted as a beachhead with which to reach additional targets. Table 3.2 lists several primary and secondary targets, as derived from NISTIR 7628 Infrastructure diagrams. Please note that this list is far from complete: it is intended to highlight the number of systems that can be used as targets and attack vectors throughout the Smart Grid.

Table 3.2 Possible Targets and Vectors

System	Target	Additional Physical & Logical Assets
Advanced metering infrastructure	AMI headend	Other AMI systems: • Meter data management system • Customer information system • Load management system • Demand-response management system Customer systems: • Outage management system • Energy services interface/HAN gateway • Smart meter Distribution systems: • Distribution management system
Advanced metering infrastructure	Meter data management system	Other AMI SYSTEMS: • AMI headend Service provider systems: • Billing Distribution systems: Distribution management system
Advanced Metering Infrastructure	Distribution management system	Other AMI systems: • AMI headend • Meter data management system • Load management system • Demand-response management system Distribution systems: • Distribution SCADA Transmission systems: • Transmission SCADA

Table 3.2 Possible Targets and Vectors (Continued)

System	Target	Additional Physical & Logical Assets
Advanced metering infrastructure	Customer information system	Other AMI systems: • AMI Headend • Load Management System • Demand-Response Management System Distribution Systems: • Distribution Crew / Field Tools
Transmission	Transmission SCADA system	Other transmission systems: • Transmission RTUs • Transmission IEDs • Wide area measurement • PMU / PDC • Operator displays • Energy management system Distribution systems: • Distribution management system • Distribution RTUs • Distribution IEDs Bulk generation Systems Plant control systems
Transmission	Energy management system	Other transmission systems: • Transmission SCADA • Wide area measurement • Operator displays Distribution systems: • Distribution management system Bulk generation systems Plant control systems
Distribution	Distribution SCADA	Other distribution systems: • Distribution management system • Distribution field devices • Distributed generation & storage management • Bulk storage management • Metering/billing/utility back office systems Transmission systems: • Transmission SCADA Service provider systems: • Billing • Customer information system • Customer systems: • Energy services interface • HAN gateway

(Continued)

Table 3.2 Possible Targets and Vectors (Continued)

System	Target	Additional Physical & Logical Assets
Distribution	Distribution management system	Other distribution systems: • Distribution SCADA • Operator displays • Bulk storage management • Metering/billing/utility back office systems • Load management systems • Geographic information systems Transmission systems: • Transmission SCADA • Energy management system Service provider systems: • Billing • Customer information system Customer systems: • Customer energy management system • Energy services interface • HAN gateway

The interconnectedness of the Smart Grid is a particular challenge because of the potential ability for an attack to propagate easily between them—therefore almost any system becomes a viable target for attack. This is especially concerning when you can draw a line from a customer's in-home EMS, through the Distribution Management System, to T-SCADA systems all the way to the Bulk Energy Control System and G-SCADA. This large-scale distribution of systems makes it challenging to effectively segment these systems resulting in an architecture that makes is relatively easy for an attack to move between systems. It is therefore equally as important to manage and (where possible) mitigate "horizontal propagation" through the use of compensating security controls and countermeasures (see Chapter 6, "Securing the Smart Grid").

If any one of these target systems is connected to the Internet, of course targeting these systems becomes easy, which is why *every* major cyber security standard, regulation, or guidance document recommends that systems are never connected *directly* to a public network. While private or leased-line WANs are increasingly uncommon, the use of Virtual Private Networks (VPNs) over the shared WAN communications infrastructure (aka public networks) provides appropriate transport layer security and access controls. However, as recently as February 2012, the ICS-CERT released a report on the increasing threat to industrial control systems, citing the primary causes of concern as "… Internet accessible ICS configurations, vulnerability and exploit tool releases for ICS devices, and increased interest and activity by hacktivist groups and others."[3] The report went on to clearly state its intent "to inform critical infrastructure and key resource (CIKR) asset owners and operators of recent and ongoing activity concerning increased risk to CIKR assets, particularly Internet accessible control systems."[3] Unfortunately, this guidance is necessary as ICS components in many industries continue to be insufficiently protected from Internet access. Combined with Internet search tools such as Shodan, which help identify Internet-connected devices by the services that they use, these devices are not only easy to hack, but also they are easy to find.

If systems are properly removed from the Internet, more traditional scanning will be needed to locate targets. However, in the Smart Grid, nothing is as easy as it seems. A SCADA server, a Phasor Data Concentrator (PDC), a recloser or some other Smart Grid device may be connected to an industrial grade Ethernet switch, segmented behind a router, a firewall and maybe even an Intrusion Prevention Systems (IPS). However, things get more difficult in the Smart Grid because there is a good chance that a purpose-built device will also utilize long-range or even global wide area network connectivity as a means of distribution communications or synchronization—such as a phasor measurement unit (PMU)'s C37.118 protocol, GPS-based network time protocols, satellite, microwave, radio, mesh wireless, and others. Further complicating things, we see a proliferation of devices utilizing integrated remote access servers in order to make it "easier" for technicians to obtain remote access to substation or field devices. While the business justification is sound (it is costly and time consuming to send technicians into the field when an issue could be resolved remotely), these systems become strong pivot points for cyber attacks. The easily accessible networks (wireless) are used to exploit the device, gain root, or admin access, and then use that device as the launching point to other systems—including other devices on the wired, wireless, and even serial networks. In other words, the entire system is at risk of compromise via the weakest component in the extensive, composite architecture.

So, while common attack methodologies apply to the Smart Grid—scan for a target, enumerate the target, identify vulnerabilities, and then exploit those vulnerabilities—the attack surface is much larger, and the number of inbound attack vectors is high. In addition, when application-layer protocols are used over TCP/IP, additional tricks can be used to identify and enumerate the participants in those protocols.

Scanning transmission and distribution infrastructure

Depending upon the nature of the target, the steps required to scan a Smart Grid target may require little if any variation from the standard hacking playbook, or they may be able to leverage scanning and enumeration techniques that are specific to world of SCADA and industrial controls. For example, if a T-SCADA server or gateway is built using commercial off-the-shelf components and a standard Windows OS, these systems can be easily identified using Nmap, enumerated via a vulnerability scan, and exploited using any number of relevant exploits within the Metasploit framework. If the target is running SCADA software, performing any sort of process automation, or communicating using a known industrial control protocol, there may be additional steps that can be taken to scan and enumerate deeper into the industrial control environment. In the context of the Smart Grid, this means that substation automation servers can be used to enumerate field devices, protection systems, and other devices, potentially mapping the entire grid.

To recap common scanning techniques, a tool (such as Nmap) is used to discover all endpoints on a TCP/IP network. Scanning a network typically begins with broad attempts to identify network devices and hosts using a ping sweep and then leveraging additional capabilities of the Internet Control Message Protocol (ICMP) to determine additional information, such as the network mask (which allows you to derive subnet information), open TCP and UDP ports (which allows you to identify operating services, as most services map to well-known ports). In industrial networks, network scanning works in much the same way. However, the results of the scan can indicate if the device is a SCADA or process control device by looking for common ports: port 102 is used by IEC 61850 messaging, C37.118 uses 4712 and 4713, 502 is Modbus TCP, 530 is RPC, 593 is HTTP RPC, 2222 or 4818 is Ethernet/IP, 4840 or 4843 indicates OPC UA over TLS/SSL, port 20000 is used by DNP3, ports 34,962 through 34,964 are used by Profinet, etc.[4]

So if you see a device communicating on port 502, it can be inferred that it is using Modbus TCP, and if you see ports 2222 or 44818, that the system is using the Common Industrial Protocol (CIP) over EtherNet/IP. Data seen on port 102 can be assumed to be substation automation controls or messaging, while port 4713 can be assumed to be a PMU measurement. It can be further inferred that a device using these ports as well as common "enterprise" ports and services like HTTP is a SCADA system, HMI, controller or other industrial control system asset.

With this knowledge, the scanning can continue at another level, using the identified industrial network protocol to further investigate the system. This works because most industrial protocols used in the Smart Grid and other control environments are based on a client-server messaging model. These models require that requests and acknowledgements be sent between devices, including information about the clients, their operating state, values within their registers (such as a phasor reading from a PMU or a power consumption reading from a smart meter), etc. It is therefore possible to perform a DNP3 request sweep in the same way that you perform a ping sweep. The requests solicit responses from active clients, identifying all of the DNP3 clients within the system.[5]

Again St****t has exemplified, the disruptive potential of this type of scanning. Once the St****t payload establishes itself into the Siemens PCS7 system, it was able to enumerate the Profibus devices remotely via the S7 communications driver, allowing it to "listen" to its surroundings and adapt accordingly. In the case of St****t, malicious code was only written to the PLC once a specific target device was identified, which it achieved by looking at the device identifiers within the Profinet packets. Profinet, like all industrial protocols, is used to communicate values and commands to these devices, so listening to the protocol can also determine the specific operational settings of that device.[6]

Today, it's easy. There are SCADA-specific scanning modules available within the widely used Nmap and Metasploit framework tools. On September 17, 2012, python code was made available online via https://code.google.com/p/plcscan/, providing a dedicated scanner for Modbus and S7 devices. These auxiliary modules simplify the fingerprinting of SCADA devices, directly from within the same tool that provides enumeration and exploit modules targeting those same systems. While not all inclusive at the time of this writing (at this time, there are 32 SCADA-specific exploit modules within Metasploit as well as 108 Nessus plugins to assess SCADA components for known vulnerabilities), the presence of such tools is indicative of a growing trend. SCADA and ICS systems used within the Smart Grid or other industries can no longer assume "security by obscurity," as the efforts of both black hat and white hat security researchers focus more heavily on industrial control. While researchers are still, for the most part, focusing their attention on the Windows-based platforms typical of the Server and HMI components, more and more research is shifting to the embedded controllers and endpoints that typically utilize non-Windows components.

Leveraging automation systems for enumeration

The protocols used by substation automation systems can also help to enumerate a target. Substation automation is, essentially, a function of T-SCADA and D-SCADA, utilizing the same protocols discussed above. This approach was used by a Project Basecamp researcher to enumerate an EtherNet/IP system. By capturing and analyzing CIP traffic, detailed knowledge about the device can be extracted from the CIP, including vendor and object identifiers, service requests, and more.[7] Basecamp was performed in a laboratory, with a known target device and readily available documentation, but the same process could have been performed to enumerate a device communicating on port 2222, as discovered by an Nmap scan.

Each industrial protocol utilizes its own function codes, and some proprietary function codes may be used on specific devices (necessitating some reconnaissance). However, by obtaining the vendor and device IDs, it is possible to research the exact device. In many cases, specific functions are documented online. In other instances, specific ICS devices have known vulnerabilities, and perhaps even exploit code—all available on the Internet. It should be noted that, while documentation typically exists for "open" protocols, the encryption or obfuscation of these protocols is often used by vendors. The resulting vendor-specific proprietary protocols—including the S7 protocol by Siemens, Honeywell's Control Data Access (CDA) protocol, and others—retain a somewhat greater degree of obscurity. These protocols are still susceptible to attack, however, despite efforts to maintain obscurity, additional efforts to obtain information about the protocols may be necessary.

Vulnerability

Once a target has been identified and enumerated within the Smart Grid, there are several specific attack methodologies that can be used to penetrate key systems, often by exploiting vulnerabilities in the same SCADA and control protocols used by transmission and distribution management systems, substation automation, EMS, etc.

Some of these vulnerabilities are specific to a device and require effort to identify and exploit. However, more and more Smart Grid systems are being analyzed and a growing number of disclosed vulnerabilities against these systems are being made publically available—often with corresponding exploit code. Worse still, as is the case described above, there are certain "vulnerabilities" that are inherent within the protocols used by these systems. These are not bugs or unintentional vulnerabilities that are the result of bad coding. They are simply the result of a command and control protocol that is functioning as designed. Unfortunately, this means that these vulnerabilities cannot be easily resolved because they are not specific to a single product or even vendor. To fix an inherent insecurity with a protocol like Modbus, for example, it would require significant re-engineering of the protocol itself, which in many cases would require a coordinated multi-vendor industry effort. While some organizations have done this—such as OPC UA and OPC XI, two variations of a "secure" OPC implementation—there is the added challenge of adoption. Similarly, the IEC has made efforts to secure substation infrastructures via the IEC 62351 standard, which recommends secure transport methods for TCP/IP-based substation communications. However, even if a protocol is made secure, the large installed base of legacy devices using the legacy protocols will ensure that many vulnerable systems will remain in the field, waiting to be exploited. Regardless of whether the vulnerability is product specific or inherent in the protocol operation, a vulnerability within the Smart Grid infrastructure can be exploited in numerous ways, including Man-in-the-Middle and network replay attacks. If a server is rooted, any variety of payloads can be executed within the Smart Grid.

Devices-specific vulnerabilities

Many Smart Grid devices possess vulnerabilities that can be determined through analysis and reverse engineering of that device. For example, by utilizing a variety of open source development and debugging tools a specific device can be fully analyzed—from surface vulnerability testing to code extraction, decompiling, and reverse engineering. The goal is to identify weaknesses in the development such as heap or stack overflows, which could allow malicious code to be executed by the target system. Many white hat tools and agencies exist to facilitate this process, such as Wurldtech Security Technologies, makers of the Achilles Test Platform, and the ISA Security Compliance Institute (ISCI). Achilles is a purpose-built testbed for the analysis of real-time and embedded devices using protocols including GOOSE (IEC 61850 messaging), RPC, EtherNet/IP, MODBUS/TCP, ZIGBEE (widely used in advanced metering and other in-home systems), OPC UA, and others.[8]

Again, the Basecamp disclosures of early 2012 included several device-specific vulnerabilities, resulting in several published exploits that can be used to target specific Smart Grid devices. From the banner of one such auxiliary Metasploit module:

```
# This module implements a CLI backdoor present in the General
Electric D20 Remote Terminal.
```

```
# Unit (RTU). This backdoor may be present in other General Electric
Canada control systems.

# Use with care. Interactive commands may cause the TFTP server to
hang indefinitely, blocking.

# The backdoor until the system is rebooted.
```

This module and others like it makes security assessment within a control environment easier, but also provides a powerful tool to attackers. As mentioned earlier, there are currently freely available Metasploit modules, NSE scripts for Nmap, dedicated scanning tools such as Modbus.py and other methods of Modbus scanning, enumeration, and exploitation.

Leveraging known vulnerabilities

Reverse engineering device code is an effective but resource-intensive method of identifying new vulnerabilities. For a large cyber weapon such as St****t, the use of zero-day vulnerabilities can ensure the successful delivery and execution of a malicious payload. However, in the post-St****t world, there are many well-known, fully disclosed ICS vulnerabilities. At the time of this writing, there are disclosed vulnerabilities for 3S, 7 Technologies, ABB, Advantech, AGG, Arbiter, ARC Informatique, AREVA, Atvise, Automated Solutions, AzeoTech, Beckhoff, Broadwin, Certec, Cisco, Cogent, COPA-DATA, Control Microsystems, Ecava, Emerson, Fultek, GarrettCom, General Electric, Honeywell, Intellicom, Iconics, Inductive Automation, InduSoft, Innominate, Invensys, IOServer, IRAI, Kessler-Ellis, Korenix, Koyo, Measuresoft, Microsys, Moxa, Ocean Data Systems, Open Automation Software, Optima, ORing, OSIsoft, PcVue, Pro-face, Progea, Real-Flex, Rockwell Automation, RuggedCom, SafeNet, Samsung, ScadaTEC, Schneider Electric, Schweitzer, Sielco Sistemi, Siemens, Sinapai, SpecView, Sunway, Technomatix, Tridium, Unitronics, VxWorks, Wago, WellinTech, Wonderware, and xArrow.[9]

Many of these vulnerabilities have been exploited either in a proof of concept environment or through the development of actual exploit code, making it extremely easy for intermediate hackers to develop new attack variants against these systems. At the time of this writing, there are 32 SCADA- and ICS-specific exploit modules for Metasploit. Metasploit includes modules to exploit systems from 18 vendors, including large ICS vendors such GE, Rockwell Automation, Schneider, and Siemens. Some of these modules extend beyond a single vendor, such as the ControlLogix Ethernet/IP exploit disclosed by Digital Bond in February of 2012. This module exploits inherent vulnerabilities in the Ethernet/IP, and therefore potentially impacts any or all products using Ethernet/IP. The ODVA currently indicates that there are 285 member companies, clearly indicating the prevalence of the Ethernet/IP. In addition, a more recent disclosure of 3S Software Gmbh's CoDeSys Control Runtime system could impact 261 additional ICS vendors and their controller products.[10] Any of these systems, if used within the Smart Grid, represent a vulnerable attack surface, and a vector through which many aspects of the grid can be attacked.

Inherent vulnerabilities in industrial protocols

As mentioned, many industrial protocols are vulnerable by design: the protocols themselves are designed to provide command and control, and often lack any compensating measures (such as encryption or authentication) to limit how that command and control capability is utilized. In 2012, the control system cyber security consulting and research firm Digital Bond initiated Project base Camp, which in their own words is "a research effort by Digital Bond and a team of volunteer researchers to highlight and demonstrate the fragility and insecurity of most SCADA and DCS field devices, such as PLC's and RTU's." The result was published vulnerability and exploit research against inherent vulnerabilities in General Electric, Schneider Electric, Koyo, Schneider Electric, Schweitzer Electronics, and Wago devices.[11]

Basecamp was and is a highly controversial project within the ICS cyber security community. According to Digital Bond, "Project Basecamp is attempting to be a Firesheep Moment for PLC's. The team has, not surprisingly, found many vulnerabilities in the PLC's, but perhaps more importantly have identified "insecure by design" issues that are actually much easier to leverage to affect the availability and integrity of a process ..." The key to making this a Firesheep Moment for PLC's is providing tools so any engineer, IT type, security professional, or anyone with a bit of computer skill can demonstrate just how fragile and vulnerable these PLC's are. It's beyond, PLC's are vulnerable. Basecamp provides the tools to show an executive just how easy it is to take down the SCADA or DCS."[11]

The "firesheep moment" is a reference to Eric Butler's Firefox extension that enabled HTTP session hijacking: an event that immediately raised HTTP security concerns by putting the tools in the hands of the community. However, with the criticality of the target industries at stake, Basecamp was condemned by many in the community as an act of irresponsible disclosure due to the fact that it failed to consider the impact of these vulnerabilities to the customers who have them deployed within their industrial processes. At the same time, many cyber security firms close to Basecamp lauded its initiative and desire to promote action.

One such example specifically exploited the EtherNet/IP to control a Rockwell Automation ControlLogix system. However, it should be noted that it was not a ControlLogix vulnerability that was exploited, but the underlying protocol, and as such this exploit is highly relevant due to the prevalence of the EtherNet/IP in industrial control systems. Basecamp researchers used a variety of network monitoring and reverse engineering tools to identify EtherNet/IP functions and object identifiers. As a result, several attack methods were disclosed[7]:

- *Forcing a system stop:* By sending a CIP command to the device, this attack effectively shuts off the CIP service and renders the device dead. This puts the device into a "major recoverable fault" state.[7]

- *Crashing the CPU:* This attack crashes the CPU due to a malformed CIP request, which cannot be effectively handled by the CIP stack. Again the result is a 'major recoverable fault' state.[7]
- *Dumping device boot code:* This is a CIP function that allows an EtherNet/IP device's boot code to be remotely dumped.[7]
- *Reset device:* This is a simple misuse of the CIP system reset function. The attack resets the target device.[7]
- *Crash device:* This attack crashes the target device due to a vulnerability in the device's CIP stack.[7]
- *Flash update:* CIP, like many industrial protocols, supports writing data to remove devices, including register and relay values, but also files. This attack misuses this capability to write new firmware to the target device.[7]
- Note that the Flash Update attack identified under Project Basecamp loosely mimics the behavior of St****t, which wrote new logic to a Siemens PLC in a similar fashion using the Profinet protocol. Surprisingly, many of these types of attacks are possible across many other ICS protocols, as they represent predefined function codes within the protocol.

Another example of inherent vulnerability involves the rash of recent vulnerabilities within the Siemens Simatic system. The Simatic Step 7 system is an "integral component part of the centralized Totally Integrated Automation Portal engineering framework. Thanks to complete integration into the centralized engineering framework, SIMATIC STEP 7 V11 has a uniform operator input concept across all automation tasks with shared services (e.g. configuration, communication, diagnostics), as well as automatic data consistency."[12] So, the Totally Integrated Automation (TIA) framework, like many SCADA system architectures, provides configuration, communication, and diagnostic capability. The TIA framework is based upon International Organization for Standardization Transport Service Access Point (ISO-TSAP), a protocol based on RFC 793 (Transmission Control Protocol) and RFC 791 (Internet Protocol) that make up TCP/IP. ISO-TSAP is therefore easy to monitor, record and manipulate—up to including the engineering and injection of new packets.[13]

ISO-TSAP is plain text, subjects to overflows, and gives absolute control over the SIMATIC system, allowing a manipulated, replayed, or injected packet to manipulate the configuration, communication, or diagnostics capabilities of TIA. This essentially allows TIA to inject malware into a Siemens SIMATIC system.[13]

Because ISO-TSAP is clear text, important information about the devices, commands and the process as a whole can either be directly extracted or derived from monitored packets.[13] Just as with EtherNet/IP, therefore, TIA can be used to obtain sensitive information such as:

- Intellectual property of the process (i.e. the industrial control "recipe").[13]
- Device identifiers, commands, and other information (for use in scanning and enumeration).[13]
- Diagnostic information about the system.[13]

> **NOTE**
>
> While this chapter focuses on attacks, and therefore upon vulnerabilities and exploits, it should be noted that Siemens has addressed many of the issues discussed here. In June 2012, Siemens released a family of communication processors providing point-to-point encryption and authentication between TIA components, and added additional integrity features to the S7 application code. As always, consult your vendor with questions or concerns about device or protocol vulnerabilities, as an important part of any cyber security assessment.

Turning a vulnerably into a compromise

When a vulnerability is identified—either through reverse engineering or through the disclosure of a vulnerability by another researcher—it can be used to build a targeted exploit. Even if a disclosed vulnerability does not include sample exploit, information about the vulnerability can allow an attacker to craft an attack to compromise the target system. SCADAhacker.com illustrates this process using the seven-Technologies IGSS (Interactive Graphical SCADA System) platform. In early 2011, researcher Luigi Auriemma published a service vulnerability of the IGSS platform.[14]

The IGSS system like most SCADA system provides graphical representation of a process. The user interface of the console provides both monitoring and control capability, allowing the operator of the console to trip protection relays, step-up or step-down voltages, etc. It also provides access to the necessary engineering toolkits or Software Development Environment (SDE) to create new logic.[15]

The vulnerability disclosed by Luigi Auriemma includes proof of concept code that proves the vulnerability without any malicious effect. Specifically, the exploit proof of concept code uses the IGSS_8b.dat to send a packet that executes the calculator.exe tool, causing the calculator to open on the console server. While the POC is benign, it is possible to take this same vulnerability and craft a malicious payload that can be executed in place of calculator.exe. In the SCADAhacker.com example, the Meterpreter tool (part of the Metasploit framework), is used to generate a payload and also to drop this new payload onto the IGSS server. Once a new payload is in place, the IGSS_8b.dat sends a packet to execute the new payload—effectively infecting the target with malware using the same disclosed vulnerability.[16]

In SCADAhacker's example, the payload is designed to establish a Meterpreter session to allow further exploitability via Metasploit. For example, Metasploit could be used to:

- Install callback malware, to establish persistence even a system is rebooted.[16]
- Scrape the server for credentials, providing hashes of all passwords, which can later be cracked or can be passed along as is to break further authentication.[16]
- Escalate privileges to provide greater control. Unfortunately, because many SCADA systems run as root or admin, full escalation can be achieved via a compromised SCADA system).[16]

- Create a remote VNC session to provide remote desktop access to the SCADA server providing unrestricted access to change configurations, alter operational graphics, and send commands to control devices.[16]

This last action effectively "pops the HMI," bringing the human-machine interface capability of IGSS console to a remote hacker's computer or laptop. Rather than launching a harmless calculator application, the vulnerability was used to obtain absolute command and control over the SCADA environment, where the attacker can do essentially anything he or she pleases.

Attack tools

There are many tools available, most of which are designed for use by security teams to test for and resolve specific vulnerabilities, or to perform in-depth security assessment tests. However, these same tools can easily be used by a malicious agent to facilitate all stages of a cyber attack. Most are well-known, general-purpose cyber security tools, although recently some Smart Grid specific tools have also been developed. It is important to become familiar with these tools and what they can do against the networks and systems of the Smart Grid.

General tools

Many commonly available tools are available to test for vulnerability and exploitability of digital information systems. Much has been written about tools such as Nmap for network scanning, the Social Engineering Toolkit (SET) for social engineering attacks, Nessus, Nexpose, and OpenVAS for host fingerprinting and vulnerability assessment, etc. In addition, frameworks for penetration testing and exploitation area also available. Metasploit, perhaps the best known exploitation toolkit, combines social engineering, scanning, enumeration, vulnerability assessment, and a variety of exploitation capabilities into a common framework. Metasploit includes several auxiliary modules for scanning and enumerating the systems used by generation, transmission, and distribution SCADA, making it particularly relevant to Smart Grid cyber security. Other penetration testing toolkits, such as Immunity's Canvas framework, which also include SCADA exploits. Gleg Ltd., a Moscow-based security firm, maintains the Agora SCADA+ Pack for Canvas. This toolkit promises 100% coverage of public vulnerabilities, bugs, zero-day SCADA exploits, weak point analysis of SCADA, industrial PCs, smart chips, and industrial protocols.[17] Nearly all of these tools and frameworks are available either as open-source or available in a "community" no-charge version.

Smart meter tools

Two tools are now available to hack smart meters through optical interfaces: SecureState's "Termineter" and InGuardians' "OptiGuard." The former is open-source, extensible and readily available to anyone, while the later is being provided in a controlled manner to those who need it in the industry—primarily the smart meter vendors and their customers, who are trying to deploy more secure metering in today's Smart Grids.

Both tools operate in a similar manner and leverage the use of optical diagnostics interfaces on most smart meters. These interfaces—designed to facilitate field crew activities at a home—combine the American National Standard Protocol Specification for ANSI Type 2 Optical Port (ANSI C12.18) and the American National Standard for Utility Industry End Device Data Tables (ANSI C12.19) to provide a common method for accessing predefined data tables within a smart metering infrastructure. ANSI C12.18 includes specifications for requesting information from a meter, identifying service parameters, reading and writing to a meter, logon and security specifications, and accessing meter table data.[18] Meter data tables include a wealth of information, including information about meter identity, meter manufacturer, operating mode, configuration and status; measurements and measurement parameters of the meter; and a variety of diagnostics capabilities including a variety of configuration and procedure commands.[19]

Termineter and OptiGuard work by combining knowledge of the C12.18 and C12.19 protocols with an ANSI type 2 optical probe, allowing the device to penetrate or test the optical diagnostic ports on smart meters supporting C12.18 interfaces.[20] Once a meter is accessed, almost any parameter can be read, presenting a clear privacy issue (see Chapter 4, "Privacy"). In addition, many field service capabilities ranging from configuration changes to firmware updates can be initiated. This makes it possible to steal data from a meter, sabotage service to a meter, or install spyware or other malware.[21]

The limitations of C12.18 do present some challenges to a would-be hacker. For example, you have to be standing very close to a meter to establish a C12.18 optical connection. This limits the usefulness of these tools for any sort of large-scale cyber attack. However, individual meters are still widely accessible, and so its feasible an attacker could simply walk up to a meter—especially in rural areas—and hack the device.

Some of these limitations could also be overcome. For example, weaponizing tools using long-range infrared transmitters and receivers, an attacker could sit comfortably in a vehicle parked on the street. The attack itself could take several forms, anything from a brute force attack to obtain access, to a network capture and replay attack. Simply damage a meter and wait for the technician to show up. If the Smart Grid is working as designed, the failure will be identified and will trigger a ticket to dispatch a field service technician. Once the technician is onsite, capture the optical communications and later replay the tech's authentication and replay attack the meter once the technician is offsite.

Attack methods

Once one or more Smart Grid assets have been discovered, and a target has been selected, there are many ways to execute a cyber attack. Depending upon the vulnerabilities of the target, these attacks could be very straightforward or may require a more sophisticated or indirect approach. Man-in-the-Middle attacks remain effective in many areas of the Smart Grid, as do network replay attacks. If a system can be penetrated and malware can be deposited (on disk or in memory), tools such as Metasploit's Meterpreter can be used to provide remote access to Smart Grid consoles and controls, install keyloggers or keystroke injectors, manipulate control bits within industrial protocols, or almost anything.

In some cases, the information that is available can be used as reconnaissance for further cyber attack capability. In many cases, systems can be attacked directly using disclosed exploits, and knowledge of a system is all that's required. If an attack is successful persistence can be established, enabling an attack to gather intelligence over time. In systems that make up a nexus between other systems (such as a substation gateway), a persistent presence can also be used to launch secondary attacks against other portions of the Smart Grid. This puts other systems at risk, such as data historians or other supplemental systems. Each successful attack can be used to gain access to more critical systems, up to and including bulk generation control systems.

In other cases, the information may be used to blend cyber and physical attacks. For example, determining when someone is at home by monitoring in-home energy signatures over time and then breaking into the home. In some cases, causing a localized failure in power delivery—by remotely disconnecting a smart meter, for example—could be used to bypass home security systems. Larger scale service disruption could be used to effect a power outage, allowing physical access to secure areas during the outage, or preventing quick response to a larger cyber incident by eliminating power from emergency response centers, SOCs, and other tactical monitoring stations.

Man-in-the-middle attacks

A Man-in-the-Middle (MITM) attack refers to an attack where the attacker inserts himself between communicating devices and snoops the traffic between them. The attacker is actually connecting to both devices, and then relaying traffic between them so that it appears that they are communicating directly, even though they're really communicating through a third device, which is eavesdropping on the interaction. To perform a Man-in-the-Middle attack, the attacker must be able to intercept traffic between the two target systems and inject new traffic. If the connection lacks encryption and authentication—as is often the case with industrial protocol traffic—this is a very straightforward process. Where authentication or encryption is used, a Man-in-the-Middle attack can still succeed by listening for key exchanges and passing the attacker's key in place of a legitimate key. It is relatively easy to intercept "secure" sessions (HTTPS, SSL, TLS). The biggest challenge to a successful Man-in-the-Middle attack is successfully inserting oneself into the message stream, which requires establishing trust. In other words, the attacker needs to convince both sides of the connection that it is the intended recipient. This impersonation can be thwarted with appropriate authentication controls. The attacker can present an invalid certificate to one device using SSL, connect to the target device, and establish a valid session. The first device is sending data encrypted, but the Man in the Middle is decrypting, inspecting, and then re-encrypting the traffic prior to delivering it to the second device. Unfortunately, many industrial protocols authenticate in clear text (if at all), or authenticated using weak (self-signed) certificates facilitating Man-in-the-Middle attacks within the various industrial controls systems throughout the Smart Grid.

Replay attacks

Initiating specific process commands into an industrial protocol stream requires an in-depth knowledge of industrial control system operations. However, because most industrial control traffic is transmitted in plain text, it is possible to capture packets and simply replay them to inject a desired process command into the system. For example, when capturing packets in a laboratory environment, a specific command can be initiated through a console, and the resulting network traffic can be captured, and when these packets are replayed, they will perform the same command. When commands are in clear text, it's simple to find and replace a command from within captured traffic to create custom packets that are crafted to perform specific tasks. If traffic is captured from the field, authentications can be captured as well allowing an attacker to authenticate to a device via a replay attack, providing an authorized connection through which additional recorded traffic can be played back. In other words, the target device has been essentially rooted, and the attacker has absolute control. If the device is a PLC or other process automation controller such as the controller functions found in more advanced substation gateways, the behavior of an entire system could be altered. If the target is an IED, specific registers could be overwritten to inject false measurements or readings into a system.

Security researcher Dillon Beresford demonstrated a PLC replay attack at the 2011 Black Hat conference in Las Vegas, NV. The attack began by starting a Siemens Step 7 console and connecting to a PLC within a laboratory environment. Various commands were then initiated to the PLC via the Step 7 console while traffic was being captured. This traffic included a valid Step 7 to PLC session initiation, allowing the recorded traffic to be played back against any supported PLC to replay those same commands in the field.[13]

Replay attacks are useful because of the command and control nature of an industrial process control system. Because commands exist to enable or disable security, alarms, and logging features, a replay attack can easily render a target system helpless. Industrial protocols also enable the transmission of new code (for firmware or logic updates), allowing a replay attack to act as a "dropper" for malicious logic or malware. At the 2011 Applied Control Systems Cyber Security Conference, researcher Ralph Langner described how simple it can be to write malicious ladder logic: with just 16 bytes of code, a logic bomb can be inserted at the front of existing logic that will place the target PLC into an endless loop—preventing the remaining logic from executing and essentially "bricking" the PLC.[22]

For the subtle manipulation of automated Smart Grid services, knowledge of industrial control system operations is still required. However, much of the information needed to attack a PLC can be obtained from the device itself. For example, in Beresford's case, packet replay was used to perform a PLC scan. Using S7 device requests via SIMATIC to probe a device, Beresford was able to obtain the model, network address, time of day, password, logic files, tag names, data block names, and other details from the targeted PLC.[13]

If the goal is simply to sabotage a system, however, almost anything can be used to disrupt operations: a simple replay attack to flip the coils in a relay switch is enough to break most processes.[13] In fact, malware designed to flip specific bits can be installed on Smart Grid assets to manipulate or sabotage that asset: if only read values are manipulated, the device will report false values; if write commands are also manipulated, it would essentially render the protocol functionality useless for that device.

Popping the HMI

One of the easiest ways to obtain unauthorized command and control of a system is to leverage the capabilities of a human-machine interface (HMI) console. Whether an embedded HMI within a substation, or the centralized command and control capability of SCADA, EMS or other systems, the most effective way to manipulate those controls is via their console interface. Rather than attacking via the network using Man-in-the-Middle or replay attacks, a known device vulnerability is exploited to install remote access to the console. Specifically, by using Metasploit to exploit a target system, and then using Meterpreter to install a remote VNC server, the desktop of the target system is returned to the attacker's PC. Now, the HMI, SCADA or EMS console is fully visible to and controllable by the attacker. This allows the hacker to directly monitor and control whatever that console is responsible for, remotely. There is no knowledge of industrial protocols needed, no specific experience in ladder logic, or control systems operations—only the ability to interpret a graphical user interface, click on buttons, and change values within a console that is typically designed for ease of use.

Blended attacks

Many attacks involve more than single exploits against a single vulnerability. Rather, more sophisticated attacks will use a blended threat model. According to SearchSecurity, "A blended threat is an exploit that combines elements of multiple types of malware and usually employs multiple attack vectors to increase the severity of damage and the speed of contagion."[23]

In the past, blended attacks typically contained multiple types of malware that were used in succession: a spear phishing attack to attack systems behind a firewall that would then drop a remote access toolkit (RAT) and might also propagate through the corporate network using additional exploits.

Recently, blended threats have evolved to a much greater degree of complexity. This was first observed with St****t, a single complex and mutating malware framework that is capable of behaving in multiple ways depending upon its environment. St****t propagated using multiple zero day exploits, allowing it to spread quickly through enterprise networks, including exploits associated with removable media, allowing St****t to more easily spread to "air gapped" networks such as a SCADA or industrial control environments. All along the way, St****t analyzed its environment, looking for specific targets, and either adapted (to initiate the next stage of the attack) or deleted itself (to hide its tracks) depending on what it found. We therefore have a single malware framework that mutated and performed different enumeration and attack activities depending upon its environment—it was clearly the most sophisticated example of malware of its time. In addition to its complexity, St****t earned notoriety because it spanned all three zones of the "3 × 3" security model (see Chapter 5, "Security Models for SCADA, ICS, and Smart Grid") to discover, penetrate, and sabotage a very specific industrial control: the enrichment of uranium.

Now, the concept of a blended attack residing within a self-contained, mutating payload has been taken even further. In June 2012, Kaspersky labs released information about Skywiper (more commonly known as Flame, one of the modular components of Skywiper). Skywiper is an even more sophisticated piece of malware, capable of "sniffing network traffic, taking screenshots, recording audio conversations, intercepting keystrokes, and managing other tricks that can compromise PC security and users' private data."[24] Investigations revealed that, like St****t, Flame had been active for years prior to being discovered. The malware was actively mining sensitive data and returning it to a sophisticated command and control infrastructure consisting of over 80 domain names, and using servers that moved between multiple locations, including Hong Kong, Turkey, Germany, Poland, Malaysia, Latvia, the United Kingdom, and Switzerland.[25]

Evidence points to connections between St****t, Duqu, and Skywiper, which explains its sophistication as a natural evolution of this new breed of weaponized cyber attack. Skywiper is modular, and the breadth of modules within Skywiper allows it to be used for a broad range of purposes. According to McAfee's security research laboratories, it is capable of, but not limited to, espionage functions such as scanning network resources, stealing information as specified, communicating with command and control (C&C) servers over SSH and HTTPS protocols, detecting the presence of more than 100 security products (antivirus, antispyware, firewalls, etc.), using both kernel and user-mode logic, employing complex internal functionality, injecting code and key processes, and concealing its presence. It can even create screen captures, record voice conversations, transmitting this back to the C&C infrastructure using multiple encryption methods.[26]

Over a dozen modules are present with Skywiper, including Flame, which handles AutoRun infection routines, "Weasel" and "Jimmy" which handle disk and file parsing, "Telemetry" and "Gator," which handles command and control routines, "Suicide" for self-termination, and exploit modules such as "Frog" password stealer, "Viper" screenshot stealer, and "Munch" network packet capturer.[26] Skywiper seems to be focused on espionage rather than sabotage: at the time of this writing, no modules dedicated to manipulation or sabotage of Smart Grid or other systems have been detected. However, the modular nature of Skywiper would certainly allows the threat to include more damaging modules as needed, no doubt leveraging the "Gadget" update module to further evolve the malware into a directed cyber weapon. When a creative attacker is able to combine modules of both St****t and Flame, he could in fact create advanced, customized malware targeting many Smart Grid architectures and systems.

Gauss, the newest sophisticated attack as of this writing, is also reminiscent of both St****t and Flame. However, rather than targeting industrial control systems or the industries that utilize them, Gauss focused on obtaining information from the banking industry. While not an example of a threat to Smart Grids *per se*, Gauss is indicative of a trend toward espionage versus data theft, using increasingly more sophisticated tools.

The trend toward targeted attacks using sophisticated, blended threats like these is of concern to the Smart Grid because the systems that make up the Smart Grid are so open and vulnerable. When many Smart Grid systems are visible on the Internet, it's almost certain that the presence of a persistent threat will uncover vulnerabilities

---

NOTE

Industrial control protocols, PLCs, and other embedded devices are not the only vulnerable systems that are highly interconnected within a Smart Grid. Many of the SCADA, EMS, and other systems are Windows-based server applications, and can be targeted and hacked using "normal" enterprise penetration techniques. Some of these, such as Data Historians, are by their nature highly connected to the industrial control networks and devices, communicating over almost every protocol, and connecting to almost every ICS interface. These systems are also widely connected to many desktops through the normal enterprise architecture, making this system a natural "bridge" between the publicly accessible and the private ICS networks. One recent vulnerability that was disclosed puts the market leader in data historians—the OSIsoft PI System—at risk. PI, due to its ubiquitous presence in most industrial automation systems (including Smart Grid), makes it a tempting target. PI interfaces many systems, collecting and historizing data from over 400 industrial control system devices and protocols. PI is built upon a solid core of Microsoft technology and unsurprisingly uses OPC DA as one method for messaging within the PI system. It is this OPC DA interface that renders the PI system exploitable. "The PI OPC DA interface does not correctly validate the OPC input messages before performing further processing. By sending additional valid packets, an attacker could partially control corruption to force the arbitrary freeing of a memory address. This could allow the attacker to cause a crash or to execute arbitrary code."[27]

Then, it becomes a matter of leveraging the capability of that server to cause mischief: theoretically misreporting process values or even potentially injecting malware over any of the many interfaces with which PI communicates.

Luckily, the "standard" systems that run on modern operating systems and modern server hardware are also easier to secure, as described in Chapter 6, "Securing the Smart Grid." It should be further noted that OSIsoft self-reported this vulnerability after they utilized the resources of ICS-CERT to provide a rigorous common assessment of their system to identify and correct security issues. Furthermore they have taken additional measures to protect the PI system and can provide further guidance on PI server security. As always, check with your vendor first before making assumptions about cyber security, and validate suspected vulnerability with controlled penetration testing.

in these systems—or reconnoiter the information needed to uncover such vulnerabilities—and then further propagate among and between them. Of even greater concern is that many of these systems can be difficult to monitor, providing a relative safe haven for resident malware to hide dormant.

A common theme when discussing advanced attacks such as St****t, Flame, and Gauss is the mutability and adaptability of the malware. These attacks are designed to provide a command channel back to a remote site, but the beauty of the malware lies in their ability to conceal themselves, updates themselves, propagate to new systems and adapt to their environment. This allows the malware to establish persistence. Persistence can be used for prolonged espionage: stealing more and more information over time. It may also be used as a launching point for a secondary or tertiary attack phase. For example, after stealing data about a national grid infrastructure—including energy generation and utilization trends, outages and how they are handled, etc.—the malware could either activate a dormant module, or it may receive a new module or functionality through an update from the malware's command and control framework. Consider the following functional example of a persistent, mutli-stage attack against a Smart Grid:

1. An advanced malware payload is distributed by redirecting the web request of a vendor technician through a malicious server, using the Kaminsky DNS exploit. The vendor's technician downloads a firmware patch for a field device, but is actually receiving a counterfeit patch that contains malware.
2. The technician arrives on site, passes background checks, and his or her laptop passes a virus scan (because the malware is a zero-day virus that has no effective detection signature to date).
3. The patch drops a small payload into the project files of a substation automation controller, infecting field devices throughout the distribution system. This is done using an identified vulnerability in the industrial protocol used between them. At the same time, the malware attempts to propagate through the network from the technician laptop, establishing a persistent rootkit and opening a command and control channel back to a remote site. Since this is a targeted attack, the remote site would not be previously identified as malicious and reported as such by many threat intelligence systems.
4. The C&C channel may or may not be able to connect, depending upon the degree of network security and logical network separation that is place between the substation and other systems. In this example, there are open network connections to T-SCADA, D-SCADA and EMS systems that co-reside in a common data center.
5. At this stage, the gateway, field devices, RTUs, and other interconnected systems are infected. Depending upon which environment the virus resides in, new modules become active, and unused code is removed to conceal its presence. We now have a malicious framework operating in a coordinated manner within all zones of the grid system being attacked, from T&D automation, energy management, protection, metering, and even in-home systems such as HEMS and HAN-connected smart appliances.

6. Now the damage can be done: it can be pure reconnaissance, the theft of private information, or a coordinated attack designed to manipulate whole areas of the grid—all while hiding its actions from both human operators and management applications.

7. Once established, this persistent threat could further scan and enumerate other areas outside of the transmission system that it infected: breaching advanced metering systems to steal customer personal identity information (PII) and financial information, or to monitor home energy profiles to learn more about a specific target user, from what is in their refrigerator to what they're watching on TV (see Chapter 4, "Privacy Concerns with the Smart Grid").

Is this type of complex, staged attack realistic? Again, the answer has been proven by example. The S*****t virus combined clever code and forward thinking to provide detailed network enumeration that could easily act as a roadmap into and throughout target networks. With each new host infection, S*****t appended information to an encrypted data file as the malware propagated, which was then transferred home via the established C&C channel. This file provided an effective "road map" of how the malware reached its target, as well as how it propagated. This detailed network enumeration could be used to uncover other areas of attack and should the virus spread between multiple systems within a Smart Grid (as in the example provided above) could easily be used to map out sophisticated attacks against almost any system within the grid infrastructure, starting with whatever "weak link" the attacker is able to first identify and penetrate.

Setting phasors to kill

Unlike in Star Trek, the phasors referred to in transmission and distribution systems are simply measurements and are not harmful in and of themselves. However, because tripped lines in power transmission could cascade and cause outages similar to the 2003 blackout in Northeastern United States, synchronized phasor measurement has been a primary goal of newer, smarter grids.[28] Could phasor measurement units (PMUs) be manipulated by a cyber attack to cause damages inline with the weapons of Gene Roddenbury's fictional universe? Hardly, but because PMUs communicate digitally over a broad internetwork, they can be hacked, and this can lead to the exact type of cascading outage that they are intended to prevent.[28]

Using measurement systems as a target or vector for cyber attack is a bit less straightforward than installing malware, command and control callbacks, stealing data, etc. Because PMUs are very purpose-built devices, designed to obtain and communicate specific measurements, there is little damage that can be done outside of interrupting or manipulating these measurements. Unfortunately, the manipulation of phasor readings can cause damage to a transmission or distribution system, causing potential over-voltages or under-voltages on T&D lines or driving power out of phase. Specific lines could be targeted using EMS and DMS systems. Attacks could be highly specialized—such as jamming the GPS communications required to synchronize time across PMUs—or very general, such as installing malware within a PMU that alters phasor measurements as they are transmitted to a PDC.

Phasor measurement manipulation could cause anything from loss of efficiency (putting T&D profitability at risk) to potential transmission line or generator trip, which could in turn lead to arcing or other serious risks to health and safety.

Researchers at the University of Texas and Northrup Grumman have shown how GPS spoofing can be used against phasor measurement units to manipulate the timing of a PMU. The hack works by spoofing a GPS and broadcasting a falsified GPS signal. Because PMU are based upon GPS time synchronization, spoofing therefore introduces a timing offset to the target PMU, and creates a corresponding change in the phase angle measured by the PMU.[28]

As with most highly distributed systems, PMUs rely upon a degree of centralization, and the Phasor Data Concentrator (PDC) is also a likely attack. There are no known instances of how a targeted attack against a PDC might be able to alter various distributed PMU data, although theoretically the same impact could be achieved in this way as by directly manipulating individual PDCs.

Attacking generation facilities from the grid

Discussions on Smart Grid attacks almost always originate from the Internet or from the utility's business systems, spreading through to control facilities and ultimately into the grid. However, in the above example, the threat started in the field and worked its way into the control room from there. To the best knowledge of the authors, the first attack of this type occurred in an industrial manufacturing facility, where a corrupt plant device spread malware through the process and control networks to the company's business systems. While details of this attack are not publically disclosed, this highlights the primary concern of Smart Grid cyber security that attacks can originate from almost any area, and propagate to almost any other. Often, the insider isn't properly considered when designing their cyber security architecture: they are assumed to be trusted and all communications are allowed. This is a problem. If it is possible to inject code into a smart meter using infrared interfaces, through the advanced metering infrastructure to D-SCADA and T-SCADA severs via Windows vulnerabilities, and from there to business systems obtaining real-time information from the SCADA systems, there is no longer any security through separation nor security through obscurity. At the same time, per DoS attacks on distribution facilities to initiate truck rolls and deplete utility manpower resources. If secondary systems—such as coolant feeds and controllers—are accessible, shut down these systems to cause secondary faults in order to keep primary systems offline longer. Attacks originating in the field demand attention to securing the purpose-built and embedded devices and the communications between them, and also make a strong case for strengthening security of aggregation or concentration points in the field—such as AMI headends, substation gateways, and of course SCADA. They also reinforce the basic security premise within industrial networks of denying by default all communications, and only allow specific, known traffic between devices. This is difficult for many to understand, but in ICS design, it is all about managing trust and relationships—trust no one inherently! Some methods of implementing this type of hardening will be discussed in

Chapter 6, "Securing the Smart Grid." However, field-based attacks also present significant concerns and implications for supply chain management.

What about secure protocols?

The vulnerability of the Smart Grid to attacks originating through field devices has been seen in the wild. For example, in September 2012, Telvent, a major Smart Grid software vendor owned by Schneider Electric, was hacked. The breach of their corporate network resulted in the installation of malware as well as access to project files.[32] While Telvent responded quickly with mitigation measures, this type of breach raises supply chain concerns. If a device manufacturer is breached and infected with sophisticated malware, there is a risk that attackers could have a persistent presence on the engineering workstations and systems of the vendors creating the field devices. This type of attack could both utilize the supply chain to gain access

---

NOTE

There has been considerable effort by standards organizations to provide the technical specifications and standards required to secure device communications within power systems management and substation automation. IEC 62351 (see "Protocols" in Chapter 2, "Smart Grid Architectures") defines the technical specifications "to provide end-to-end transport security for the communications between software applications."[29] The standard relies heavily on the use of TLS to protect against eavesdropping (via encryption), Man-in-the-Middle attacks (via authentication), spoofing devices (via certificate node authentication), and replay attacks (via encryption).[29] However, while the implementation of TLS is a step in the right direction, compliance with IEC 62351 (or any standard) does not correlate to absolute security of a Smart Grid.

As recently as September 2012, there have been exploit capable of extracting authentication from secure communications, such as with the CRIME (Compression Ratio Info-leak Made Easy) exploit that extracts credentials from compressed SSL traffic by changing characters in attacker-controlled data and comparing the compressed data against legitimate requests to figure out specific encrypted values of authentication cookies.[30] Broader TLS exploits such as CVE-2009-3555 which "allows Man-in-the-Middle attackers to insert data into HTTPS sessions, and possibly other types of sessions protected by TLS or SSL."[31] This vulnerability, though three years old at the time of this writing, and with a published mitigation available since 2010, is still widely unpatched today. So, like with any software implementation there is risk that the implementation of TLS into Smart Grid systems is itself susceptible to attack through unintended vulnerabilities.

For substation automation, IEC 62351-6 provides specifications for the extension of 61850 GOOSE and sample measured values (SMV) PDUs to include a hash, used to protect the message and ensure its integrity.[29] This is important to protect these multi-cast messages. If current GOOSE and SMV messages are implemented without this extension, it becomes trivial to eavesdrop on messages, or even spoof or manipulate messages.

Also consider that secure communications are initiated based upon a degree of trust in the host device: if the device itself is compromised, authenticated communications with valid certificates can be established from that device. This is why the security models discussed in Chapter 5, "Smart Grid Security Models" include host security, communication security and application, or data security considerations.

to target an ICS system at a client site, or to exfiltrate critical intelligence that could be used to compromise a client site through additional means.

According to Telvent, "OASyS DNA is a real-time SCADA [service] solution that bridges the gap between an enterprise network and activities in the field, delivering real-time data for critical business and operations decisions. It combines the systems your business already relies upon with technological solutions from our many software suites, our trusted partners and even our competitors. It seamlessly integrates every tool you need under a single umbrella of centralized, standardized hardware and software."[33]

In other words, OASyS is like many SCADA systems in that it is a command and information nexus. Other leading ICS vendors like ABB, Emerson, Invensys and Honeywell to name a few offer similar services. The security implications of this or similar SCADA software being compromised within the supply chain is severe (this topic will be discussed in depth in Chapter 8, "Securing the Supply Chain"). The OASyS DNA system integrates information collected from Telvent SCADA, Schneider distribution management system, outage management, and other systems.[33] This reinforces that almost any SCADA communication system is not only a tempting target on its own, but also an inbound vector to many other systems. If malware were to find its way into this or other similar SCADA systems from other manufacturers, it could be used as a sleeper agent to infiltrate almost any system throughout the Smart Grid.

A sophisticated attack and successful breach of a device manufacturer could provide remote command and control necessary for hackers to embed malware directly within the machines of program developers and engineers. At that point, project files, patches or other software delivered by the vendor to the end user could represent an inbound attack vector—a problem exacerbated by the fact that vendors typically have permissions necessary to modify systems within customer deployments.[32] It should be noted that Telvent has taken measures to mitigate the risks associated with this breach. Always consult your vendor to obtain the latest information about vulnerability or breach disclosures, and validate vulnerability concerns via controlled penetration testing or suspect systems.

SUMMARY

There are many systems that interconnect to make a "Smart Grid," and all are susceptible to either a variety of general purpose attacks, and/or to specialized attacks that prey upon the distributed and easily accessible industrial protocols that are used within automation, measurement, metering and other specialized systems. While some devices are more secure than others (see Chapter 2, "Smart Grid Network Architecture"), the "weakest link" can be used as an attack vector into other devices due to the highly interconnected nature of the Smart Grid. Whether using common tools such as Metasploit, common techniques such as Man-in-the-Middle or network replay attacks, or specialized threats such as GPS spoofing against the synchrophasor infrastructure, the Smart Grid is vulnerable and accessible to a variety of attacks.

References

1. Peterson Dale, editor. *S4 Proceedings series (digital bond's SCADA security scientific symposium, 2007–2010)*. Miami, FL: Digital Bond Press; 2010.
2. William H, Bartley PE. Analysis of transformer failures In *International association of engineering insurers 36th annual conference*. Stockholm; 2003.
3. ICS-CERT. *ICS-ALERT-12-046-01– increasing threat to industrial control systems*. US Department of Homeland Security; February 15, 2012.
4. Knapp Eric D. *Industrial network security: securing critical infrastructure networks for Smart Grid, SCADA, and other industrial control systems*. Massachusetts: Syngress; August 29, 2011.
5. Franz Matt. DNP3 recon. *Digital bond* [document from Internet]; October 18, 2006. <http://www.digitalbond.com/index.php/2006/10/18/dnp3-recon/> [cited December 23, 2010].
6. Falliere Nicolas, Murchu Liam O, Chien Eric. *Symantec*. W32.St****t Dossier, Version 1.4; February 2011.
7. Santamarta Ruben. *Attacking controllogix*. Digital Bond Project Base Camp.
8. Wurldtech Security Technologies. *Achilles test platform product profile* [Document on the Internet]. <http://www.wurldtech.com/cyber-security-products/achilles-testplatform/product-profile.aspx> [cited August 27, 2012].
9. ICS-CERT. *ICS-CERT advisories and reports archive* [document from the Internet]. <http://www.us-cert.gov/control_systems/ics-cert/archive.html> [cited October 20, 2012].
10. ODVA. [document on the Internet]. <http://www.odva.org/default.aspx?tabid=102> [cited August 27, 2012].
11. Digital Bond. *Basecamp* [document on the Internet]. <http://www.digitalbond.com/tools/basecamp/> [cited August 12, 2012].
12. Siemens AG. *SIMATIC STEP 7 V11—controller software in the TIA portal* [document on the Internet]. <http://www.industry.siemens.com/topics/global/en/tia-portal/controller-sw-tia-portal/pages/default.aspx> [cited September 5, 2012].
13. Beresford Dillon. *Exploiting siemens simatic S7 PLCs*. Prepared for Black Hat USA+2011. Las Vegas, NV; 2011.
14. Offensive Security. *7-technologies IGSS 9.00.00.11059 multiple vulnerabilities* [document from the Internet]; March 22, 2011. <http://www.exploit-db.com/exploits/17024/> [cited September 1, 2012].
15. Langil Joel, Byres Eric. *Analysis of the 7-technologies IGSS security vulnerabilities for industrial control system professionals*. Tofino Security, SCADAhacker.com; March 28, 2011.
16. Langil Joel. *Exploitation 101: turning a SCADA vulnerability into a successful attack* [document on the Internet]. <http://www.scadahacker.com/videos/igss-video.html> [cited July 28, 2012].
17. Gleg, Ltd. *SCADA+ Pack* [document from the Internet]. <http://gleg.net/agora_scada.shtml> [cited September 4, 2012].
18. ANSI C12.18-2006, *Protocol specification for ANSI type 2 optical port*. American National Standard Institute, Inc.; May 2, 2006.
19. ANSI C12.19-2008. *American national standard for utility industry end device data tables*. American National Standard Institute, Inc.; February 24, 2009.
20. Fisher Dennis. *Termineter security framework for smart meters released*. ThreatPost [document from the Internet]; July 20, 2012. <http://threatpost.com/en_us/blogs/

termineter-security-framework-smart-meters-released-072012> [cited September 1, 2012].

21. Menn Joseph. *Web-connected industrial controls stoke security fears*. Reuters. San Francisco [document from the Internet]; July 22, 2012. <http://in.reuters.com/article/2012/07/23/us-blackhat-industrialcontrols-idINBRE86M14R20120723> [cited September 1, 2012].

22. Lagner Ralph. Forensics on a complex cyber attack—lessons learned from St****t. In *Presentation at the 2011 applied control solutions (ACS) conference, September 20*, Washington, DC; 2011.

23. SearchSecurity. *Definition: blended threat* [document from the Internet]. <http://searchsecurity.techtarget.com/definition/blended-threat> [Cited September 4, 2012].

24. Mlot Stephanie. *Kaspersky uncovers new details of Flame malware* [document on the Internet]; September 18, 2012. <http://www.itproportal.com/2012/09/18/kaspersky-uncovers-new-details-of-flame-malware/#ixzz26pUY2u8P> [cited September 18, 2012].

25. Kaspersky Labs. *Virus news: Kaspersky lab experts provide in-depth analysis of flame's C&C infrastructure* [document from the Internet]; June 4, 2012. <http://www.kaspersky.com/about/news/virus/2012/Kaspersky_Lab_Experts_Provide_In_Depth_Analysis_of_Flames_Infrastructure> [cited September 18, 2012].

26. Walter Jim. *Flame attacks: briefing and indicators of compromise*. McAfee Labs; May, 2012.

27. US-CERT. *ICS-CERT advisory ICSA-12-201-01—OSISOFT PI OPC DA interface buffer overflow*; July 19, 2012.

28. Shepard Daniel P, Humphreys Todd E, Fansler Aaron A. Evaluation of the vulnerability of phasor measurement units to GPS spoofing attacks, In *Sixth annual IFIP WG 11.10 international conference on critical infrastructure protection*. Washington, DC; March 19–21, 2012.

29. Technical IEC Specification TS 62351-1. *Power systems management and associated information exchange—data and communications security Part 1: Communication network and system security—Introduction to security issues*. International Electrotechnical Commission (IEC): Geneva, Switzerland; 2007.

30. Goodin Dan. *Many ways to break SSL with CRIME attacks, experts warn*. ArsTechnica [document from the Internet]; September 17, 2012. <http://arstechnica.com/security/2012/09/many-ways-to-break-ssl-with-crime-attacks-experts-warn/> [cited October 1, 2012].

31. CVE-2009-355. *Mitre. 2009* [document from the Internet]. <http://cve.mitre.org/cgi-bin/cvename.cgi?name=CVE-2009-3555> [cited October 1, 2012].

32. Zetter Kim. *Maker of Smart-Grid control software hacked*. Wired [document on the Internet]; September 26, 2012. <http://www.wired.com/threatlevel/2012/09/scada-vendor-telvent-hacked/> [cited September 27, 2012].

33. OASyS *SCADA: Standardized, centralized SCADA solutions from Telvent* [document on the Internet]; 2012. <http://www.telvent.com/en/business_areas/smart_grid/solutions_overview/smart_grid/smart_operations/oasys-scada.cfm> [cited September 27, 2012].

Privacy Concerns with the Smart Grid

INFORMATION IN THIS CHAPTER:

- Personal data
- Privacy risks associated with the Smart Grid
- Privacy impact assessment

"These patterns can be useful for analysing our energy use for energy conservation but, together with data from other sources, the potential for extensive data mining is very significant."[1]
Giovanni Buttarelli, assistant director of the European Data Protection Supervisor.

Personal data

The above quotation refers to comments raised by the European Data Protection Supervisor raising his concerns about the massive amount of personal data that can be accessed without appropriate safeguards. Indeed, there have been numerous concerns related to the potential threat of personal data by Smart Grids. Consumer acceptance of the grid "depends upon the development of legal and regulatory regimes that respect consumer privacy, promote consumer access to and choice regarding third-party use of their energy data" according to a recent US Department of Energy report.[2]

As we analyze the proposed risks to consumer privacy, and effectively the implications to personal data, we should firstly consider what we mean by the term "personal data." There are of course many different descriptions of the term personal data; invariably, they do refer to the text as outlined by the UK Data Protection Act:

UK Data Protection Act—Basic Interpretive Provisions

Effectively, what the above text refers to is, can a living individual be identified from the data, or, from the data and other information in the possession of, or likely to come into the possession of, the data controller?[3]

Using this premise as the basis to assess the privacy implications of the Smart Grid, it is likely that there will be data that can identify a living individual originating from the metering infrastructure. Moreover as has been identified in the quote from the European Data Protection Supervisor, without the implementation of appropriate safeguards, there will be massive amounts of personal data easily accessible by authorized and potentially unauthorized parties.

Privacy risks associated with the Smart Grid

Smart Grids provide many benefits to its stakeholders; in particular, consumers are given control and transparency over their energy usage. In practical, terms what this allows includes (but not limited to) as follows:

- Ability to login into their energy account and view how much energy they are using based upon information reported from their smart meter.
- Allow smart devices to adjust energy consumption based upon their preferences, and the price of energy (e.g. utilize off-peak pricing).
- Receive alerts based upon grid outages via the preferred communication channel as outlined in their profile preferences.
- Allow the grid operator to accurately identify the source of disruption, thus allowing for rerouting, and subsequently minimizing the time and impact of disruption.

The above consumer benefits are only a small subset of available examples. One thing, that is perfectly clear, is that to realize these benefits there will be a need to utilize personal data, in other words data that identifies the consumer. Consider that in Italy, for example, in 2009, it was reported that 85% of homes already had a smart meter in each home[4] that of course puts the earlier quote into context whereby there will be a massive collection of personal data (note: the author(s) make no statement on the specific implementation of the Italian Smart Grid deployment, merely to illustrate the amount of personal data collected).

Earlier chapters discussed the technical components of the Smart Grid, but it is important to consider that these systems will collect personal data. Although specific implementations may have additional components capable of collecting and processing personal data, the following represents the core devices at the center of privacy concerns related to the grid.

Smart Meters: One of the key objectives of the meter is to record the energy consumption of the consumer, and report this back to the operator/energy company. As we mentioned earlier, one of the main consumer benefits is to report energy usage in a very granular fashion, where, for example, they could well report consumption in near real-time.

One could ask the question, well so what? Does it really matter if anybody knows how much energy you are consuming? Well, the impact on privacy is that it allows a third party to establish a profile of the activities being undertaken at a property. For example, if there is no usage of energy at specific times in the day, it may be an indication that property is vacant. Now ask the question, does it really matter? Do you really want third parties to know at what time your home is potentially vacant? Moreover, the level of granularity goes beyond simply on or off. For example, a third party may even be able to estimate the number of individuals at a given property.

Consumer Appliances: Not only are the meters capable of capturing usage by consumers, the appliances that are now "smart" also have the opportunity to capture and reveal a wealth of information. According to the National Institute of Standards and Technology (NIST); NISTIR 7628, "Guidelines for Smart Grid Cyber Security: vol. 2, Privacy and the Smart Grid[5]," it is possible to utilize Nonintrusive Appliance Load Monitoring (NALM) techniques to not only reveal usage patterns about individual appliances, but also identify individual appliances using libraries of known patterns. Indeed, an Italian research study from 2002 using data from 15 min intervals was able to pinpoint the use of washing machines, dishwashers and water heaters with an accuracy rate over 90%. Furthermore, this degree of accuracy is only likely to increase as more signatures become available.

This degree of accuracy is presented in graphical format in Figure 4.1.

Perhaps, letting third parties know about the appliances you use in your home is not an issue. It is not as though your medical records are being shared publicly? However, there have been a number of "worst cases" and in some cases farfetched scenarios presented that have raised some significant concerns by consumers. Some of these examples include the use by law enforcement to review the energy consumption of properties to determine whether, for example, marijuana is being grown! While this may seem one of those scenarios, we class under the farfetched category, consider that in Ohio, there

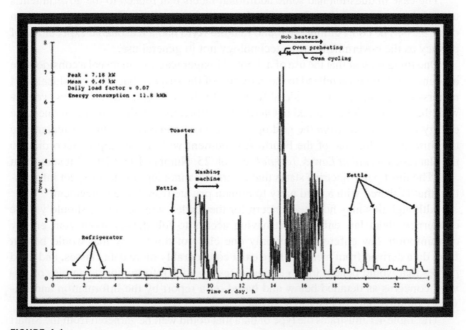

FIGURE 4.1

Power usage to personal activity mapping—from NISTIR 7628.

are at least 60 subpoenas filed by law enforcement seeking customer's energy records from power companies.[6] This technique is confirmed as effective by enforcement, and according to a spokesperson from American Electric Power, they commented "We're obligated when we get these requests. There's not an option to say no." Ultimately, the net result is that law enforcement are provided with information about the subscriber, including the billing details. It would be fair to say that when the grid becomes ubiquitous, more detailed information is available that the number of subpoenas is likely to increase. While this example may seem perfectly reasonable, and for those of you that are not marijuana growers, the risk that the Smart Grid can allow law enforcement the opportunity to undertake non-intrusive, real-time surveillance is of little concern. However, this particular use case does represent a very interesting precedent, the case in question is *Kyllo v. United States*; in this particular case, the government used the monthly energy records for its case against a suspected marijuana grower to demonstrate that the power usage of the suspect was deemed as excessive and in line with that of a marijuana growing operation. The case, however, demonstrated a very interesting precedent pertaining to the privacy interest under the Fourth Amendment. This contains a "search and seizure" provision that requires warrants before the government can invade one's internal space. In this particular case, the Supreme Court stated.

"We think that obtaining by sense-enhancing technology any information regarding the interior of the home that could not otherwise have been obtained without physical intrusion into a constitutionally protected area, constitutes a search [and is] presumptively unreasonable without a warrant."[7]

The case in question had some additional facets that related to the government's use of thermal imaging to determine the areas of the house that were hotter than other parts. The court ultimately found that the Kyto had a reasonable expectation of privacy as the government used a technology not in general use.

One thing is clear that the use of a thermal imager was able to reveal a considerable amount of information related to the activities of the suspect, but if we consider smart meters—they can reveal considerably more. In this particular case (and as we saw with the statistics demonstrated in Ohio), law enforcement will invariably request the energy usage records from the grid operator/energy company. In this particular case the third-party doctrine of the Fourth Amendment will clearly apply. According to the Harvard *Journal of Law & Technology* vol. 25, Number 1 Fall 2011,[8] it states that

"The third-party doctrine states that a person cannot legitimately expect information that is shared with a third party to remain private from law enforcement."

Although this may not be a concern for the reader, why of course should you be concerned about law enforcement having access to full details about your energy consumption, law enforcement is only one class of third party that would benefit from data derived from meters. There exist considerably more data classes, and third parties that would benefit from gaining access to such information, examples of privacy concerns as detailed below and based on a report by the Information and Privacy Commissioner of Ontario, Canada.[9]

The Table 4.1 illustrates the type of data that could well be garnered from the Smart Grid, and this data could well become valuable to third parties beyond law enforcement. We will discuss the supply chain within the Smart Grid elsewhere in the book,

Table 4.1 Privacy Concerns

Component	Technology or Application	Privacy Questions	
End User Components	Smart Meters	Remote connect/disconnect of meter	Will disconnection of power be based on any new sources of energy consumption data created by the use of smart meters?
		Meter detects meter bypass	While this technology will reduce theft, will it produce false positives and expose innocent individuals to possible fines or criminal proceedings?
		Data Collection, Communication, and Storage	Will data collection and communication be secure? Will the utility develop proper policies and procedures for maintaining data privacy?
	In-home appliances that communicate with the utility operator * Highly sensitive		Will information from the home regarding specific appliance use or disuse be relayed directly to the utility?
	In-home devices that communicate usage information to the customer		Will these devices also share data with third parties, and if so, on what basis?… With the consent of the customer?
	Consumer access to energy-related information		Will access to this information (e.g. username and password) be kept private and secure—not disclosed to or captured by third parties?
	Automated feeder equipment		Will the automated system communicate directly with smart meters and potentially disclose personal information regarding electricity use in the home?
Electricity Distribution Component	Fault detection		When detecting faults in the Smart Grid, will systems have access to personal information regarding electricity use in real time, without direct interface with the consumer?
	Load management		Will the utility company shut off appliances within the home without the consent of the occupant? Will tenants have less privacy vis-a-vis landlords who participate in load management?
	"Load" or demand information communicated to smart generators		Will generators have direct access to electricity demand information, and if so, could individual household electricity be discernible?
Electricity Generation	"Distributed" or "on-site" generation		When on-site generation is provided back to the power system, will customer information be kept private and secure?
	Plug-in hybrid electric vehicles		Will a charging vehicle's location be shared with the utility operator? In "authenticating" charged vehicles for billing purposes, will the authentication scheme, by necessity (privacy by design) address the privacy and security issues? What role will batteries play on the Smart Grid? Will there be restrictions on charging during peak demand? Will batteries exchange power with the grid?

but with regards to privacy, the concerns are very high for consumers where sensitive data could be made [legally] available to organizations outside of the energy supplier, grid operator, and of course law enforcement. One simple example may be insurance companies, where an insight into the behavior of consumers could well impact insurance premiums. Although the possibility of the insurance provider utilizing energy consumption to set premiums may seem somewhat far fetched, it is worthwhile considering that the grid operator may look to develop information it collects as a revenue stream. Consider also the attractiveness of such a rich repository of valuable information to those individuals that may seek to access data they are unauthorized to access.

Of course the release of individual, personal data will be covered by privacy legislation, and this was highlighted by the Article 29 Working Party opinion[10] on Smart Grids which stated; *"Where personal data are contained in the information generated and disseminated by a smart meter, the Working Party determines that Directive 95/46/EC applies to such processing."* Therefore it is expected that without some form of explicit consent, the grid operator/energy supplier cannot release this information to authorized third parties. Note, the caveat there? Authorized third parties. If you have a database with millions of records that are of economic benefit to many, then it does make the system considerably more attractive to malicious individuals looking to get the data for re sale. This becomes an unintended consequence of the Smart Grid, where the simple collation of such valuable data, makes it more attractive for malicious individuals to try and retrieve the data to sell on. This is out of scope for this book, mainly because the controls for protecting this data are covered by multiple books elsewhere (this will likely be within the IT domain).

As mentioned earlier, it is expected that the data will not be about the individual and therefore not covered under the scrutiny of data protection legislation. What is likely to be sold to authorized third parties should be anonymized. When we say authorized, however, we are likely to be referring to that authorization being provided by the operator, and not the consumer. This of course should not cause any privacy concerns, right? Well not quite.

The challenge we face with the release of very large volumes of data is the issue of inference. Of course, we make a very big assumption that the data cleansing routine is of sufficient quality so as not to inadvertently reveal personal information. However, if we assume that obfuscation of personal data fields is of sufficient quality, then we are faced with the inference challenge. In a nutshell, this refers to the ability to derive data that may be sanitized from the collation of multiple data sources. A simple example is those records which fall outside of normal, or average consumption, and is a technique we saw used by law enforcement to infer marijuana growth. The field of analytics for the Smart Grid is anticipated to grow enormously, and Pike Research estimates that the market for software and services that can mine intelligence could reach a cumulative $11.3 billion between 2011 and 2015.[11] Of course, this figure in itself is not indicative of burgeoning privacy considerations and indeed, there could be tremendous value to the consumer in the operator in identifying intelligence that could be passed to the consumer. For example, recommendations on energy consumption that could save money; we noticed that your washing machine is used always during peak hours, but by doing your washing an hour later then you could save twelve dollars per month. However, what may be less desirable are a plethora of electronics manufacturers inundating consumers with details of their latest products with detailed prior knowledge about the devices and their consumption within the home, without prior consent. This concept of Big Data, and the ability to infer certain things about consumers are already uncovering things about consumers that somewhat blur the line of ethics. A recent example related to shopping habits reveals this in striking detail, whereby in a recent NY Times[12] article, it was revealed that the US retail shopping organization "Target" were able to identify their customers that were likely expecting a baby. Simple indicators such as women buying larger quantities of unscented lotions at the start of their second trimester, as well as purchases of other indicating products, all suggested the customers that were likely pregnant. Indeed, the company built a "pregnancy prediction" score that predicted the likelihood of the data subject being pregnant based on the various products purchased together. This allowed the company to send coupons based on the stages of pregnancy (note: they were able to predict the due date). The implications of this degree of accuracy were demonstrated approximately a year after the pregnancy prediction was developed as cited below:

"A man walked into a Target outside Minneapolis and demanded to see the manager. He was clutching coupons that had been sent to his daughter, and he was angry, according to an employee who participated in the conversation.

'My daughter got this in the mail!' he said. 'She's still in high school, and you're sending her coupons for baby clothes and cribs? Are you trying to encourage her to get pregnant?'

The manager didn't have any idea what the man was talking about. He looked at the mailer. Sure enough, it was addressed to the man's daughter and contained advertisements for maternity clothing, nursery furniture and pictures of smiling infants. The manager apologized and then called a few days later to apologize again.

On the phone, though, the father was somewhat abashed. 'I had a talk with my daughter,' he said. 'It turns out there's been some activities in my house I haven't been completely aware of. She's due in August. I owe you an apology.'"

Now of course there is no suggestion that Smart Grid analytics can indicate whether consumers are expecting a baby. However, what this example demonstrates is that here you have a commercial organization being aware that a girl was pregnant before her own father, and that the field of analytics is able to infer that level of accuracy simply based on a series of purchases. Although this example is entirely unrelated to the type of data that can be garnered with Smart Grids, it demonstrates the power of analytics and how "creepy" the conclusions it can draw. Furthermore, when it comes to Smart Grids there are three factors we know for sure:

1. The field of Smart Grid analytics is predicted to grow to monumental proportions.
2. Third-party organizations will most certainly be interested in gaining access to such data.
3. There will be financial benefits for operators who are able to "sell" such data to third parties.

When you combine these three factors, it is evident that the implications regarding the privacy of consumers may well be significant, and of concern. Of course if handled appropriately, there should not be this degree of concern. After all, what consumer wouldn't want to know ways to save money? Or should I have said… what operator wouldn't want to know ways to make money! However, a simple privacy notice is not sufficient, electronic distribution today only provides the opportunity to accept or reject. Reject in many cases is simply being prevented from utilizing the service; therefore, allowing some constructive feedback option is essential.

Moreover, what the above example does demonstrate is that there may be privacy concerns when at first glance there may not appear to be any issues. There is a great deal of research being conducted to determine the amount of information that can be garnered from Smart Grid deployments. One such example[13] was presented at the hacker conference, the Chaos Computing Congress by researchers Dario Carluccio and Stephan Brinkhaus under the title "Smart Hacking for Privacy." The title of the presentation does of course give the game away with regards to the content; however, the level of detail they were able to derive from their research was certainly surprising. By signing up with a company known as Discovergy to have a meter installed in their chosen location to conduct the research, they were able to identify a number of privacy concerns. Their research uncovered numerous security flaws that included the ability for their data and passwords to be intercepted, as they were transmitted in clear text, they also found that the smart meters were monitoring power usage, not in the fifteen-minute intervals suggested as standard earlier in this chapter, but rather in two-second intervals. We had previously discussed the privacy implications associated with fifteen-minute intervals, but the researchers then asked the question, what level of detail could be garnered from considerably smaller intervals? The outcome of their work found that not only are there likely signatures for the devices within a consumer's home but also the research found that there are also likely to be signatures for movie or a television show based on the brightness levels for particular scenes. We had previously considered the need for security controls to protect the usage data from unauthorized third parties and suggested that they are out of scope for the book as this topic is extensively covered in other publications. However, just because it is covered elsewhere, its importance should not be underestimated. Carluccio and Brinkhaus found the historical records of meter usage were easily obtainable from the company's systems despite the design only allowing access for the previous three months. The CEO of Discovergy, who was at the presentation, took to the stage and defended the polling interval as necessary in order to notify consumers if they had left their home with an iron left on, but had promised to make the polling interval configurable for their customers who are concerned with privacy issues.

Therefore operators should most certainly undertake an assessment to consider the privacy implications with any implementation. Who knows, as investment continues in the field of analytics, and as the data sets do get richer, it may well be likely to predict pregnancies.

Privacy impact assessment

As has been already discussed, there are potentially some considerable privacy concerns with regards to Smart Grid deployments. It therefore becomes important to ensure that a more detailed assessment is undertaken, invariably this assessment is comprised of a privacy impact assessment (PIA), a process designed to analyze the privacy implications within a given system. A privacy impact assessment or data protection impact assessment (DPIA) is a recommended action through a number of authoritative sources. For example, Expert Group 2 of the EC Task Force on Smart Grids is in the process of developing a DPIA template that can be then used by operators; in addition, vol. 2 of NISTIR 7628 recommends the following: "Conduct an initial privacy impact assessment before making the decision to deploy and/or participate in the Smart Grid."

Undertaking a privacy impact assessment (or DPIA) is necessary for not only satisfying legal requirements, but according to the UK Information Commissioner's Office (ICO),[14] there are many other reasons:

- *Identifying and managing risks:* Conducting an exercise to identify potential privacy risks early in any project demonstrates good governance and business practice. Equally, from a security perspective, it is likely for risk assessments to be conducted in the early phases of projects, and a PIA may be considered part of this broader risk exercise.
- *Avoiding unnecessary costs:* The concept of "privacy by design" is an effective foundation toward ensuring that systems have the appropriate safeguards to reduce privacy risks. By undertaking an assessment early to identify potential privacy risks, it reduces the likelihood of after-market solutions being bolted on after the system has been deployed. Not only is this more likely to be cost effective, it will certainly allow the project team to consider any safeguards as part of the project budget. In comparison, unexpected costs after deployment will more than likely be after the setting of any project budgets.
- *Inadequate solutions:* Identifying risks early allows the opportunity and time to source appropriate safeguards. According to the Information Commissioner's Office, the bolt-on solutions "devised only after a project is up and running can often be a sticking plaster on an open wound, providing neither the same level of protection for the individual nor organization that privacy risks have been identified and adequately addressed." The same incidentally applies to security, whereby like privacy, integrating the controls into the design of solutions is key to the deliver of any implementation.
- *Avoiding loss of trust and reputation:* There are no assurances that conducting a PIA will entirely prevent privacy issues within any system deployment. However, the ICO, as well as numerous global authoritative sources, do feel that it reduces the likelihood. What is clear is that if an organization experiences a privacy breach and has not conducted any form of privacy impact assessment (PIA), then this will likely be seen negatively by the Data

Protection Authority (DPA) that would consider this with regards to any puni-
tive action.

- *Informing the organization's communications strategy:* This is related to the loss of trust and reputation and allows any potential risks to identified and correlated with the communications plan.
- *Meeting and exceeding legal requirements:* Conducting a PIA provides the opportunity to ensure that any privacy risks are identified early, and therefore, implementing the appropriate controls that will allow for ensuring the implementation adheres to legal requirements. This applies even when engaging with a third party, whereby the operator still is responsible for ensuring that appropriate controls are in place to protect personal data.

One of the first steps in any Smart Grid deployment is to ask the question whether the system being deployed processes any personal data. This forms part of the necessity test when determining whether an impact assessment is indeed required. Although there are likely to be numerous definitions of the term "process," broadly speaking this should include any actions related to the collection, storage, retrieval, communication, or modification of personal data. According to the Article 29 opinion on smart metering, "it is established that the Directive 95/46/EC places obligations on the data controller with regard to their processing of personal data." In a smart metering/grid context, there is recognition that there are likely many organizations that can take on the role as the "data controller," but once it has been determined the role of the controller has been assigned, they are bound by the legal requirements of the appropriate Data Protection Authority.

Upon completion of the necessity test, it is then necessary to undertake an exercise to consider the privacy risks to the data subject. We had earlier cited some examples of potential risks, for example, the profiling of data subjects based on the analysis of their energy consumption. To support the risk management process, other factors may want to be considered, such as the potential impact from the risk being realized, as well as the probability of the impact occurring in the first place. These are important fields as part of the overall process because it does allow for the prioritization of any remedial actions.

Upon the identification of any risks, a management exercise is undertaken to consider the steps taken to manage them based on the priorities. There exist a series of options:

- *Risk Acceptance:* The overall risk owner of the system accepts the risk as it is.
- *Risk Transfer:* The identified risks are transferred to a third party.
- *Risk Mitigation/Reduction:* An exercise is undertaken to identify potential controls that can reduce the identified risks to an acceptable level.
- *Risk Avoidance:* The risk owner decides not to implement the system and therefore avoids the potential for the risk to be realized entirely.

As detailed earlier, one of the objectives of the PIA is to demonstrate that due diligence has been undertaken regarding the processing of personal data. Therefore, it will be necessary to present more information than simply presenting risks, and the management actions as follows:

- *Overall Risk owner:* The individual accountable for the presentation of the assessment.
- *Justification:* Outline the reasons for the decision to undertake the risk management process.
- *Date:* When the assessment was approved.
- *Date of next review:*
- *External Review:* Any details of this document being reviewed (with comments) from third-party review. This may include the Data Protection Authority (DPA).

Upon completion of the previous process, there may well be some amount of outstanding risk or residual risk. These residual risks are "the risk remaining after the risk treatment." It is important to monitor and address these residual risks on a regular basis to ensure they do not exceed the risk appetite of the data controller. Upon completion of the impact assessment process, the Smart Grid system should be ready for deployment. The assessment should be signed and presented to the Data Protection Officer (DPO) and regularly reviewed.

While we have regularly referred to the grid operator being responsible for carrying out the impact assessment, there are many other stakeholders within the Smart Grid that are likely to have the obligation for conducting such assessments. One such example may well be the operators of charging stations for electric vehicles. This is because in this example, there will be personal information that will be captured for the purposes of charging. The vehicle itself will initially identify itself with the charging station, which in turn will calculate the parameters for the requested charge and submit that to the distribution or sub-distribution system operator. This will lead to the development of the charge plan, although it is worth noting that the charge station operator may calculate the charge plan and send this to the distribution operator. This process does require specific personal details, for example, the charge operator requires electric vehicle information such as the requested amount of energy, when the vehicle intends to depart, and the state of the battery. In addition, there will be customer-specific information that is also likely to be processed, this will include customer name, address, and possible financial information to determine how the charge plan will be paid for. Such information is relevant to determine the charge plan that may/may not be accepted by the distribution operator. Using this very high-level and simplistic example, the privacy risks to the electric vehicle driver are that it will be possible to uniquely identify the vehicle owner where they are physically located and their intended departure time at a minimum.

There is no suggestion that the PIA, or even a DPIA for that matter will eliminate risks. Also, as we experience the proliferation of smart meters in our homes, it is also more than likely that considerable research will be conducted to determine what additional information can be garnered. Just as we saw with the earlier example with the ability to detect what movie you may be watching, there are likely to be equally surprising results in the future. It is therefore imperative that not only security and privacy controls built from design, but that privacy assessments are conducted regularly to keep up with the evolving threat landscape, and research activities. There is real concern from consumers about smart meters, with some individuals taking very severe actions to stop meters being installed on their homes. For example,[15] Thelma Taormina recently posted signs on her home that read, "No smart meters are to be installed on this property." When a center point energy worker ignored this advice attempting to replace her old electricity meter, Taormina drew here gun on the individual demanding they leave the property. She later commented,

> *"Our constitution allows us not to have that kind of intrusion on our personal privacy. They'll be able to tell if you are running your computer, air conditioner, whatever it is."*

Consumers are clearly, and based on recent research quite rightly very concerned about the privacy implications associated with smart meters. Be under no illusion, failure to protect our personal data, and behavioral data has the ability to not only slow down meter deployments but also possibly stop the rollout altogether.

References

1. Williams Diarmaid, Power Engineering International. *European data watchdog puts spotlight on smart meters* [document on the Internet]; July 2012. <http://www.powerengineeringint.com/articles/2012/07/european-data-watchdog-puts-spotlight-on-smart-meters.html> [cited July 2012].
2. Vijayan Jaikumar, Computer world. *Energy department warns over Smart Grid privacy* [document on the Internet]; October 2010. <http://www.computerworld.com/s/article/9191220/Energy_Department_warns_over_smart_grid_privacy> [cited July 2012].
3. Information Commissioner's Office, *Key Definitions—guide to data protection* [document on the Internet]; <http://www.ico.gov.uk/for_organisations/data_protection/the_guide/key_definitions.aspx> [cited July 2012].
4. Scott Mark, Bloomberg BusinessWeek. *How Italy beat the world to a smarter grid* [document on the Internet]; November 2009. <http://www.businessweek.com/globalbiz/content/nov2009/gb20091116_319929.htm> [cited July 2012].
5. *"NISTIR 7628 Guidelines for smart grid cyber security: Vol. 2, Privacy and the smart grid* [document on the Internet]; <http://csrc.nist.gov/publications/nistir/ir7628/nistir-7628_vol2.pdf> [cited July 2012].
6. Narciso Dean. The Columbus dispatch. *Police seek utility data for homes of marijuana-growing suspects* [document on the Internet]; February 2011. <http://www.dispatch.com/content/stories/local/2011/02/28/police-suspecting-home-pot-growing-get-power-use-data.html> [cited July 2012].

7. IT Law Wiki. *Smart Grid privacy considerations.* <http://itlaw.wikia.com/wiki/Smart_Grid_-_Privacy_Considerations#cite_note-5> [cited July 2012].

8. Sonia McNeill. *Harvard J Law Technol* 2011;**25**(1). *Privacy and the modern grid* [document on the Internet]; Fall 2011. <http://jolt.law.harvard.edu/articles/pdf/v25/25HarvJLTech199.pdf> [cited July 2012].

9. Information and Privacy Commissioner, Ontario, Canada. *Smart privacy for the Smart Grid: embedding privacy into the design of electricity conservatio*n [document on the Internet]; November 2009. <http://www.ipc.on.ca/images/resources/pbd-smartpriv-smartgrid.pdf> [cited July 2012].

10. Article 29 Data protection working party opinion on smart metering [document on the Internet]; December 2011. <http://idpc.gov.mt/dbfile.aspx/WP_183.pdf> [cited August 2012].

11. Fehrenbacher Katie. Gigaom. *Big data meets the Smart Grid* [document on the Internet]; August 2011. <http://gigaom.com/cleantech/big-data-meets-the-smart-grid/> [cited August 2012].

12. Duhigg Charles. NY Times. *How companies learn your secrets* [document on the Internet]; February 2012. <http://www.nytimes.com/2012/02/19/magazine/shopping-habits.html?pagewanted=1&_r=1&hp> [cited August 2012].

13. Wisniewski Chester. Naked security. *Smart hacking for privacy* [document on the Internet]; January 2012. <http://nakedsecurity.sophos.com/2012/01/08/28c3-smart-meter-hacking-can-disclose-which-tv-shows-and-movies-you-watch/> [cited August 2012].

14. Information Commissioner's Office. *Privacy impact assessment handbook* [document on the Internet]. <http://www.ico.gov.uk/upload/documents/pia_handbook_html_v2/html/1-Chap1-2.html> [cited July 2012].

15. Sodahead.com. *Woman pulls gun to prevent smart meter installation* [document on the Internet]; July 2012. <http://www.sodahead.com/united-states/woman-pulls-gun-to-prevent-smart-meter-installation/question-2816327/?page=5&postId=89495167#post_89495167> [cited August 2012].

Security Models for SCADA, ICS, and Smart Grid

INFORMATION IN THIS CHAPTER:

- NISTIR 7628 Smart Grid cyber security architecture
- EU M/490 and the SGCG reference architecture for the Smart Grid
- IEEE 2030-2011 Smart Grid power system, communication technology, and information technology reference diagrams
- ISA-62443: zones and conduits and Smart Grids
- Mapping security requirements to Smart Grid environments
- A simplified Smart Grid reference model

Many cyber security models exist, including several—such as those presented within NIST and ISA guidance documents—that are highly relevant to critical infrastructure. But what about the Smart Grid? The Smart Grid is a meta-system that is built via the interconnection of many smaller systems. Some are business systems; some are industrial control systems. Some are built for SCADA and automation, some for measurement, some for control, and some for safety. Some are industrial in nature, while others are commercial or consumer oriented.

All of the publically available reference models are valuable, and it is highly recommended that these standards be studied in detail by anyone attempting to fully understand the intricacies and complexities of Smart Grid system interoperability (see Appendix B, "Recommended Reading"). NISTIR 7628 is the poster child for the sophistication of the Smart Grid, while the IEEE 2030 simplifies things by looking at power, information and communications systems separately. The Smart Grids Coordination Group's reference architecture, built in accordance with European Mandate M/490, offers a simplified model while extending the architecture to differentiate between distributed generation and bulk generation.

Understanding interoperability is important because it's the necessary first step to determining boundaries and implementing security controls. The concept of "zones and conduits" (best known from ISA-62443), is much easier to implement in simpler, more isolated systems. However, though highly applicable to the Smart Grid, defining zones and conduits within a complex meta-system like the Smart Grid is hardly trivial. The "enclave" model, documented in "Industrial Network Security," takes a different approach: rather than grouping assets based on security concepts (as is the case in ISA 62443), this model groups assets based on functional concepts—specifically the asset's functional role within one or more digital systems. This approach is similarly appropriate yet also difficult to deploy in a highly interconnected system such as the Smart Grid. The "enclave" model requires defining functional groups and securing them internally as well as securing the connections between groups:

> *"Functional groups need to be defined. While simple in concept, this can be a difficult and time consuming process. It begins by logically grouping networks, assets, the operations that they perform, and even the users who are responsible for those operations. These overlapping groups are then examined to identify the common denominators between systems. The result is an enclave: exclusive collections of only those systems that are necessary to perform a specific function.*
>
> *Once defined, the enclave then needs to be secured. Ideally, every enclave would be secured to the highest degree possible. Realistically, costs and other factors make this goal unattainable. Therefore it is also necessary to identify those enclaves that represent the highest risk to safety and reliability, so that the strongest perimeter defenses can be implemented where they are needed the most (understanding the criticality of an enclave may be required for regulatory compliance purposes as well). Perimeter defenses may consist of firewalls, network IDS and IPS devices (NIDS and NIPS), router access control lists (ACLs), application monitors and/ or similar security products—all of which can and should be configured to isolate the defined members of an enclave."*[1]

One reason that multiple security standards are referenced here is that no "one size fits all," especially as we consider the unique security and privacy requirements of the Smart Grid at a global level. The model itself is less important than the fundamental concepts upon which they are built. Whether you subscribe to the philosophy of security-based or function-based separation, it is imperative that *appropriate separation* of Smart Grid systems occurs. Once groups are defined, by whatever means, the careful control over how data are communicated and utilized between systems is the most important consideration pertaining to Smart Grid cyber security—whether it is called a "conduit" or an "information path" or a "network connection" or a "flow," etc. is largely irrelevant so long as that digital intersection of Smart Grid systems is properly controlled, managed and protected.

There are many relevant standards, recommendations, and guidelines for the secure implementation of communication networks, Smart Grids, industrial control systems, information exchange, etc. —not all of which are mentioned within this book.

It should also be noted that many common recommendations are defined differently between such references. Where possible, common terms from relevant standards are used in this text, for purposes of clarity. This does not imply or suggest that this book or its authors are backing any one standard *per se*. Rather, these terms are used to convey the concepts from which they are derived as clearly as possible.

But how can a highly interconnected system such as the Smart Grid be realistically separated into zones or enclaves? The more interconnected a system becomes, the more difficult it becomes to logically group assets, the more difficult it becomes to enforce the separation of those groups of assets, and the more difficult it becomes to secure the communications between groups. At the same time, it also becomes more important to do so.

The first step to applying this or any model to a Smart Grid is to identify the assets, prioritize the assets, and understand how they are used, and how they should interconnect (if at all). This includes understanding concepts of trust, criticality, and dependencies as they relate to assets and groups of assets (systems). Only once this level of understanding is obtained can you effectively segment the Smart Grid into its component enclaves, zones, domains, groups, levels, etc.

However, there still the question of how each domain or zone works, and what the specific security challenges of that zone might be. By applying the concepts defined within the "three by three" cyber security model for critical infrastructure—a model developed by security company McAfee, Inc. to tailor security technology to the specific qualities of critical infrastructure networks—a more practical understanding of how to *apply* security can be obtained. The endpoints, networks, and applications used within each zone represent their own vulnerabilities, and therefore three levels of security must be implemented to protect each. The up-front security planning required can be challenging, but the added effort allows the correct security measures to be implemented in each area, and it becomes possible to identify where and how specific security products and technologies should be implemented within a Smart Grid (see Chapter 6, "Securing the Smart Grid").

NISTIR 7628 Smart Grid cyber security architecture

NISTIR 7628 addresses the same risks discussed throughout this book. From NISTIR 7628, "With the implementation of the Smart Grid has come an increase in the importance of the information technology (IT) and telecommunications infrastructures in ensuring the reliability and security of the electric sector. Therefore, the security of systems and information in the IT and telecommunications infrastructures must be addressed by an evolving electric sector. Additional risks to the grid include the following:

- The increased complexity of the grid could introduce vulnerabilities and increase exposure to potential attackers and unintentional errors;
- Interconnected networks can introduce common vulnerabilities;
- The increased vulnerabilities to communication disruptions and the introduction of malicious software/firmware or compromised hardware could result in denial-of-service (DoS) or other malicious attacks;
- Increased number of entry points and paths are available for potential adversaries to exploit;

- Interconnected systems can increase the amount of private information exposed and increase the risk when data are aggregated;
- Increased use of new technologies can introduce new vulnerabilities; and
- Expansion of the amount of data that will be collected that can lead to the potential for compromise of data confidentiality, including the breach of customer privacy."[2]

This is a departure from the more myopic view of many energy-sector cyber security discussions, recommendations, and standards, which tend to focus on energy generation rather than the entire grid and focus on reliability of generation facilities rather than the security of the broader infrastructure that constitutes the "grid" and its supporting systems. "In its broadest sense, cyber security for the power industry covers all issues involving automation and communications that affect the operation of electric power systems and the functioning of the utilities that manage them and the business processes that support the customer base."[2]

Figure 5.1 (reprinted from NISTIR 7628 Figure 2-2) illustrates the initial complexities introduced by the disparate stakeholders, influencers and customers of the Smart Grid (i.e. "actors"). With each actor (meaning a group with similar objectives and application dependencies) comes additional concerns of security awareness, policy, and governance that supersede physical and technical cyber security controls.

To further complicate matters, these actors (and the systems they influence) do not operate in isolation: Figure 5.2 (reprinted from NISTIR 7628 Figure 2-3) further illustrates the complexity of the Smart Grid by mapping the interconnections between systems.

The NIST IR 7628 guidance is comprehensive, consisting of three volumes—all of which are meticulously researched and articulated—outlining the requirements and inter-relationships between bulk generation, transmission, distribution, customer, service provider, operations, and marketing actors. In addition, NIST has published the Special Publication 1108R2, the "Framework and Roadmap for Smart Grid Interoperability Standards," which is a revision 2.0 as of this writing. NIST SP 1108 does not provide the same level of detail around architectural interconnectivity, but otherwise aligns with NISTIR 7628's model.

EU M/490 and the SGCG reference architecture for the Smart Grid

Standardization Mandate M/490 is a mandate of the European Standardisation Organisations (ESOs) to support European Smart Grid deployment and requires (among other things) the provision of "a technical reference architecture, which will represent the functional information data, flows between the main domains and integrate several systems and subsystems architectures."[3] Based on this mandate, the European Committee for Standardization's Reference Architecture Working Group

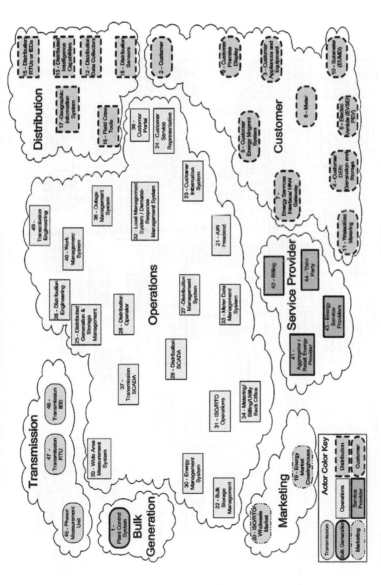

FIGURE 5.1

NIST's composite high-level view of the actors within each of the Smart Grid comains (reprinted from NISTIR 7628 Part 1 Figure 2-2 as public information)[2].

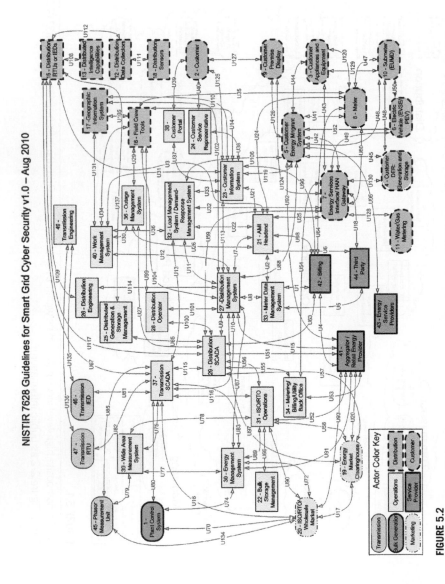

FIGURE 5.2

NIST's Smart Grid logical reference model (reprinted from NISTIR 7628 Figure 2-3 as public information.)[2]. Also printed in Chapter 2, "Smart Grid Architecture," and reprinted in Appendix B, "Reference Diagrams" for convenience.

of the Smart Grid Coordination Group (SGCG) developed the Smart Grids architecture model (SGAM) framework. The SGAM is a five-layer architectural model (Business, Function, Information, Communication, and Component layers) that "allow[s] for a representation of interoperability viewpoints in a technology neutral manner, both for current implementation of the electrical grid as well as future implementations of the Smart Grid."[4] The EU model builds upon the NISTIR 7628 model in a few key ways:

1. It extends 7628 to include a new domain for "distributed energy resources" (DER) to more comprehensively define Smart Grid architectural zones ("actors" in NIST terminology), as illustrated in Figure 5.3.
2. It applies the five layers to the defined zones to establish a three-dimensional representation of interoperability, as illustrated in Figure 5.4.
3. It incorporates the GridWise Architecture Council (GWAC) interoperability categories, which defines and separates interoperability requirements into organizational, informational, and technical categories.

As can be seen in Figure 5.3, the architecture itself maps out the different zones in a five by six grid, showing the interconnectivity between zones in a much more straightforward manner than NISTIR 7628. This is also a logical extension of the "3×3" model discussed below under "Mapping Security Requirements to Smart Grid Environments" and illustrates in Figure 5.7, and it clearly separates zones that are dependent upon field devices, process automation, substation controls, operations, etc. as they pertain to the Smart Grid. The model is very articulate in its representation of the different zones stakeholders, and functions within a distributed Smart Grid system and makes it easier to understand how the different layers of interoperability apply across zones, as illustrated in Figure 5.4.

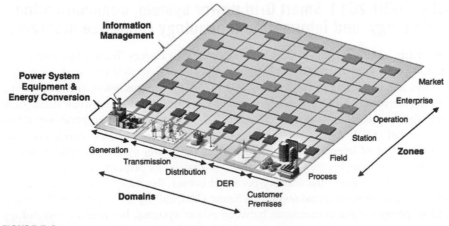

FIGURE 5.3

SGAM domains and zones (reprinted with permission from Figure 5.6 of the SGCG report on reference architecture for the Smart Grid).

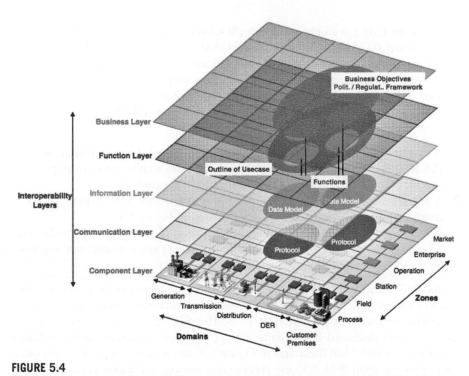

FIGURE 5.4

The SGAM framework with interoperability layers (reprinted with permission from Figure 5.7 of the SGCG report on reference architecture for the Smart Grid).

IEEE 2030-2011 Smart Grid power system, communication technology, and information technology reference diagrams

The IEEE "Guide for Smart Grid Interoperability of Energy Technology and Information Technology Operation with the Electric Power System (EPS), End-use Applications, and Loads" again models the Smart Grid, the various actors and influencers, and the interconnection between systems. One major difference between IEEE 2030 and other standards is its intent: "The IEEE 2030 Smart Grid interoperability reference model (SGIRM) is a reference tool to provide stakeholders with a common understanding of interoperability criteria from the power system, communications, and information technology perspectives."[5]—that is, its primary concern is one of interoperability rather than security per se. However, the IEEE again recognizes the diversity and interconnectedness of the Smart Grid, calling it a "System of Systems" and mapping out the connections between power systems, information technology systems, and communication systems. IEEE 2030 uses similar actors (referred to as "domains") as NISTIR 7628: bulk generation, transmission, distribution, customer, service provider, control and operations, and markets. Primary mappings of specific domain entities however are limited to three main categories (power systems, information technology and communication technology), versus 7628, which maps entities separately for electric storage, electric transportation, distribution grid management, advanced metering, and other subsystems of the Grid. This makes the IEEE mappings slightly less comprehensive than NISTIR's, mostly due to the perspective on interoperability of systems.

ISA-62443 (also known as ISA-SP99): zones and conduits and Smart Grids

The International Society of Automation (ISA) Standards and Practices (SP) committee 99 originally developed a road map for the creation of a series of standards, guidelines, and technical reports focused entirely on security for industrial automation and control systems more commonly known as SCADA or DCS. Prior to the final ratification of the majority of the documents within the series, the designation was officially changed to ISA-62443. The idea behind this renumbering was to aid in the eventual adoption of the standard by the International Electrotechnical Commission (IEC) making it a globally recognized standard.

Because the Smart Grid uses industrial automation extensively throughout generation, transmission and distribution, ISA SP99 security recommendations are highly relevant. ISA-62443 is based upon the physical and logical location and separation of the systems being protected, which again is highly relevant. The standard applies the important "zone and conduit" model to a provided reference architecture to identify which systems by necessity or function work as a group (zones) and how they should be separated from other groups or zones (conduits).[6] Figures 5.5 and 5.6 show the ISA-62443 reference architecture in a multi-plant environment, where it can be clearly seen how this model isolates functional groups and provides a single, controllable connection path between them.

What Figure 5.5 does not show is that it may be necessary to further subdivide a zone into multiple "subzones" which allow further segmentation of assets based on common criteria. To accomplish this, ISA-62443 considers that the first allocation of zones could be based on the physical grouping of assets (for example, a remote substation). Next, additional subzones are created that provide for a logical grouping of assets in order to apply a specific set of security requirements to these assets based on the desired level of protection.

A good example of this is to consider that the same types of security controls cannot be applied to embedded devices (PLCs, RTUs, IEDs) that would be applied to Windows-based devices (servers, HMIs). Therefore, this leads to natural subzones that provide the capability to implement primary and compensating security measures based on the subzone's characteristics (which are shared amongst all the members in the subzone). In the case of the Windows-based asset subzone, application control technology may be used to mitigate the risk of malware, while the embedded device subzone may focus more on deep packet inspection technology to

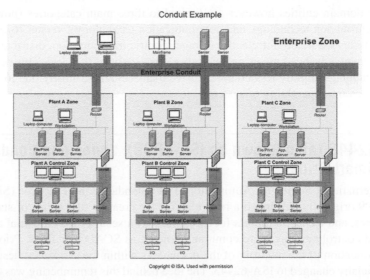

FIGURE 5.5

The ISA-62443 reference model for multi-plant zone separation (source: ISA-62443[6]).

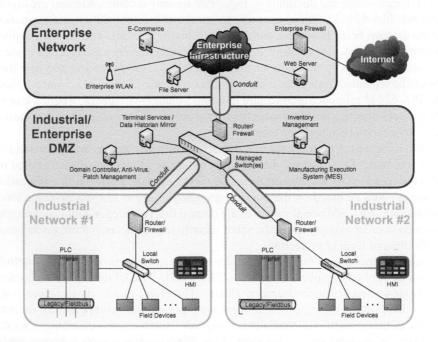

FIGURE 5.6

An ISA-62443 representation of zones and conduits (source: ISA-62443[6]).

limit functional access (and in turn malicious commands) from reaching these assets. ISA-62443 also focuses on the importance of assets to the reliable operation of the system, separating assets by level of criticality. This is a common requirement among many critical infrastructure security standards and guidance, as it prevents attackers from breaching less important (and presumably less secured) systems and then pivoting from those systems to more important targets.

The challenge, again, is the diversity and interconnectedness of the Smart Grid. In many Smart Grid deployments, functionality that should exist across several dedicated assets may be combined—measurement systems, controllers, gateways, RTUS, etc. being integrated into a single physical asset. In some cases, if these functions were broken out into dedicated assets, they might be placed into separate zones with different security levels. For example, a substation gateway provides remote connectivity, interconnects business, substation and field services, provides automation control, protocol translation, *and* measurements. These types of multi-function device are common due to the various economic benefits of device convergence, but they present a challenge to the zone/conduit model. To accommodate this, these highly integrated devices must be very carefully deployed and managed to ensure that the proper degree of separation is accomplished.

In other words, where possible separate Smart Grid systems into zones and carefully control the connections or conduits between them. Many systems within a Smart Grid are separated physically (such as the devices and systems within a substation yard), while some are separated logically (such as a T-SCADA system which connects to many substations and most likely resides in a centralized physical data center), so the reference model shown in Figure 5.5 may be overly simplified. Knowing that pure separation may not be obtainable, introduce as many additional security measures as possible, consisting of both policies (administrative measures) and products (technical measures), to make sure that the devices involved are secure from malware, that the applications are being used as intended, and that data isn't being manipulated.

Using the example of an electric transmission facility, as illustrated in Figure 5.7, we might separate T-SCADA systems from other SCADA or business systems within the data center. There might also be separation between protection systems and other devices located within a given substation yard. We can then focus on implementing security measures not just on devices within a zone, but on the conduits that connect these zones. In reality, however, the introduction of substation automation requires significantly greater segmentation if the intention is to prevent an attack from pivoting between zones. Gateway systems, as mentioned earlier, provide SCADA and automation capability, pass-through network connectivity to substation devices (via integrated remote access servers) and network connectivity to a centralized SCADA server or servers. We therefore have single physical devices that span multiple zones, requiring special consideration.

One way that ISA-62443 can be helpful here is in how it treats communications or "conduits" between zones and the assets contained within these zones. As in the example above, it is clear that gateway systems accept and direct communication

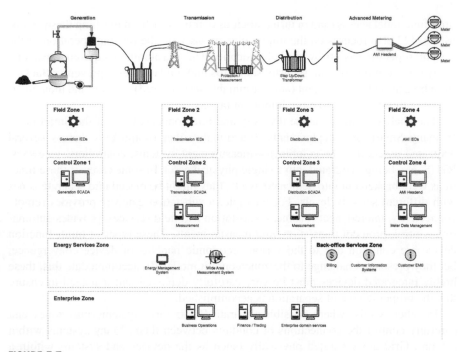

FIGURE 5.7

Examples of zone separation in a Smart Grid (not inclusive).

flow to/from a large number of devices/systems, many which are likely located in multiple zones and/or subzones. These conduits that exist between zones actually contain communication "channels" that represent the actual data flow between these systems. In keeping with the ISA-62443 approach, these channels should share the same security level (or requirements) as the conduit that contains them. So when we look more deeply into the design of conduits into substation yards through gateway servers, it may be necessary to actual establish more than one security conduit that offers different levels or protection based on the channels they contain. At first, this may seem overly complex—why not just implement everything at the highest security level? The problem is that with increased security and complexity also come increased cost in terms of both equipment and maintenance and support costs. This does not consider the common vulnerabilities that can now be introduced due to misconfiguration or other errors in implementation. Consider a simple VPN concentrator. Most are licensed based on the number of concurrent tunnels established through the appliance. When you consider the potential quantity of endpoints within the Smart Grid, it becomes obvious that these figures could significantly impact cost. Therefore, the intent would be to identify and protect each conduit based on its relative security requirements. Some conduits may require simple site-to-site encryption and authentication, while others may require the additional security that comes with content inspection and threat management.

The answer to this challenging scenario of zone separation lies in securing the individual services provided by the gateway at the host level. In a sense this is effectively implementing security to the conduits interconnecting assets, and not just the assets themselves, by providing unique access controls, authentication and authorization for each. Ideally, the gateway itself will provide strong anti-malware controls to prevent root-level exploitation of the device. Even better, the multiple functions will also reside in unique and protected operating environments or "sandboxes," using products such as Microsoft's Hyper-V or VMware's vSphere Hypervisor, such that the compromise of any one operating environment will not impact another. This is even possible within embedded systems such as controllers and field devices, using embedded Hypervisor technology, such as the Wind River Hypervisor, although this effort needs to originate from the device manufacturer and cannot be implemented by the operator.

The simplest way to segment a Smart Grid into zones or enclaves is to treat the Smart Grid as multiple systems rather than a single conglomerate system. We know that Smart Grids possess four unique architectural areas— generation, transmission, distribution and metering—so these can be easily approached individually. We also know that there are functional differentiators, such as protection systems versus automation systems, or remote access facilities versus end-user interfaces. Attempting to limit segmentation by architecture versus security requirements versus function will result in clear overlaps, which is why there are multiple security models and standards—each of which also overlap. Separating functional groups within each architecture (the "enclave" model) also poses problems. Using this model, there is a multitude of identified security enclaves, as illustrated in Table 5.1.

Even in this simplified table, over twenty enclaves are identified. To make cyber security realistic, a method of simplifying this approach is needed.

Table 5.1 Security Enclaves

	Generation	Transmission	Distribution	Metering
SCADA	X	X	X	
Automation	X	X	X	
Protection	X	X	X	
Measurement	X	X	X	X
Business systems	X	X	X	X
Line or load management		X	X	
Remote access systems	X	X	X	X
End user access				X

Mapping security requirements to Smart Grid environments

Having a reference model to work from is invaluable, and the models discussed so far all have merit. But what does this mean in terms of actually implementing security controls? Each domain or zone or actor in the Smart Grid has its own technical requirements for cyber security, its own challenges, and its own unique threats, vulnerabilities and associated risk. To help answer this question, the "3 × 3" security model was introduced in 2012 by one of this book's authors, Eric D Knapp, in conjunction with the McAfee Critical Infrastructure business unit. This model was developed as an attempt to simplify the many diverse systems used across a variety of critical infrastructures (including but not limited to Smart Grids) so that common cyber security countermeasures could be appropriately mapped to these complex requirements, and so that gaps in existing cyber security technologies could be more easily identified. The resulting model shows three unique environments, each of which requires its own special cyber security considerations.[7] They are as follows:

- Business networks, or "the Enterprise environment."
- SCADA networks, or "the control room environment."
- Device networks, or "the field environment."

Each of these environments was architecturally similar and often utilized the same assets and management systems across industries.[7] For example, a defense manufacturer might utilize the same robotic manufacturing system as an automotive assembly line, which in turn is the same as a substation automation system or coal-burning generator. While the generalization of every critical infrastructure into common architectures is purposefully oversimplified, the generalization itself is an accurate one and helps to differentiate between the technical aspects—and therefore the security challenges—of each area.

For example, business networks are very diverse by nature. They evolve rapidly, with machines being upgraded or refreshed often, patches being applied diligently, and new applications and services being installed almost daily. There is also the need for high levels of communication and collaboration, resulting in many necessary communication paths both within and outside of the organization. Countless resources are available to discuss the Enterprise, and so little time will be devoted to it here except to make the clear statement that the Enterprise is as much a part of the critical infrastructure as the SCADA and device networks are. Because corporate IT teams and ICS operations teams are often managed separately, there is a common practice of thinking of the network infrastructure as being similarly separated, and therefore, the Enterprise is often overlooked by operations, and the SCADA and device networks are often overlooked or ignored by IT. In truth, they are highly interrelated. In the Smart Grid, the billing systems are an excellent example: they utilize real time data from the AMI and are accessed by corporate sales and finance departments. To ignore these types of interconnected business systems is to render effective Smart Grid cyber security ineffective.

In contrast to business systems, the SCADA network is very different. While there are direct commonalities—each use Ethernet and TCP/IP predominantly, and leverage Windows as the primary OS, for example—the nature of these systems is very different. The main differences come from the operational paradigms of an industrial control environment, where safety, reliability and production efficiency are paramount, and where ROI is measured against production versus cost. The result is an infrastructure that is built around stability and longevity, which in turn means that the Windows systems will differ widely from those in the business network. Instead of planning a migration to Windows 7 or Windows 8, these systems are facing vendor enforced end-of-life issues with Windows NT Server and Windows 2000 platforms. Uptime requirements also present challenges to system upgrades or replacements, and even to regular patching. As a result, the individual PCs and servers within a SCADA environment are both more vulnerable and also more difficult secure using standard off-the-shelf security products such as anti-virus or host intrusion prevention systems (HIPS). Even if these tools can be implemented successfully, the servers may have very limited CPU and memory resources, making it difficult to perform a scan against large virus definition files, resulting in less frequent (and therefore less protective) infrastructure scanning. What makes industrial control system architectures even more difficult to secure is that unlike business networks that are almost exclusively Windows-based desktops and servers (with the exception being network-attached printers and multi-function devices), industrial systems have a majority of network-connected devices running embedded operating systems with vendor-specific application software. Many traditional security controls used on business systems cannot be applied to industrial control system components.

The SCADA network is also similar to the Enterprise, using Ethernet as the predominant communication technology and TCP/IP as the predominant communication protocol. However, while Ethernet and TCP/IP are used, they are used to carry real-time industrial protocols, such as Modbus/TCP, Profinet, EtherNet/IP, DNP3 and others. This introduces two important differences between Enterprise and SCADA networks.

First, this means that the networks—though they may be designed using similar hardware and facilities—function very differently. The Ethernet network in a SCADA system will be highly sensitive to latency and jitter, due to the real-time nature of the industrial protocols—many of which rely on precise synchronization. This makes in-line network detection using traditional Intrusion Detection or Prevention Systems (IDS/IPS) difficult. The second is the network becomes an extension of the "command and control" capability of the SCADA servers, because the industrial protocols in use are designed to convey messages and response between a command and control client-server system, with (typically) little authentication or other integrity controls in place. This means that, just as with the SCADA endpoints, the SCADA network is both more vulnerable and more difficult to protect than its Enterprise counterpart.

The biggest difference, however, is in the applications. Business applications are designed around specific functions, such as maintaining a database of customer information, sharing files within or between workgroups, etc. In contrast, a SCADA application is designed to create, implement, monitor and control all industrial processes. An equal, yet separate component of the SCADA application infrastructure are the complex configuration files used to customize the application to a particular manufacturing process, and allow common equipment to be used in a wide range of industries. The configuration files contain the core of a given automation system, and include hardware configuration, operational graphics and schematics used on the HMI, custom application programs, individual controller programs (such as ladder logic or function block diagrams), and often field network device configuration databases (essential with newer "smart" devices). As with the industrial network communication protocols, these SCADA systems are essentially "command and control" applications—exactly the type of application that a hacker is (in most cases) attempting to obtain through the installation of malicious code.[7] This is why the use of Meterpreter to "pop an HMI" is a common attack method; the HMI already provides the needed control; the hacker simply needs to gain access to it (see Chapter 3, "Hacking the Smart Grid").

The third environment, the process control network—which may be referred to as the field network, the plant network, the device network, the industrial control network, or the process network depending upon the specific industry that you are dealing with—is made up of the devices that run in automation: PLCs, RTUs, IEDs, and other single-purpose devices. Again, these systems are interconnected using real-time, industrial protocols that convey commands between master or control devices (such as an HMI) and slave devices (such as a PLC, RTU, or IED). They are also responsible for transporting information and measurements from the automated system to HMI consoles, the SCADA servers, and data historians. The assets themselves are typically embedded devices running an embedded operating system. This presents an even greater challenge—not only are these systems vulnerable to attack, but also they are extremely difficult to defend. Host security of these devices is often entirely dependent upon the device manufacturer, as there is (typically) no mechanism for an end user to install security software onto an embedded device.

The networks in this environment consist entirely of industrial control protocols—and present the same challenges as in the SCADA network environment—but despite the common use of Ethernet, the physical network layer within the process control network varies widely from the copper and fiber optic Ethernet networks that are ubiquitous in the Enterprise (10/100/1000baseTx and 10/100/1000BaseFx). Cellular, satellite, radio (VHF/UHF), microwave, and other specialized networks are often in use to interconnect broadly distributed systems—making it extremely difficult to utilize commercial off-the-shelf (COTS) cyber security products in these environments. Finally, the application or data tier of this environment consists of programmable logic—the automation processes that are defined by the SCADA systems and then used by the embedded infrastructure to carry out the intended automated process.

Today, the security of this third environment is an exercise in compromise. While endpoint, network and data security controls exist, it is very difficult to implement them everywhere. The specialized and heterogeneous nature of these environments

At the time this book was being written, only a handful of embedded control system devices were available with any sort of integrated security technology. The most common security technology included in these devices was limited to strong authentication to consoles or user interfaces and SSL/TLS for management data. Only a handful of products included any sort of VPN (for point-to-point encryption and endpoint authentication), host firewall, intrusion detection, application whitelisting, or other "advanced" security technology. It is the belief of the authors that more secure devices will become a market-driving feature among embedded control devices, and that more embedded devices will include strong(er) security controls in the future.

demands specialized tools. Where host security products and technologies exist, the challenge is further exacerbated by the embedded nature of these devices, which require the support of the device manufacturers. In most cases host security controls in this environment will need to be implemented by the vendor.

Of course, where an embedded process control device cannot be secured directly, it remains possible to secure the access to these devices via compensating controls. Typically this would be done using a network-based security device capable of understanding and protecting industrial control systems and protocols, such as specialized industrial control system firewalls or intrusion prevention systems. At the time of publishing, there was a new class of security appliances emerging on the market that not only offer standard Layer 3 encryption capability of IP packets using IPsec Encapsulating Security Protocol (ESP), but also provide the ability to encrypt the data payload only portion of a Layer 4 segment on IP and MPLS networks. This effectively allows network services such as class of servive (CoS) and other important L4 header information to remain in clear text and be maintained through the service provider network while the payload itself is encrypted. Put another way, ICS specific application layer protocols (transported over IP) can now have their payloads (or data) encrypted and sent across public networks, insuring data protection and endpoint authentication on both sides—a key technology in enabling the Smart Grid.

It is also possible to monitor and control the data being used by, and produced by, each of these three zones. With sufficient activity monitoring, anomaly detection products can be used to detect abnormal and potentially malicious behavior. Obviously, care must be given to the "appropriate" use of encryption in order to allow appropriate packet inspection that could otherwise hide malicious payloads. Therefore, the "3 × 3" model is most useful for mapping host, network and data security controls to business, SCADA and plant environments—providing nine unique security challenges against which security controls can be applied, as illustrated in Figure 5.8: endpoint security, network security, and data security enterprise, SCADA and embedded control systems.

Each point in the resulting matrix represents unique security challenges, and each requires special consideration when deploying cyber security measures. Not to be overlooked is that—because an attack can easily migrate from one area to the next (see Chapter 3, "Attacking the Smart Grid")—it is equally important to monitor all nine areas as a cohesive whole. This can represent a challenge of its own due to the need for strong network separation and access controls between zones

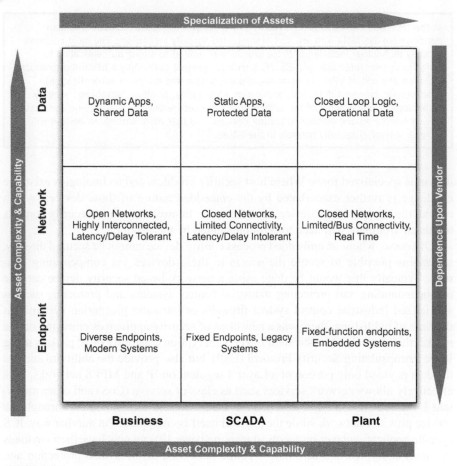

FIGURE 5.8

The McAfee "3 × 3" security model for critical infrastructure cyber security (source: McAfee, Inc. an Intel Company[7]).

(see Chapter 6, "Securing the Smart Grid"). Complicating matters further, there are multiple areas in a Smart Grid to which the "3 × 3" model can be applied, and as shown above, many of these areas are interconnected, creating another dimension of zone definition and separation.

Applying the "3 × 3" cyber security model to Smart Grids

The Smart Grid is made up of many interconnected systems, making it extremely difficult to architect a single security model around the "Smart Grid" as a whole. However, by thinking of the Smart Grid as a conglomerate of component functional groups, the 3 × 3 model can be applied individually to each group. In Figure 5.9,

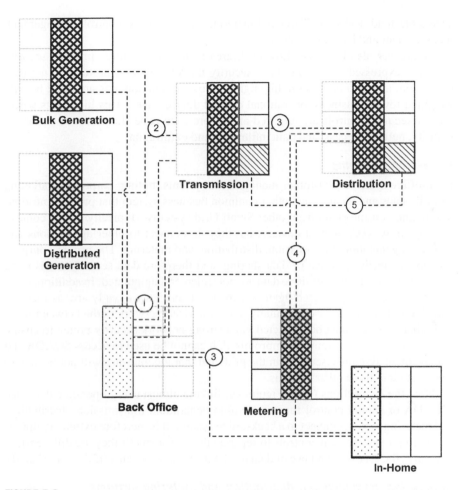

FIGURE 5.9

Extending The McAfee "3 × 3" security model to accommodate Smart Grids.

the following functional groups are illustrated: back office, generation, transmission, distribution, and metering, and in-home systems. Each of these areas (with the exception of back office systems) consists of business functions, command functions (SCADA, EMS, etc.), and control functions (the embedded devices or "plant").

The challenge to cyber security is introduced when these systems are interconnected openly. Various SCADA and management servers will likely be collocated in one or more data centers. Just as likely, these systems will be interconnected via Ethernet, and while a security perimeter will be established around this network, the communication of devices within the network will be largely trusted. Figure 5.9 shows clearly that without a strong degree of access controls between *all* individual systems, there will be easy communications between any point (including highly accessible field devices in T&D and metering) and SCADA, control, management, measurement and business systems.

Figure 5.9 also illustrates how each area maintains the three primary security concerns expressed within the 3×3 security model: endpoint protection, network protection, and data protection, highlighting how certain domains are more heavily weighted toward business, operational or field device zones. This highlights where greater security controls are required and where each zone should focus on device security, network access, and data infiltration and exfiltration.

Back-office systems

Back-office systems—customer management systems, billing, corporate marketing and PR, sales and finance, and other common business system that provide information to and consume data from other Smart Grid systems—typically do not connect directly to SCADA or field devices, but they do connect to other applications and servers in generation, transmission, distribution, and metering. The primary purpose for this connectivity is one of data sharing, and therefore data security needs to be protected to ensure that sensitive data are not stolen or manipulated. In addition, these systems need to be protected against malware (they likely already are, as they are valuable enterprise IT assets). Finally, the authorized network paths between these and other services must be protected via a strong network security policy to ensure that if a back office system is compromised, it cannot be used to access SCADA and management systems elsewhere in the grid, and that the malware will not be able to propagate into these other systems.

Note the connections (1) in Figure 5.9, linking almost every operational service (SCADA or similar control function) within generation, transmission, distribution, and metering system connect to a back-office system. It is therefore extremely important to implement logical controls to separate these systems (if they are different), or to control the access to and use of data used within these systems (if they are shared).

Generation, transmission, distribution and metering systems

Most of the systems used within these domains are command and control management systems: SCADA systems, distribution management systems and demand response systems, meter data management systems, etc. These systems provide key operational capabilities within their domain and provide control over subordinate field devices (RTUs, IEDs, etc.)—all while providing important information to back-office systems. Separating these systems from the back-office systems is a good start, but each of these systems also requires a similar degree of separation from each other. Each must also be separated from other zones within its own functional group, to prevent malware from moving between SCADA systems, management systems, and other "command" infrastructure components—as well as to prevent threats from entering the business areas of each zone from these command environments.

In Figure 5.9, connections (2), (3), and (4) between the operational (SCADA) zones of these systems are illustrated to highlight how the infection of one domain can easily propagate into neighboring domains.

As proven by real-world examples, malware is capable of moving from SCADA to industrial control systems such as PLCs and HMIs, so again all three areas of security are required: endpoint to protect these command components, network protection to control access to them and limit network based exploits, as well as data protection to prevent theft of data or (perhaps more important in these environments) the injection of false data to manipulate or sabotage the control environment.

However, the Smart Grid also introduces several interesting back channels, such as between field devices shown in connection (5) in Figure 5.9. In this example, distributed phasor measurement units (PMUs) communicate to a central system (the PDC). While the PMUs do not communicate directly with each other, they are interdependent upon a common globally available (via GPS) time source for synchronization. Other field devices, such fault indicators, may also interconnect with each other as well as a headend unit of management systems, via GSM or other wireless network.

Generation, transmission, and metering embedded devices

Embedded systems include programmable logic controllers (PLC), remote terminal/telemetry units (RTU), intelligent electronic devices (IED), single-purpose process HMIs, power protection systems, transformers, reclosers, PMUs, Volt/VAR systems, and almost any field device within the Smart Grid that is not a server-based system. In many cases, these devices are also not typically based on a Windows OS. These devices represent the third environment of the "3 × 3" model and are, as previously mentioned, more difficult to secure. However, these systems are susceptible to attacks and must be secured both to (a) protect the devices from direct manipulation or sabotage, and (b) to prevent the use of these widely accessible field devices as an inbound attack vector to other more lucrative systems such as SCADA and back-office systems.

With the exception of distributed measurement (connection (5) in Figure 5.9), most field devices interconnect only with other devices within the same domain, and with corresponding management systems.

A simplified Smart Grid reference model

Putting all of this together, a new reference model for Smart Grid cyber security can be used to apply the same "zone and conduit" or "enclave separation" security methodology outlined by ISA-62443 and other cyber security standards. While no one architecture is universally applicable (all Smart Grid deployments will different substantially due to their inherent complexity), this reference model illustrated in Figure 5.10 provides a solid foundation upon which to plan, design, and implement the cyber security controls discussed in Chapter 6, "Protecting the Smart Grid." Note that this reference model is not intended to be all-inclusive: it has been simplified to make it more understandable and so that it can be referenced heavily within Chapter 6 without undue distraction.

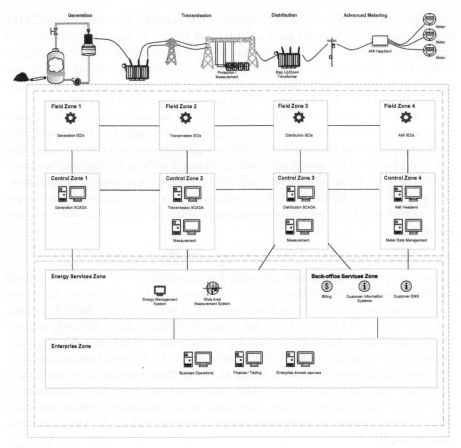

FIGURE 5.10

A simplified Smart Grid reference model for cyber security. Also reprinted in Appendix B, "Reference Diagrams" for convenience.

SUMMARY

While cyber security methodologies based upon the separation of asset groups and the control of group interconnectivity—such as the methodologies of ISA-62443's "zone and conduit" and the McAfee "3 × 3" cyber security model—are good practice in general, they can be difficult to apply to a system as broad and highly interconnected as a Smart Grid. By carefully mapping a Smart Grid's architecture to these methodologies, an adequate security methodology can be achieved, and a workable reference model can be built. This reference model is a useful tool for security planning and implementation, and has been used extensively in Chapter 6, "Protecting the Smart Grid."

References

1. Knapp Eric D. *Industrial network security: securing critical infrastructure networks for smart grid, SCADA, and other industrial control systems.* Massachusetts: Syngress; August 29, 2011.
2. *The smart grid interoperability panel—cyber security working group. NISTIR 7628 guidelines for smart grid cyber security. Smart grid cyber security strategy, architecture, and high-level requirements*, vol. 1. US Department of Commerce, National Institute of Standards and Technologies; August 2010.
3. M. Sa´Nchez Jime´Nez. *Smart grid mandate M/490 EN: standardization mandate to european standardisation organisations (ESOs) to support European smart grid deployment.* Brussels: European Commission Directorate-General for Energy; March 1, 2011.
4. CEN, CENELEC, ETSI. *SGCG report on reference architecture for the smart grid external version V2.0. SGSC Reference Architecture Working Group (RAWG)*; August, 2012.
5. IEEE Standards Coordinating Committee 21. IEEE Standard 2030™-2011. *IEEE guide for smart grid interoperability of energy technology and information technology operation with the electric power system (EPS), end-use applications, and loads.* NY, USA: IEEE. September 10, 2011.
6. American National Standard ANSI/ISA–99.00.01–2007. *Security for industrial automation and control systems, Part 1. Terminology, concepts, and models.* NC: Research Triangle Park; October 2007.
7. Knapp Eric D. *Industrial control systems cyber security proof of concept. Presented at the department of homeland security industrial control systems joint working group spring conference*, Savannah, Georgia; May 9, 2012.

Securing the Smart Grid

- Implementing security control within Smart Grid endpoints
- Establishing strong boundaries and zone separation
- Protecting data and applications within the Smart Grid
- Situational awareness
- Use case: defending against Shamoon

The consequences of a cyber attack against the Smart Grid range from espionage to sabotage, and from petty theft to larger privacy concerns. However, one thing is certain, and that is that there is considerable risk of digital foul play. So, how can the Smart Grid be protected against this risk of cyber attack? By understanding Smart Grid architecture (see Chapter 2, "Smart Grid Network Architecture"), attack methodologies (see Chapter 3, "Hacking the Smart Grid"), and a basic cyber security model (see Chapter 5, "Security Models for SCADA, ICS, and Smart Grid"), we can start examining where and how to implement specific countermeasures. In this chapter, point security products and technologies will be discussed throughout all areas of the Smart Grid architecture, from generation to metering and everything in between. While no one product or technology is certain to stop all attacks, when used together in a defense-in-depth posture across all areas of the Smart Grid, it is possible to greatly minimize the risk of a successful cyber attack. This approach creates multiple layers of protection that enable the architecture to remain resilient even when a small number of security defenses are violated—effectively creating a sort of fault-tolerant security environment.

However, despite the degree of endpoint, network and data security that is established, vulnerabilities will still remain as new exploits and more sophisticated, blended attacks will continue to arise. It is therefore necessary to—above all else—establish appropriate monitoring of all Smart Grid systems to obtain situational awareness. Today's log and event analysis tools are capable of looking at the bigger picture: collecting events from implemented security countermeasures and comparing it to network activity, user activity, application activity and even global threat activity.

By looking at the entirety of a system's digital behaviors, areas of risk can be identified, blended attacks can be detected, and in many cases suspicious or dangerous trends can be identified. The importance of establishing situational awareness cannot be underestimated due to the sheer volume of information that is relevant—both within each discrete domains and zones, and within the larger conglomerate system that is "the Smart Grid."

Implementing security control within Smart Grid endpoints

There are several methods of securing a device or endpoint against a cyber attack. Common technology-based methods include as follows:

- Access control/data access control.
- Anti-virus.
- Application whitelisting or dynamic whitelisting.
- Change control or configuration control.
- Database security.
- Endpoint encryption.
- Host data loss prevention (DLP).
- Host firewall.
- Host intrusion detection systems/host intrusion prevention systems (HIDS/HIPS).
- System hardening.

How and where these controls are implemented will vary based upon the endpoints that require protection. We can generalize this to a degree by zone: for example, field devices will typically be comprised of embedded or fixed-function devices, which may not be accessible by an end user for the installation of new software. For this reason, it may be more appropriate to focus security controls on the conduit(s) that connect to these field zones. However, the protection of field devices remains an important challenge that needs to be addressed within the industry as a whole. This generalized approach is illustrated in Figure 6.1, which illustrates specific endpoint security technologies and where they are suitable within the Smart Grid reference architecture.

Field zone protection

Field devices are often embedded systems: usually designed around low cost and low power consumption. Therefore, these devices will typically require security countermeasures that consume less memory, utilize fewer CPU resources, and have a smaller footprint. While the protection of these devices is paramount, the Smart Grid owner or operator will (typically) be unable to alter these devices, or install any commercially available cyber security countermeasure. Rather, the onus falls to the device manufacturer to build cyber security into these devices within the factory. Many device vendors are starting to investigate (and even implement) certain controls as

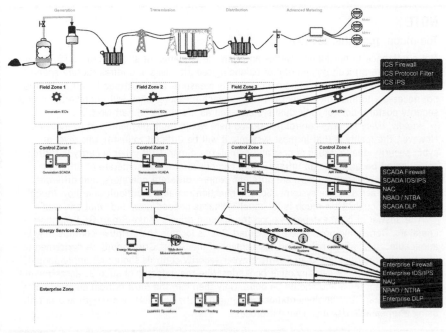

FIGURE 6.1

Applying endpoint security controls to the Smart Grid reference model.

part of their product development cycle. This is a positive trend, as the protection of the field devices would go a long way toward removing the inherent vulnerabilities that are present in most control environments. In addition, many commercially available technologies are highly significant and applicable to field device protection. Consider application whitelisting. Application whitelisting is one of the more popular software security solutions for embedded devices for these reasons. Unlike blacklist technology, which defines a rapidly growing list what is *bad*, whitelisting defines a finite list of known *good* applications and blocks everything else. "Applications" here refers to executables, including DLLs and other system functions, making it extremely difficult for malware to circumvent. The biggest advantage in an embedded system is, of course, that the whitelist rarely changes, minimizing or even eliminating the need to update the security profile on the embedded device (anti-virus, in contrast, must be patched frequently, with over 8 million new malware samples collected in $Q2$ of 2012, and over 90 million unique malware sample known to date in total.[1]). Application whitelisting is highly suitable for many embedded devices, which by their nature provide a fixed function: no application other than those that originate in the factory should ever be enabled on these devices (embedded devices using VxWorks or a similar real-time operating system are an exception due to the way "applications" function in these systems; however the concept of locking down authorized code and preventing the execution of unauthorized code still applies).

> **NOTE**
>
> Too much, too little, too late?
>
> Not a reference to the Johnny Mathis and Deniece Williams hit single from 1978, but to the even more difficult conundrum of balancing security risks and infrastructure spend. It is important to note that while many security measures are described herein, and it is not necessary to implement them all. Rather, each measure taken will improve the overall security posture, both of individual systems and as the whole "Smart Grid."
>
> Ideally, every security control mentioned here would be implemented at every level. However, the reality is that in most systems, it will be difficult to justify this level of cyber security due to issues of cost and complexity. Smart Grid cyber security is further complicated because—as an infrastructure comprised of a conglomerate of different interconnected systems—there are different owners, different operators, and different stakeholders across these systems. So, the question remains a difficult one: how much security is enough? How much is too much? What is needed now, and what can wait?
>
> The answer of course depends upon the specific drivers of the Smart Grid planners and operators. Depending upon where the Smart Grid is located, prescriptive controls may be applicable. In addition, risk-based assessment of the Smart Grid should be performed to identify and prioritize those areas where cyber security controls should be implemented. This book cannot, nor can any other book, describe the outcome of such as assessment—the assessment must and should be done. Only then can the most critical elements of a particular Smart Grid implementation be secured to the appropriate strength and priority using a repeatable risk management process.

However, it is important to remember that there are exceptions to all rules: some systems in the field, such as feature-rich gateways, may run on standard computing platforms using commercial operating systems, making it not only possible to install secure software, but also making much more important to do so.

It's also important to watch the field device vendors closely, as more security countermeasures are being designed into these devices from the factory. Several device vendors—including the makers of the real-time operating systems (RTOS) that are often used on fixed-function devices, the industrial control vendors designing field assets, and even the chipset vendors who are designing the silicon used within these devices—are working with security vendors and researches to implement a greater degree of protection. Many field device vendors have implemented secure coding and design practices, while others are addressing compensatory features to limit vulnerabilities, protect against exploit, or provide secure communication capability. At the DHS's 2012 Spring Industrial Control System Joint Working Group conference, RTOS makers Wind River and security research firm Wurldtech presented a joint initiative to embed vulnerability detection signatures directly into the RTOS, essentially providing an embedded host deep packet inspection capability into fixed-function devices.[2] Another example is that of major ICS and electric utility vendor Siemens who in Summer 2012 released new enhanced communication processors for their Windows PCs and S7 line of PLCs providing an effective method of point-to-point authentication between command and control devices. Other vendors are supporting this positive trend as well, and as more security becomes built in to these devices by design, the less onus is on the end customer to secure the devices themselves after the fact (if that is even possible at all).

Control zone protection

As shown in Figure 6.1, as we move further in from the field and into the substations, we see more sophisticated devices: SCADA servers, measurement and data management servers, AMI headends, and similar server-based systems. These devices are fully owned and operated by the end user and thus any security countermeasure—once fully vetted and tested by the vendor—can theoretically be installed. Again, however, there are certain technologies that fit better than others.

- Application whitelisting again solves the patching and resource problems associated with traditional anti-virus and is therefore recommended on all systems.
- Anti-virus is useful as well, although on many servers where application whitelisting technology is used, anti-virus serve more as an auditor of the whitelisting solution than as an active security measure, provided the whitelisting application is capable of detecting both memory- and filesystem-based malware. Anti-virus scans should never detect malware on a whitelisting endpoint and therefore will produce useful reports to that effect.
- A method of controlling configurations and system changes—often referred to as change control, change management or configuration management systems—provides added protection by preventing the secure state of an endpoint (obtained through the use of the other countermeasures listed here), from being changed or manipulated back into an untrusted state. Some solutions will detect changes and report them to a security information and event management system (SIEM), while others may actively prevent changes.
- Above and beyond the protection of third-party security products discussed so far, full system hardening is recommended, by removing all unnecessary applications and services from the host. Also, separation of services (either to dedicated hardware or to individual virtual machines if virtual data centers are utilized) is recommended to prevent cross-contamination should a system become compromised. One of the fundamental principles used in hardened industrial systems is that of "least privileges" which denies or removes everything except that which is specifically required to accomplish a given function.
- Host IDS or Host IPS is also recommended. While signature-based host detection may still be challenges due to the same patching challenges that anti-virus faces, the class of server typically found in these zones will provide the greater horsepower needed to perform deep packet inspection, detect inbound anomalies, and other tricks common to HIDS and HIPS platforms— making them useful beyond "typical" DPI inspection and detection.
- Host data loss prevention (DLP) enables sensitive data to be tagged and monitored, so that attempts to exfiltrate these data via an application, via the network or by removable media can be alerted and/or blocked. This is important

> **CAUTION**
>
> Some more advanced application whitelisting systems may also be able to prevent new data from being written directly into memory, which is useful for protection against memory attacks such as buffer overflows. As is typical in a Smart Grid, however, additional caution may need to be taken when implementing these types of advanced cyber security controls. Some Smart Grid communications may utilize application layer protocols that write directly to memory by design, and the prevention of this activity could cause a communication failure. Similarly, if software is utilized to prevent changes, extra consideration should be given to intentional changes in project files or other file structures that may be a necessary function of some systems. Remember that within the SCADA and control environments, availability is the primary objective, and any software that could potentially impact operations should always be fully tested and vetted by both the end user as well as the vendor of the system or server being protected.

considering the risk that data within the substation can present: almost any information extracted from a SCADA system, for example, can be used as reconnaissance toward a larger threat.

- Event logging, though not a security control *per se*, is also an important consideration. Any information—from system utilization, network activity, security events, authentication activity, et al.—that can be provided by a host and utilized to great benefit by centralized monitoring tools such as security information and event management (SIEM) systems. The rule of thumb is if there's any chance that a given piece of information may be relevant, log it.

Service zone protection and back-office systems

As we get to centralized SCADA systems, historians, data concentrators, and back-office systems such as billing and customer management systems, the capabilities of the servers increase, as does the value of the data created by (or utilized by) these systems. In these cases, the same security countermeasures utilized in the control zone apply. However, there is an increased reliance upon the integrity of data and less on availability since we are moving away from real-time control to more transaction-based information. The increased volume of information (as a result of centralization) also indicates the use of supporting database(s) to store and manage that data. It is therefore important to give additional consideration to data integrity and information assurance tools, including database security solutions, database auditing, and data loss prevention tools in these areas.

Establishing strong boundaries and zone separation

The term "boundary" or "perimeter" is misleading, as it implies that there is a specific thing that needs to be secured. In fact, a "boundary" is likely to consist of many network connections, between many devices—the "wires" within the "conduit."

Ideally, there would be only one such physical connection—the ISA-99 "conduit"—between systems that contains the necessary communication paths—the "wires." In this way, the conduit can be easily demarcated on both ends with a security gateway (a VPN, firewall, intrusion detection system, etc.). In a system as complex as a Smart Grid, however, that ideal is difficult to achieve as there are so many interconnected systems, blurring the proverbial "perimeter" and making network security a much greater challenge. There may be multiple wires, and multiple conduits—enough so that managing and controlling them all can be extremely difficult. It is therefore extremely important that any excess connectivity (any extraneous interfaces, ports or services) should be eliminated so that (a) the legitimate can be sufficiently protected, and (b) those protections cannot be inadvertently circumvented via an unintentional "back door." Figure 6.2 illustrates specific network security technologies and where they are suitable within the Smart Grid Reference Architecture.

The problem is that there is a need for strong network security—including encryption and authentication—between critical systems, but only a small subset of the substation, control room, data center, and field devices support this natively. To further complicate matters, commercially available TLS isn't always the best solution, because the added overhead may interfere with real-time communication (Layer 2 encryption makes more sense here, although TLS may be required by those intending to comply fully with IEC62351.). Even then, the process of encryption can also

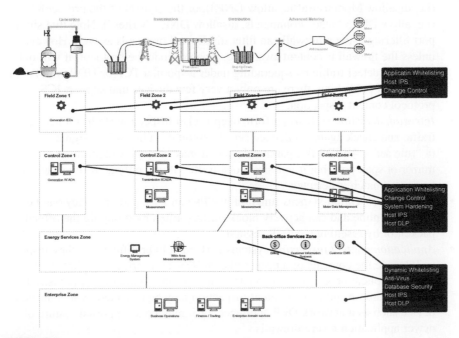

FIGURE 6.2

Applying network security controls to the Smart Grid reference model.

put blinders on security monitoring and situational awareness tools. The solution, therefore, lies in careful compromises, and in compensatory measures.

One such compromise is of risk vs. visibility: if the network connection is critical it should be secured as strongly as possible, using encryption and authentication. A strong network VPN or security gateway is a good choice here. However, if traffic is encrypted in transit, make sure that the traffic can still be monitored at either end. This will prevent a compromised device from gaining free reign to transmit exploits and malware across a connection that is "invisible" to security tools.

Compensating controls

Compensating network security controls has been around for a long time, and includes devices such as firewalls, intrusion detection and prevention systems, network access control systems, and similar devices. Firewalls, either host- or network-based, should be used promiscuously to filter out unauthorized network connections where possible. However, authorized traffic can be used to exploit a system, so firewalls should always be supplemented with some sort of monitoring or inspection technology as well:

- *Industrial protocol filters* monitor industrial protocols such as Modbus, DNP3, 61850, and others, and filter traffic based upon the protocol being used (i.e. disallow Modbus traffic, allow DNP3), or the content of the protocol (i.e. allow DNP3 "read" commands, disallow DNP3 "writes"). Note that simple port filtering using a firewall can filter disallowed protocols as well. However, unless the firewall is content aware (i.e. it can decode the protocol) it will not be able to detect traffic masquerading under a spoofed TCP or UDP port. As of the time of publishing, there are only a very few devices that support ICS protocol content inspection.
- *Intrusion detection systems* perform deep packet inspection (DPI) on network traffic and check against a defined set of exploit or vulnerability signatures (a "rule set"). An IDS is a passive device: it may be deployed inline or on a mirror or span port, but it will not block traffic: it will only alert if and when a signature match is detected.
- *Intrusion prevention systems* function just like an IDS, and only they can be deployed inline and can actively block traffic—often by dropping the offending packet, or by resetting the TCP session.
- *Application content inspection* systems perform a hybrid function: they inspect and decode the contents of a packet like an IDS, or a series of packets within a given application session, and analyze the contents similar to an Industrial Protocol filter. Application content inspection may be provided by a dedicated device such as a network DLP appliance, or it may be a supported feature of newer application-aware firewalls.
- *Transport layer security* is increasingly supported by those devices intended for use in substations automation, thanks to IEC 61850 and IEC 62351.

However, TLS can also be established as a compensating measure around those devices that do not comply with the TLS requirements of 62351. Network-based encryption (usually via a VPN appliance) also provides the benefit of facilitating lower-cost network inspection. That is, data across otherwise vulnerable communication paths can be encrypted (to protect against eavesdropping, replay attacks, man-in the-middle attacks, etc.), while the decrypted traffic within the secure network can still be inspected using IDS or IPS technology to ensure the integrity of the communication (to protect against network-based exploits). Data integrity is also provided as a standard piece of the encryption process, preventing potential manipulation of data in transit (effectively preventing "garbage" from being introduced into an encrypted payload).

It's important to remember that, without costly hardware tools, encrypted traffic is extremely difficult to inspect. Therefore, if a communication path is encrypted using a network appliance or other tool, the traffic should by inspected before encryption (i.e. within the "safe" side of the demarcation). If the encryption occurs at the host, the host itself must be secured to ensure the integrity of the sessions it participates in—otherwise an infected endpoint could authenticate and send encrypted exploits without risk of detection. Application whitelisting is a good fit here, as it offers the best degree of protection against malware at the endpoint.

Of course, it won't be possible to protect all connections, especially in remote areas. It's also not always possible to implement just any commercial off-the-shelf (COTS) security tool. Many substations, for example, present extreme temperature conditions and high levels of electromagnetic interference (EMI). Space may be limited, or other physical or environmental conditions might prevent installation. Luckily, many network security tools today can be virtualized. This allows the firewall, IDS, IPS, and/or other tools to be installed as software upon an industrial computing system—ideally one that already exists and is implemented in the target area. While not as strong a solution as dedicated, purpose-built appliance, virtualization offers more flexible deployment options and (typically) lower cost—an important consideration as you attempt to implement network security deeper into the grid where it may not be cost-effective to implement large numbers of dedicated hardware appliances, but where virtual appliances may be easily deployed. Note that virtualized systems should not be allowed to violate established zone separation. Virtual machines should be assessed as if they were physical devices, and virtual connectivity should be assessed as if they were "normal" network connections.

Advanced network monitoring

A monitored network connection can be used to aide security in several ways. Often, anomalous behavior can indicate that some sort of cyber attack is underway. In other scenarios, anomalous behavior may be an indication that a breach has occurred and additional infection stages are in process. Network behavior and anomaly detection (NBAD) tools are devices dedicated to this type of analysis and detection, and can often block against suspect traffic as well, like an IPS. Similarly, by feeding network flow information to a SIEM or log management tool, anomalies may be detected after the fact. One advantage to this method is that multiple flows can be compared—against each other and against other security events—to detect more complex threats such as multi-vector attacks, low-and-slow attacks, and blended attack scenarios.

Another useful tool for network monitoring and analysis is a network forensics tool such as Netwitness Investigator or Solera Networks' DeepSee products. These tools capture all network traffic, storing it as a base of forensic evidence that is extremely useful to investigators should a breach occur. Network packet capture does require an investment in storage, but the return can be well worth it, especially if used by an advanced cyber security team.

Data loss prevention (DLP) is better known for securing financial information in the banking industry, or patient information in the medical industry, but is just as applicable to the Smart Grid. DLP provides detection of sensitive information—both at rest and in motion—and can prevent this information from being stolen. In terms of the Smart Grid, DLP has a less obvious role. However, just like in other critical industries such as Smart Oilfields used by modern oil and gas companies, Smart Grids rely on sensitive information that must be protected. DLP can prevent it from being transmitted outside of a protected zone via the network, and can even prevent sensitive data from being saved to a USB drive or other removable media, printed, or otherwise extracted. This information could include the following:

- Distributed measurements from PMUs, PDCs, the metering infrastructure, etc.
- Power consumption information or other data with potential privacy concerns, from meter data management systems, AMI headends, HEMS, and other devices.
- Customer finance information from billing and payment systems.
- Energy production, load, and shed information used by trading systems.
- Purchasing records or other information containing specific device models of gateways, PLCs, and other substation and field devices, which could be used to research and develop a custom threat.

As can be seen in Figure 6.2, not every control fits in every area, and the needs of a DLP solution for back-office systems will be very different from those intended for SCADA systems. Still, there are numerous areas where security may be implemented to separate, segment and control network activity between the numerous and diverse systems of the Smart Grid.

Protecting data and applications within the Smart Grid

Protecting the data and applications being used within the Smart Grid means understanding a lot about how the Smart Grid works, and is one of the reasons this book has focused so heavily on the importance of the interconnectedness of the grid. In a Smart Grid, data protection requires as follows:

- Being aware of all the data and applications that are being used within the Smart Grid, including the following:
  - Where automation logic resides, what it controls, and how.
  - Where measurements are being taken, and how those measurements are being used.
  - Where management systems—including SCADA, EMS, and other systems—reside, what they manage, and how.
  - What business applications are being used, how they utilize or depend upon grid operations or measurement data, and how they obtain that data.
- Being aware of where repositories of data reside, and how they are stored (i.e. a database).
- Being able to collect that information in a format that is relevant to digital cyber security, even if the data spans multiple domains or zones.
- Being able to analyze and assess that data in a meaningful manner, to detect indications of cyber risk and threat.
- Being able to articulate that analysis back to the many stakeholders involved in Smart Grid operations.

This requires a very comprehensive understanding of the grid as a whole—a daunting task, but one that can be made somewhat easier through technology. This is because the same security countermeasures that protect data (SIEM, Network DLP, etc.) are first and foremost monitoring tools designed to obtain and analyze information from the network and/or from the devices within the network. By using these tools purely for information-gathering, a baseline can be established that can help identify where important data resides. For example, by monitoring network traffic with a SIEM, active information flows using industrial protocols can be discovered, in turn identifying the source and destination IP addresses of those communications—in turn, building a list of active automation devices. Monitoring database activity—using a network- or host-based database activity monitoring tool—can identify systems both inserting new data, and accessing stored data, again identifying dependent systems and applications (a network-based database monitoring tool may even be able to identify unknown databases by detecting SQL traffic to those databases, which is very useful for identifying databases that might have otherwise been overlooked).

NOTE

One of the most difficult tasks in securing industrial control system networks is that there is zero tolerance for any "false-positive" results that could negatively impact the performance of the network and its connected devices, either in terms of availability or integrity. What adds to this challenge is that in many cases, detailed knowledge of the network architecture in terms of not only connected devices, but also the communications that occur between devices is often incomplete or unknown. There are many tools that can be deployed in more traditional office networks, but these same technologies could prove to be disastrous when implemented on sensitive, time-critical ICS networks.

To help solve this dilemma, a team of researchers from Idaho National Laboratory (INL) sponsored by the Department of Energy—Office of Electricity Delivery and Energy Reliability (DOE-OE) and funded by the National SCADA Test Bed Program, initiated the Sophia project. Sophia is a passive, real-time tool for inter-device communication discovery and monitoring of active elements in an ICS architecture. Sophia monitors network traffic and extracts the source, destination, and port sets between ICS components. These "conversations" are stored in real-time to establish a list of conversations that are valid, effectively "fingerprinting" the ICS network.

Once the initial fingerprint is identified and accepted, Sophia continues to monitor and capture conversations, and is able to generate alerts on any conversation or device that is not a part of the system fingerprint. This effectively creates a form of "network whitelisting" application, where it knows what is normally allowed, and raises alerts when anything outside the norm occurs.

The data and application protection systems illustrated in Figure 6.3 include as follows:

- *SIEM* or security information and event management systems are information management systems designed to collect information from devices, networks, and applications. SIEMs are often focused on security events from network and endpoint security products (as described above), but can also collect application logs, operating system logs, and network flows (an audit of network communication details from the switching or routing infrastructure). This allows a SIEM to identify risks and threats against applications and data based on analysis of both internal system data and external global threat data.
- *Network DLP* prevents the loss or theft of data across the network by detecting specific types of data (or specific data that has been tagged or flagged in some way) that are "in motion." i.e. Network DLP can detect data that is being used by applications and traversing the network. For example, detecting when sensitive data are retrieved within a query from a remote database console, embedded in a file transfer, or attached to an email. Network DLP is very useful at the perimeters of data centers that house substation automation systems, energy management systems, and other systems that contain information that could in and of itself pose a threat to the larger operations of the grid. In other words: where the "data" originate or are used by a command and control system such as a SCADA server, where the data can be used to manipulate operations and cause a direct threat to the infrastructure.
- *Database Activity Monitoring* or "DAM" does exactly what it says: it monitors activity to and from databases, either via in-line inspection of network traffic, or via a host-based agent that monitors database activity locally. DAM is extremely useful for both monitoring and controlling the access to the data stored within a database, but it can also protect against database-specific exploits, such as Slammer, that could compromise the database server entirely.

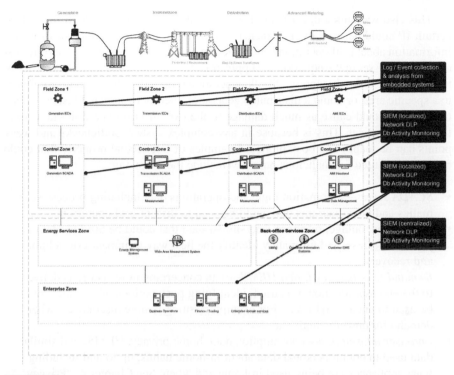

FIGURE 6.3

Applying data integrity and protection controls to the Smart Grid reference model.

Notice in Figure 6.3 that SIEM can be deployed both for local information management or centralized. This allows SIEM to be used within secure and isolated facilities, or in broadly distributed systems. This is crucial to obtaining situational awareness across zones and will be discussed further under "Situational Awareness," below.

What types of data should be protected? Some examples include as follows:

- *SCADA project files:* used by SCADA severs; certain gateways and controllers; the software development environments (SSEs) for HMI console SDEs, etc.
- *Measurement data stored within:* PDCs; meter data management systems; data historians, etc.
- *Personal data about customers or end users, stored in:* customer service/CRM systems; billing systems; the advanced metering infrastructure, etc.
- *Information about the grid, including the following:* specific device models of assets and infrastructure, from purchasing systems or from engineering diagrams; Device node information obtained from industrial protocol traffic between devices; PMU location data obtained from GPS references stored at the PDC, etc.

This also warrants a discussion of intellectual property and the theft thereof, as certain IP could be used by an attacker to threaten specific systems. For example, information about grid operations and metering could allow a malicious actor to discover weaknesses in the equation of supply, transmission, distribution, and consumption of power. Is the disruption of bulk generation required to disrupt power delivery to a specific area, or could a distributed generation facility be targeted instead? If so, the attacker could cause as much damage to the overall grid operation via a (relatively) easier target. This is because in any complex system bottlenecks and weak points can be found, and be exploited. Examples of intellectual property that could be stolen and used for malicious purposes include the following:

- *SCADA severs*—automation logic and operations data including process schematics and flow diagrams that could be used to disrupt grid operation.
- *EMS*—load, outage, response, and similar data that could be used to identify periods of stress, and ultimately identify the best way to impact grid reliability and recovery.
- *Demand response, AMI, and HEMS*—data concerning how energy is delivered to the end user and how it is used, identifying peak periods of use, etc. could be used to impact end-users. For example, issuing remote disconnects when demand for power is high, etc.
- *End-user information*—consumption data, home privacy, HEMS, and similar data used to obtain personal data about in-home habits, up to and including what appliances are being used in-home and when. See Chapter 4, "Privacy Concerns With the Smart Grid."

Situational awareness

"Situational Awareness" refers to process of perception, decision and action that enables the assessment of and reaction to a situation. In the context of cyber security, the first step (perception) requires the collection and aggregation of information from a variety of digital systems, usually by a security information and event management system (SIEM) or similar tool. The more information that can be collected, the greater the visibility the SIEM has into the environment it is protecting (i.e. the better the "perception" of the systems). Once perception is obtained, the next step is to make educated decisions based upon the situation. SIEM tools provide many automated mechanisms to make decisions about potential risks and threats to a system, and also provide a console through which a security professional can manually assess the situation as well. Automated capabilities include the following:

- Correlation of collected data against known threat patterns, to detect more complex or blended threats (e.g. multiple failed login attempts, followed by an eventually successful login attempt, followed by a network port scan originating from the same device, which may be indicative of a brute force attack).

> **NOTE**
>
> The assumption is made, of course, that a logging or security monitoring tool such as a SIEM will be used to facilitate and automate the volumes of information analysis required to obtain situational awareness in a Smart Grid. This is because the amount of data can be staggering and is definitely too much to depend entirely upon human assessment. Much of these data will originate from or be relevant to the industrial automation systems used within the Smart Grid. The monitoring and management of these data falls outside the scope of this book but is covered in the book "Industrial Network Security," by one of this book's authors, Eric Knapp.

- Calculation of baseline activity and trends, and the ability to alert when statistical deviations occur (very useful for detecting the symptoms of an attack that have affected operations).
- Tracking or "scoring" risk associated with specific assets, users, or applications and issuing an alert when risk is high.
- Filtering large amounts of data against defined criteria, and/or cross-referencing information against outside information sources such as: threat feeds; CERT activity, malware databases.

What to monitor

What needs to be monitored? For effective situational awareness within a Smart Grid, a minimum of the following should be monitored:

- All endpoint activity of the servers, gateways, controllers, field devices, etc. Essentially, if it has a network interface and is connected in any way to the grid it should be monitored.
- All network activity between any and all of these devices, obtained from the network infrastructure itself (switches, routers) and/or from network probes (network IDS or IPS is useful for this function).
- All data produced by and/or utilized within the grid, especially readings from measurement devices, device status information, protection status, phasor data, etc.

In other words, abide by the 3×3 model referenced in Chapter 5, "Security Models for SCADA, ICS, and Smart Grid" by monitoring endpoint, network, and data layers across all domains.

To actually perform this level of monitoring, a combination of log collection (from those devices and applications producing logs), event collection (from those cyber security devices that produce security events), and the direct inspection of the communication paths between devices (using network-based detection tools such as IDS, IPS, DLP, and DAM). For those devices that do not produce logs, do not utilize security countermeasures that could create events, and cannot be inspected by a network-based tool—for example, the embedded devices and field devices used within substation automation, line protection, metering, etc.—another means of information collection is required. One example of how to obtain information from these devices would be to integrate with the PDCs, SCADA servers, historians, and/or other systems that are already monitoring these devices, so that all activity can be passed to the SIEM. This will typically require customization of the SIEM, to provide the necessary integration with these specialized systems. However, it should be noted that many of these "specialized systems"—DM, EMS, HEMS, Substation Gateways, SCADA servers, et al.—will most likely produce logs of their own, relevant to the operating of that device. These logs should be collected as well, to provide awareness as to when users authenticate to the server, activity that is performed, changes that are made, etc.

Where to monitor

Based on the advice given so far, the trite answer is, "everywhere!" However, there's a broader concept of "where" that applies to the grid. For example, what domains should be monitored? What zones? Well, the answer is still trite, and it's still "everywhere!" However, the concept of domains and zones by definition means that the systems will be separated from each other, and often there will be (or at least should be) hard cyber security perimeters between them.

Therefore, in many cases the information will need to be collected locally within a domain or within a specific zone within a domain. In some cases, there will be no network path at all to a centralized facility (i.e. the mythical "air gap"), and in many cases, there will be hard security restrictions in place. For example, in nuclear generation facilities, there is a clear one-way communication requirement between secure zones and unsecure zones: if a network connection is used at all, it must only support outbound communication, so that information can be obtained from a reactor for use by business systems, but malware or malicious control cannot be sent from the insecure location back to the reactor. Local information can therefore be collected by a local SIEM that is deployed within the secure facility. The collected data can then be sent, one-way over a data diode or unidirectional network gateway, to a SIEM located centrally.

In most areas, however, establishing a secure connection for the bi-directional communication of collected data is enough. Fortunately, most SIEM tools on the market today support encrypted transfer of data when deployed in a distributed manner—many of which are actually certified "secure" under standards such as common criteria (which certifies system security) and FIPS 140-2 (which certifies secure and cryptographic boundaries).

Once information is being collected from within and between zones, simple correlation rules within the SIEM can be used to detect policy violations, for example, controllers communicating with IEDs in a separate zone, or administrators authenticating to servers in a separate domain. These types of deviations are clear indicators of risk—someone or something is behaving in a way that may seem normal but has not been explicitly allowed—but also of threats. This is because most methods used by attackers will violate these strict policy definitions. The trick is to "teach" these

> **NOTE**
>
> Segmented monitoring and situational awareness
>
> Just as monitoring can be distributed within and between different systems, zones and domains, security analysis can also be distributed. The security management tools that provide situational awareness—SIEM, log management systems, etc.—typically consist of separate components for the collection of data ("visibility") and the analysis of data ("awareness"). Most commercial solutions allow either component to be distributed, feeding back into one or more centralized location. For example, a collector appliance might be deployed across several plants to feed data back to a centralized analysis appliance.
>
> But what about areas that require a first-line defense capability? In these areas, the "analysis" portion of the solution can be distributed as well, providing the critical facility with the ability to collect *and* analyze local data. At the same time, those data can still be fed back to a central location for further analysis;—however, now there is localized situational awareness as well, to support incident detection, investigation and remediation inside of the secure facility. This type of distributed situational awareness is widely adopted in high-security facilities such as nuclear generation plants, but is also applicable within the Smart Grid, providing localized situational awareness to crews within substations, dispatch facilitates, etc.
>
> This methodology can also be extended in the other direction, feeding data up even further, to provide remote situational awareness to a trusted third party who provides managed security services.

policies to the SIEM so that it can detect the violation. This requires configuring the SIEM with domain and zone knowledge, as well as user roles and responsibilities, and any other relevant policy information. This can be done by the following:

- Establishing lists of IP addresses or IP ranges (subnets) that are authorized within a defined zone, typically by defining and populating variables within the SIEM.
- Defining access rules (this controller is only allowed to communicate with these field devices) within the SIEM, typically via correlation rules assessing network flow data.
- Establishing users, groups, and roles as actionable variables within the SIEM, typically done automatically through integration with LDAP or Active Directory, but sometimes requiring manual variable definitions.
- Defining allowed user/asset interactions, again using correlation rules to assess established user knowledge against defined zones.

Use case: Defending against Shamoon

Shamoon (W32.DistTrack) is malware that was first detected by Symantec on August 16, 2012. It was designed for data-theft and destruction, and targeted the Oil Industry. Consisting of a Dropper (the original infection that installs the additional modules of the malware), a Reporter (responsible for sending information back to the attacker) and a Wiper (which overwrites the master boot record of its target to render the system useless),[3] Shamoon was able to cause significant damage. Once the malware successfully breached a system, it spread quickly, stealing information along the way, and then leaving behind a wasteland of completely wiped systems. Because the master boot record was overwritten, system storage was effectively wiped beyond recovery, requiring that every infected machine needed to be completely reimaged, and the damage of data theft was compounded by data loss. Luckily, there were no known incidents where Shamoon interrupted the operations of a target company, but the damage to enterprise systems was severe. While Shamoon (at the time of this writing) has focused exclusively on the Oil industry, the malware could easily have targeted the business servers in any industry, including the Smart Grid.

The ICS-CERT responded quickly, issuing a Joint Security Awareness Report (JSAR-12-241-01) about Shamoon, and offering a comprehensive mitigation strategy. Looking at that mitigation strategy here, we can apply the concepts of endpoint, network, and data protection to extend the ICS-CERT's advice into a more actionable cyber security plan. Table 6.1 provides recommended countermeasures to help address each mitigation, as well as the expected result of employing that countermeasure.

Table 6.1 Mapping Cyber Security Countermeasures to the JSAR Mitigation Recommendations for the Shamoon Virus

Mitigation Recommendation (excerpted from ICS-CERT JSAR-12-241-01B)	Recommended Countermeasure	Result of Countermeasure
Implement detection for internal network traffic to match previously discovered exploit. (example: to detect Shamoon infection search for the pattern: `http://<internal_C&C_IP>/ajax_modal/modal/data.asp?mydata=<_iteration>&uid=<IP>&state=<randomnumber>`)[3]	Network IDS/IPS	Will detect and/or block inbound vulnerability, preventing infection
Implement detection for dropper files (example: the `E1RawDisk` driver to indicate Shamoon)[3]	HIDS, Host Anti-virus	Will detect a successful infection
Isolate any critical networks (including operations networks) from business systems[3]	Firewall	Will make inbound network attacks from business systems more difficult
Ensure anti-virus is up to date. ICS-CERT is aware of anti-virus reports that are not detecting some variants; however, updating signatures is still prudent[3]	Application whitelisting	Removes antivirus update requirements by utilizing a whitelist vs. blacklist approach to detection

Table 6.1 Mapping Cyber Security Countermeasures to the JSAR Mitigation Recommendations for the Shamoon Virus (Continued)

Mitigation Recommendation (excerpted from ICS-CERT JSAR-12-241-01B)	Recommended Countermeasure	Result of Countermeasure
Disable Autorun and Autoplay for any removable media device. Use Caution with USB Drives. Prevent or limit the use of all removable media devices on systems to limit the spread or introduction of malicious software and possible exfiltration data[3]	Host change control/change prevention agents	When configured to do so will prevent Autorun or Autoplay from being used on an end system
	Host DLP	Will prevent the misuse of removable media, and limit what media types or file types may be accessed by or saved to removable media
	NAC systems	Some NAC solutions allow verification of attached devices to ensure proper configuration/policy of technician or engineering laptops
Both standard and administrative accounts should have access only to services required for nominal daily duties, enforcing the concept of separation of duties[3]	SIEM	Map account/identity information to established policies and provide exception-based alerts to notify of violations
Monitor logs. Maintain and actively monitor a centralized logging solution that keeps track of all anomalous and potentially malicious activity[3]	SIEM	Will provide both advanced risk and threat detection, for the detection and discovery of incidents after-the-fact. Will also help predict incidents beforehand though anomaly or deviation analysis
Build host systems, especially critical systems such as servers, with only essential applications and components required to perform the intended function. Any unused applications or functions should be removed or disabled, if possible, to limit the attack surface of the host. Consider the deployment of software restriction policy set to only allow the execution of approved software (application whitelisting) recommend the whitelisting of legitimate executable directories to prevent the execution of potentially malicious binaries[3]	Application whitelisting	Will define the authorized executables (applications, DLLs, scripts, etc.) on a given device and prevent all other executables—including malware—from functioning

(Continued)

Table 6.1 Mapping Cyber Security Countermeasures to the JSAR Mitigation Recommendations for the Shamoon Virus (Continued)

Mitigation Recommendation (excerpted from ICS-CERT JSAR-12-241-01B)	Recommended Countermeasure	Result of Countermeasure
Implement network segmentation through V-LANs. Minimize network exposure for all control system devices. Control system devices should not directly face the Internet. Place control system networks behind firewalls[3]	Firewall, router(Note: the authors do not recommend VLANs for network segmentation, as VLANs are very easily to circumvent. Layer 3 separation is recommended, with additional segmentation via a Firewall)	A router will segment the network to restrict layer-2 identification of potential targets, making the malware more difficult to spread Firewalls should be used at all points of separation will further enforce that only desired systems and protocols are used at all perimeters
Consider the use of two-factor authentication methods for remote access or when accessing privileged root-level accounts or systems, deploying a two-factor authentication through a hardened IPsec/VPN gateway with split-tunneling prohibited[3]	VPN (2 factor)	Will prevent unauthorized remote access, and will deter man-in-the-middle and network replay attacks
Implement a secure socket layer (SSL) inspection capability to inspect both ingress and egress encrypted network traffic for potential malicious activity[3]	SSL-capable IPS, gateway, or dedicated SSL Inspection	Enables network monitoring of encrypted traffic to ensure that network exploits originating from a compromised trusted device are not being attempted over the "secure" link

SUMMARY

Developing a security plan based upon the Smart Grid cyber security reference model described in Chapter 5, "Security Models for SCADA, ICS and Smart Grid" will highlight where security controls need to be deployed. At this phase, it is possible to assess these various Smart Grid systems and components to determine where the greatest risks lie, and develop a security plan that will prioritize the security of those areas at the highest level risk. Common controls for endpoint, network and data protection are available today to support such a plan. While popular controls—such as application whitelisting, vulnerability detection via network or host IDS, NAC and SIEM—are often seen as "silver bullets," many controls are applicable and will provide the best protection when used as part of a defense-in-depth strategy. A comprehensive and mature security plan might include host and network DLP, application content monitoring, purpose-built industrial control system firewalls and protocol filters, and more.

References

1. McAfee Labs. *McAfee threats report: second quarter 2012*. Santa Clara, CA: McAfee. Inc.; 2012.
2. Kube Nate, Damisch Alexander. Mitigating industrial control systems vulnerabilities through intrusion detection systems/intrusion prevention systems signatures. In *Department of homeland security industrial control systems joint working group spring conference*. Georgia: Savannah; May 9, 2012.
3. Industrial Control System Cyber Emergency Response Team (ICS-CERT). *Joint security awareness report JSAR-12-241-01B—Shamoon/disttrack malware*. Update B. US department of homeland security; October 16, 2012.

Securing the Supply Chain

INFORMATION IN THIS CHAPTER:

- Smart Grid supply chain
- The chain in the supply chain

"Security is only as strong as its weakest link." This simple statement is a fundamental foundation of the information security industry. Simply put, the use of compromised hardware or software undoes any efforts to deliver a safe and secure system. One of the biggest challenges with the supply chain, is that these vulnerabilities are invariably outside the control of the grid operator, and most certainly the end consumer. Although this may be seen as an unlikely event, there has been recognition by the Department of Homeland Security that there have been instances where electronics sold in the United States have been preloaded with malicious programs by unknown foreign parties.

In testimony before the House Oversight and Government Reform Committee, acting deputy undersecretary of the DHS National Protection and Programs Directorate Greg Schaffer told Rep. Jason Chaffetz (R-UT) that both Homeland Security and the White House have been aware of the threat for quite some time.[1]

Indeed the recognition that the White House is concerned about supply chain attacks, and the difficulty in addressing the threat was recognized in the US Cyberspace Policy Review[2];

The challenge with supply chain attacks is that a sophisticated adversary might narrowly focus on particular systems and make manipulation virtually impossible to discover.

Although the cyber security concerns related to the supply chain do not apply solely to the Smart Grid, this threat is recognized by numerous sources including the UK Cabinet Office, in the Cyber Security Strategy of the United Kingdom[3]:

"Cyber attacks can be carried out in a number of ways:

subversion of the supply chain, where the technology supplied to an organization or individual is subtly altered (for example by implanting malicious programs) in order to make network attacks easier, or to interfere with services."

The United Kingdom and the United States are only two examples of major governments recognizing the cyber security-related threats associated with the supply chain, with many other countries implementing measures such as product certification(s) schemes, recognition within formal strategies. And quite rightly so, some examples of Cyber Supply Chain Risks were presented in the Cyber Supply Chain Risks, Strategies, and Best Practices, produced by the US Resilience Project (see Table below)[4]:

Table 7.1 Examples of Supply Chain Risks

Date	Example
September 2006	A small number of Apple Video iPods left the contract manufacturer carrying the Windows RavMonE.exe virus
October 2006	TomTom admits that a batch of devices were shipped with malware installed
September 2007	Seagate's Maxtor Basics personal storage drives were installed with a virus that hunts for gaming passwords. Drives were built under contract
July 2008	Email sent to US government employees: "Please be advised that two USB thumb drives were discovered on the 9th Floor of the Bicentennial Building. One was discovered in the men's restroom yesterday afternoon. Another was found this morning on a facsimile machine. The drives contain malicious code that automatically and silently executes when the drive is plugged into a system. The code captures certain system information and transmits it out of DOJ"
May 2009	A factory-sealed M&A Companion Touch netbook contained three pieces of malware, including a worm that spreads to USB devices and steals the online passwords of gamers. In the case of the M&A Companion Touch netbook, the malware was likely introduced when an infected USB drive was plugged into a computer at a manufacturing facility where technicians were installing drivers for the machine
March 2010	Energizer Duo USB Battery Charger software automatically downloads contaminated files from the manufacturer's website during the installation process. The malware was developed in 2007 and is suspected to have always been part of the software
May 2010	IBM hands out free USB storage devices with autorun worm malware at the Australian Computer Emergency Response Team Conference
July 2010	Replacement parts for the Dell PowerEdge servers were shipped already infected with malware that was embedded in the server management firmware
July 2011	Aldi ships an external hard drive which installs the Conficker virus when plugged into a computer
January 2012	Apple approves a fake new iPhone app, Camera+ v.4.0, which includes malware not created by the original application maker. The app was quickly pulled from the store when the verified developer confirmed they had only released v.2.4

More recently,[5] Microsoft discovered under the project name "Operation b70" that a number of new computers in China had been embedded with malware. By purchasing ten new desktop computers, and ten new laptop systems, the investigators discovered that four of these systems were infected with malware. This included the Nitol botnet that allowed cyber criminals to steal from online bank accounts, as well as take control of them.

When the compromised system was switched on, the Nitol botnet would attempt to connect to a command and control system operated by the attackers. This would allow the attackers the ability to operate the microphone or cameras of the computer; moreover, it included key loggers that would track every key the user would type.

These examples are of course, very concerning but do not appear to be directly related to the Smart Grid. A debatable point, because there may be scenarios where a grid operator employee brings a consumer device onto corporate premises that then inadvertently infect corporate systems. These scenarios are better covered in texts discussing the Bring Your Own Device (BYOD) and consumerization phenomenon. Equally, the use of brand new laptop computers and desktop computers into the organization could also introduce malware into the organization. Perhaps more disconcerting is that while the example identified by Microsoft demonstrates how the attackers utilized known malware, it would appear that this was a non-targeted attack. In other words, the intention was to infect as many systems as possible, but the relative ease in which 20% of systems were infected would infer that a targeted attack on the supply chain of a grid operator could be relatively straightforward to carry out. Also, if the attack is very targeted, then one would assume that malware which is likely to be covered by signature-based controls (e.g. anti-virus) would not be used. After all, why would so much effort be taken to attack the supply chain, when a simple AV scan can pick up the malware!

Such an example clearly demonstrates the implicit trust placed on the provision of new products, and this of course applies to not only hardware but also software. Many vendors provide the capability for customers to update the software/firmware of their purchased products but not all provide the capability to check the integrity of the software. This particular vulnerability has been recognized within the ISA 99 Standard, and this standard is focused on Security for Industrial Automation and Control Systems, and under Draft 1 Edit 4, it is advises to determine the authenticity of the patch.

"Once a patch has been evaluated and before proceeding with testing and installation, the authenticity of the patch files must be authenticated to ensure they are from a trusted source. Although rare, there still exists the risk that a patch may be obtained from an untrusted source or may have an integrity error."[6]

Smart Grid supply chain

Earlier in the book, the concept of the 3×3 model was presented. This of course is a very valuable graphical representation to explain a simplified view of the zones within an operator's environment. However, it does not explain the whole story.

In particular, it is quite likely for the composition of these zones to be reliant on third parties. For example, the management of the zone may be entirely outsourced to a third party, or parts of the zone may be. Equally, many of the components are likely to be from third-party providers, even the technical architecture of the zone is probably designed by a third party.

In order to consider the scale of the issue, we firstly need to consider the third parties in this ecosystem and build out the various dependencies. One point of note, is that initially we will consider the primary contractors, in other words those organizations with some formal, direct relationship with the operator. Later in the chapter, we will look into the subcontractor issues (and of course the subcontractor, of the subcontractor, of the primary contractor, and so on).

High transparency

This category refers to those stakeholders within the ecosystem in which the grid operator has the highest degree of transparency. In other words, all operations and all activities are completely visible to the operator. Somewhat unsurprisingly, this particular category only has one stakeholder, and this of course is the operator themselves!

Stakeholder: Grid operator

Description: When referring to the grid operator within the Smart Grid ecosystem, this could refer to a transmission system operator (TSO) or the distribution system operator (DSO). The transmission system operator (TSO) is the entity that according to the Article 2.4 of the Electricity Directive 2009/72/EC (Directive)[7]:

> *a natural or legal person responsible for operating, ensuring the maintenance of and, if necessary, developing the transmission system in a given area and, where applicable, its interconnections with other systems, and for ensuring the long-term ability of the system to meet reasonable demands for the transmission of electricity.*

The distribution system operator (DSO): According to the Article 2.6 of the Directive:

> *a natural or legal person responsible for operating, ensuring the maintenance of and, if necessary, developing the distribution system in a given area and, where applicable, its interconnections with other systems and for ensuring the long-term ability of the system to meet reasonable demands for the distribution of electricity.*

Potential Issues: Although it is worth noting that while the operator does have the remit to review all processes and procedures, the mechanisms to review all controls may not actually exist. A recent example of this was realized at the California Water Service Company in San Jose. It was reported that

> *an insider at the California Water Service Company in San Jose broke into the company's computer system and transferred $9 million into offshore bank accounts and fled the country.*

Abdirahman Ismail Abdi, 32, was an auditor for the water company, which delivers drinking water throughout the state and is located in San Jose, Calif. Abdi resigned from his position on April 27. Allegedly, that night he went back to work and made three wire transfers totaling more than $9 million from the company's accounts to an account in Qatar.[8]

What this example demonstrates is that despite having the remit to conduct all manner of assessments against the employee, for example background checks, as well as technical controls to reduce the risk of misuse, this theft still occurred. Without forming an opinion about this specific case, it does show that without appropriate controls to monitor misuse, the threat still exists regardless of the transparency afforded to the operator.

Medium transparency

In this particular category are those stakeholders that the operator has a direct, formal relationship through the provision of products or services. The level of transparency is not as high as the internal operations, but a degree of oversight is available. Note: An assumption is made here, in that the operator has placed the appropriate legal provisions to allow oversight into the activities of the third party. There is the risk that certain provisions, or required oversight is not included into formal legal contracts between the third party and the operator. In such circumstances, it is not uncommon for a contract change notification (CCN), in which the initial contract between the two parties undergoes changes. Of course, this activity is likely to incur a financial commitment on the part of the operator.

Stakeholder: End customer

Description: The consumer of the power, this includes the residential customer and business customer.

Potential Threats: The Smart Grid will allow the customer to sell energy back to the operator, and some components within the Smart Grid are likely to be owned by the customer. For example the electric vehicle. This of course does represent potential risks, with a clear financial motivation for end customers to affect the integrity of reported readings back to the operator from their equipment.

There have been numerous examples of customer tampering with electricity meters in order to modify meter readings. For example, a recent report[9] suggested that by simply using a magnet, end customers were able to tamper with smart meters deployed in Malta. The result of this simple "hack" was the opportunity to reduce energy bills by up to 75%. This particular risk has indeed been realized, where there were reports of significant revenue loss for the operator.

Stakeholder: Communications providers

Description: The communications providers are those organizations responsible for maintaining grid communications. This includes intersystem communications (for example, between meters and the collector) that are critical toward maintaining stability of the grid.

Potential Issues: The operator in this instance will likely have certain cyber security requirements when contracting the communication provider, obviously availability being one of them. The grid will need a reliable communication network, so naturally the availability of the link will need to be monitored, as well as defined within contracts under Service Level Agreement (SLA) clauses. Another requirement is for the network to remain secure, in other words one that not only scans for and filters malicious traffic, but also has the capability of isolating areas of the grid that may be infected with malware for example.

Stakeholder: Installation companies

Description: Third-party organizations are likely to be responsible for the installation and potential management of those systems within the grid. These systems may include the "core" components of the grid, but likely include those supporting facilities. Examples include, physical security equipment, fire detection and prevention equipment, heating/ventilation/air-conditioning (HVAC), and so forth.

Potential threats: Engaging third parties for installation services does potentially generate risks, for example, utilizing third parties for the implementation of those systems within the grid demands assurance that installation engineers are not implementing mechanisms that could introduce vulnerabilities into the system. Of course with a level of transparency afforded with the legal contracts between the two parties, there exists the opportunity to demand vetting procedures are applied to all installation engineers. However, without some form of independent audit, the operator will be reliant on assurances by the installation companies that all necessary procedures are adhered to.

It is inevitable that the utilization of third parties to install supporting facilities will generate some degree of risk (however unlikely this may be). For example, there have been cases where fire alarm installation organizations have been sued because their work was deemed as substandard. This has led to the insurance industry in creating alarm liability insurance. The impact of such a risk being realized is the loss of availability for sites, where a fire alarm may not have alerted authorities of a potential issue, or the sprinkler system failed to work. Equally, the installation of faulty security equipment may result in the operator not being alerted over a break-in (and again there have been court cases where security alarm companies have been sued for allegedly installing faulty equipment).

Stakeholder: Retail

Description: Organization that sells energy to the end customer.

Potential issues: The relationship between the grid operator and retailer will rely upon information, and this is imperative to transfer, for example, details of energy usage between customers for billing purposes. There will exist the risk of this data being compromised, or not being available. Such risks may manifest themselves through deliberate actions, or even unintentional actions.

Stakeholder: Information & Communication Technology (ICT) provider

Description: Organizations that provide technology for the Smart Grid, however, it is worth noting that there will be numerous subcategories associated with this list:

-    *Grid ICT:* There are those organizations that produce ICT solutions for the grid infrastructure.

- *Consumer ICT:* There will be organizations that provide products that will be owned by the end customer. For example, consider new home appliances, and these will be purchased by the consumer, but will clearly integrate with the grid, as will electric vehicles also.

Potential Issues: Earlier in the chapter, examples were provided for products that were compromised, resulting in unintended consequences. These examples provide a small insight into some of the risks associated with the ICT providers, and there is of course the risk of intentional acts of sabotage. As highlighted earlier, there is significant concern that the integrity of the grid may be compromised with equipment being intentionally sabotaged. One such (alleged) example of this was documented in efforts to disrupt the Iranian nuclear program:

> *The US-Israeli collaboration was intended to slow Iran's nuclear program, reduce the pressure for a conventional military attack and extend the timetable for diplomacy and sanctions. The cyberattacks augmented conventional sabotage efforts by both countries, including inserting flawed centrifuge parts and other components into Iran's nuclear supply chain.*[10]

These are of course a small insight into some of those stakeholders that are likely to provide a degree of transparency to the grid operator. Beyond this list, there are many more stakeholders in the Smart Grid that either will provide less or no transparency whatsoever. Moreover, some of the risks they represent to the operator may not be technical (cyber related) in nature, but, in fact, financial and reputational (e.g. data protection authority). Some of these additional stakeholders are listed below:

Standardization bodies

Energy Regulator: An independent body that regulates energy networks, with a view of ultimately protecting end customers through the promotion of competition. In the United Kingdom, the regulator Ofgem (Office of the Gas and Electricity Markets) cite their priorities and influences as follows:

- *"helping to secure Britain's energy supplies by promoting competitive gas and electricity markets—and regulating them so that there is adequate investment in the networks, and*
- *contributing to the drive to curb climate change and other work aimed at sustainable development by, for example:*
  - *helping the gas and electricity industries to achieve environmental improvements as efficiently as possible; and*
  - *taking account of the needs of vulnerable customers, particularly older people, those with disabilities and those on low income."*[11]

In the United States, the Nuclear Regulatory Commission (NRC) defined regulations that nuclear facilities have to adhere to regarding cyber security. For example, in 2009, the NRC defined regulations regarding cyber security for reactors. Moreover, in the case of the nuclear industry, there are additional regulators to the NRC, and these include the Federal Energy Regulatory Commission (FERC) and North American Electric Reliability Corporation (NERC).

At the time of writing, there has been considerable debate regarding the government oversight into US critical infrastructure providers through the US CyberSecurity Act with numerous attempts to establish some form of legislation. Regardless of the outcome of a possible bill, the impact that a regulator can have on the operator can be particularly significant. If we take the case of the NERC Critical Infrastructure Protection (CIP) requirements, simply reviewing the list of enforcements (e.g. those authorities that had a violation to the standard), the financial penalties were relatively large, but perhaps more concerning is that they are public. The NERC fines for May 2011 (based on adherence to version 3 of the CIP standard) clearly demonstrate the impact a regulator can have in the field of cyber security with 71.6% of all financial penalties CIP related. Other examples include the US Department of Energy issuing a call for electric power companies to make cyber security a top priority, with the explicit action of establishing a "cyber security governance board" whose purpose is "to oversee an internal cyber security program for protection and share information with the DoE."[12] In India, there has been significant concern about cyber threats affecting the energy infrastructure; a series of nationwide power blackouts highlighted the importance of information security controls. It is worth noting however, that the blackouts were not as a result of cyber attacks, but the event did result in a series of assessments. Subsequently, the Indian government declared their intention to align the cyber security of the energy sector with the National Critical Information infrastructure Protection Centre (NCIPC), which in addition to energy will also have oversight with other sectors. What these actions clearly demonstrate is that the regulator does have the authority to greatly impact the cyber security controls of operators, and failure to adopt the regulations can have significant financial penalties for non-compliance.

Standardization bodies: The role of standardization bodies within the information security industry is of paramount importance, particularly with the role of third parties. In particular, their prominence has risen with the advent of cloud computing, where the third-party cloud provider deals with an enormous volume of customers and cannot afford to provide clauses that support the "right to audit." This has led to the rise in third parties utilizing compliance against a myriad of standards as an attempt to assure customers that appropriate information security controls are implemented to protect valuable customer data. In terms of standards, there are many available that can be somewhat confusing, and equally their scope and impact for non-compliance does vary. In terms of applicable standards for the Smart Grid, the National Institute of Standards and Technology (NIST), advised the Federal Energy Regulatory Commission (FERC) of five standards[13] relevant for Smart Grid interoperability and cyber security. These are as follows:

- *IEC 61970 and IEC 61968:* Providing a common information model (CIM) necessary for exchanges of data between devices and networks, primarily in the transmission (IEC 61970) and distribution (IEC 61968) domains.

- *IEC 61850:* Facilitating substation automation and communication as well as interoperability through a common data format.
- *IEC 60870-6:* Facilitating exchanges of information between control centers.

IEC 62351: Addressing the cyber security of the communication protocols defined by the preceding IEC standards.

Of course, the applicable standards may well differ depending on the specific application, for example if the operator is utilizing a third party for "cloud based" services, then interoperability standards may not be appropriate. A common standard for attestation of third parties was the SAS 70 Type II audit, which in June 2011 was replaced by the American Institute of Certified Public Accountants (AICPA). In its place are three new Service Organization Control (SOC) attestation standards, SOC 1 and the associated SSAE 16, SOC 2, and SOC 3. Other common standards/ guidelines in use include ISO27001/2, NIST SP 800-53, and so on (although technically of course NIST SP 800-53 is a special publication). A detailed evaluation of the various information security-related standards is out of scope for this chapter, and indeed, the book however the reader may wish to review the library maintained by our technical editor which is available at http://www.scadahacker.com/library/index.html. It is however worth considering the role of standards within the Smart Grid; we can consider the following broad categories:

- *Mandatory standards:* Used by regulators and governing bodies to explicitly enforce information security controls onto operators. Examples of these particular standards include NERC Critical Infrastructure Protection (CIP) that is intended to *"improve physical and cybersecurity for the bulk power system of North America as it relates to reliability."*[14]
- *Contractually explicit:* When working with third parties, the contracting organization is likely to utilize standards as a means for enforcing security controls within third-party systems. Defining such standards within contracts places the explicit obligation on the contracting party to adhere to the controls within the standards. For further reading, please refer to the Department of Homeland Security, "Cyber Security Procurement Language for Control Systems."[15]
- *Guidance:* These standards are not mandatory either by the regulator/governing body or obligated by legal contracts. This of course does beg the question, why adopt such standards at all? Typically, such standards are adopted as a means for business development, for example, consider the cloud provider that wishes to entice new customers that may be worried about security. What better way to publicize to such individuals that their data will be safe than announcing compliance against well known, and universally accepted cyber security standards. Some good examples include NIST SP 800, and the Department of Homeland Security "Catalog of Control Systems Security."

Legislation authorities: This stakeholder was briefly discussed in earlier sections, with multiple authorities both national and those covering multiple national boundaries (e.g. the European Union) that are defining (or may) cyber security requirements for the grid.

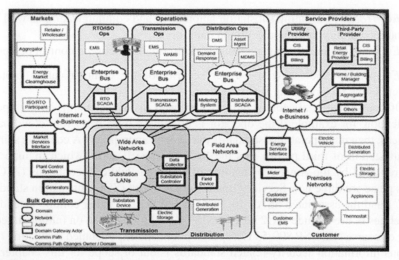

FIGURE 7.1

NIST conceptual reference diagram for Smart Grid information networks.

The above-listed stakeholders are only a short sample of the potential organizations that may operate within the grid. One thing that is particularly clear is that the ecosystem is very complex; to illustrate this point, Figure 1.0 graphically depicts a high-level overview for identifying actors and possible communication paths in the Smart Grid based upon NIST Framework and Roadmap for Smart Grid Interoperability Standards, release 1.0[16] (see Figure 7.1).

The standard also includes a series of graphical diagrams outlining a more detailed graphical representation of the various domains listed above that in some way begin to articulate the complexity of the Smart Grid.

The chain, in the supply chain

When we discuss the concept of the supply chain, this does infer that there are more than simply primary contractors involved in the process of managing data or systems. An example of the potential impact a subcontractor can have on the contracting organization of the primary supplier is demonstrated with Zurich Insurance. It was reported in 2010[17] that the UK Financial Services Authority (FSA) had fined Zurich Insurance a total of £2,275,000 when a back-up tape containing unencrypted personal details on 46,000 policy holders went missing in transit. What is particularly relevant in the case of the supply chain is that Zurich UK had outsourced the processing to Zurich Insurance Company South Africa Limited (Zurich SA). In August 2008, the FSA reported that an unencrypted back-up tape was lost during a routine transfer from a data center in South Africa to a third-party data storage facility. This tape however was lost by a subcontractor engaged by Zurich SA, who in this case was the primary contractor and had engaged without Zurich UK's written consent.

The FSA found that Zurich UK

"had failed to take reasonable care to ensure it had effective systems and controls to manage the risks relating to the security of customer data resulting from the outsourcing arrangement."

This may seem a little unfair, whereby the contracting organization would appear to have outsourced the risk, but we need to consider that while it is possible to outsource the work, outsourcing risk is not really possible. Indeed, when discussing the concept of personal data, data protection legislation generally dictates that the data controller (who is likely to be the grid operator) has the obligation to ensure that the data processor has the appropriate controls in place. What this means is that it is up to the operator to ensure that the third party has the appropriate security in place and should there be a breach, then they will need to demonstrate that they have undertaken the appropriate due diligence or face the penalties.

So, regardless of what happens, whether the impact of third-party failure to implement appropriate security is financial loss-or reputational loss. The contracting organization will still experience the impact, so the topic of the supply chain and need for assurance are of paramount importance. This has been recognized globally; more recently, the United States introduced the General Services Administration rule[18] that adds cyber security obligations for all contractors and subcontractors providing federal agencies with IT-based services. The requirement mandates that such contractors and subcontractors submit a cyber security plan that not only matches government regulations, but also allows inspectors to access the resources to ensure that they are in compliance. Moreover, the new rule requires contractors to submit such plans within 30 days of winning the contract, provide written proof that plans have been implemented within six months of winning the contract, and finally prove each year that measures remain in place. In the United Kingdom, guidance on managing information assurance within supply chains for government departments has been provided through the Supplier Information Assurance Toolset.[19] The SIAT assessment was designed to "enable Government Departments to gain a level of assurance from their major ICT suppliers with regard to securing information and particularly, personal data." The process itself utilizes a series of questions for supplier organizations that handle personal data, and this effectively becomes part of the government department's information risk management processes that they are required to review by the Cabinet Office to conduct annually.

Although such actions are useful to demonstrate the focus that organizations are placing on the security risks associated with the supply chain, one element that probably needs to be highlighted is the sheer difficulty of the overall task.

Let us consider the resource and cost associated with assessing one single supplier (of course making the assumption that the appropriate level of access necessary is indeed allowed). Multiplying this figure by the number of suppliers will undoubtedly place a burden on the internal resources of the operator. Conversely for the supplier, the challenge is supporting the multiple assessments from (potentially) every customer. This of course does not even consider the subcontractor of the primary contractor, or equally the subcontractor of the subcontractor of the primary contractor! Equally, the limitation with this approach is that any such assessment is only a point in time assessment, which is usually conducted annually. Therefore, from the minute the auditor walks out of the building, and when they return a year later, there is the potential for unsafe security practices to be adopted in the intervening 11 months and 2 weeks. Despite such limitations, such an approach is one of the most common approaches to managing security in third parties. In the future, there are initiatives to provide a more real-time, continuous assessment for technology services. Equally, the role of standards and certifications should not be underestimated. Many organizations both in the public and in the private sector are demanding for technology solutions to be accredited and certified against specific industry and/or national standards.

Every organization utilizes third parties, and this can range from everything such as simply providing cleaning services to managing every device on the network and almost everything else in between. Furthermore, the risk is not solely related to those third parties with whom the end customer is contracted to, but also the subcontractors also.

This represents a significant risk, as stated earlier, while the work can be outsourced the risk rarely is. This may seem somewhat against the foundations of risk management where there exists the opportunity to transfer risk, and we have to consider, for example, recent high-profile data losses involving third parties. Where the publicity and financial impact (through customer loss) was bore by the end customer.

It is very clear that the supply chain represents one of the biggest challenges not only the Grid, and not only to critical infrastructure, but possibly to every organization that operates in the cyber world today.

References

1. Neal Ungerleider. *Fast Company. DHS: imported consumer tech contains hidden hacker attack tools* [available on the Internet]; July 2011. <http://www.fastcompany.com/1765855/dhs-imported-consumer-tech-contains-hidden-hacker-attack-tools> [cited August 2012].
2. *US Cyberspace Policy Review: assuring a trusted and resilient information and communications infrastructure* [available on the Internet]. <http://www.whitehouse.gov/assets/documents/Cyberspace_Policy_Review_final.pdf> [cited August 2012].
3. Cabinet Office. *Cyber security strategy of the united kingdom* [available on the Internet]; June 2009. <http://webarchive.nationalarchives.gov.uk/+/http://www.cabinetoffice.gov.uk/media/216620/css0906.pdf> [cited August 2012].
4. US Resilience Project. *Cyber supply chain risks, strategies and best practices* [available on the Internet]. <http://www.usresilienceproject.org/workshop/participants/pdfs/USRP_Resources_Chapter_4_022812.pdf> [cited August 2012].
5. TechWeek Europe. *Microsoft finds Nitol Botnet malware on PCs in chinese supply chain* [available on the Internet]; September 14 2012. <http://www.techweekeurope.co.uk/news/nitol-botnet-microsoft-chinese-malware-security-cs-92741> [cited September 2012].

6. IEC/TR62443-2-3. *Security for industrial automation and control systems* [available on the Internet]; June 2012. <http://isa99.isa.org/Documents/Drafts/ISA-d62443-2-3.pdf> [cited November 2012].

7. Official Journal of the European Union. *Directive 2009/72/ec of the European parliament and of the council of 13 July 2009* [available on the Internet]; July 2009. <http://www.energy.eu/directives/Directive_internal_electricity_market.pdf>> [cited August 2012].

8. SC Magazine. *California water company insider steals $9 million, flees country* [available on the Internet]; May 2009. <http://www.scmagazine.com/California-water-company-insider-steals-9-million-flees-country/article/136923/?DCMP=EMC-SCUS_Newswire> [cited August 2012].

9. MaltaStar.com. *Tampering with smart meters to pay 75% less* [available on the Internet]; April 2012. <http://maltastar.com/dart/20120410-tampering-smart-meters-to-pay-75-less> [cited August 2012].

10. Washington Post. *US, Israel developed flame computer virus to slow Iranian nuclear efforts, officials say* [available on the Internet]; June 2012. <http://www.washingtonpost.com/world/national-security/us-israel-developed-computer-virus-to-slow-iranian-nuclear-efforts-officials-say/2012/06/19/gJQA6xBPoV_story_1.html> [cited August 2012].

11. Ofgem. *About us* [available on the Internet]. <http://www.ofgem.gov.uk/About%20us/Pages/AboutUsPage.aspx> [cited August 2012].

12. NetworkWorld.com. *Dept. of energy wants electric utilities to create "cybersecurity governance board"* [available on the Internet]; August 2012. <http://www.networkworld.com/news/2012/081012-dept-of-energy-wants-electric-261562.html?hpg1=bn> [cited August 2012].

13. NIST.gov. *NIST identifies five "Foundational" Smart Grid standards* [available on the Internet]; October 2010. <http://www.nist.gov/public_affairs/releases/smartgrid_100710.cfm> [cited August 2012].

14. North American Reliability Corporation (NERC). *Critical infrastructure* protection [available on the Internet]. <http://www.nerc.com/page.php?cid=6%7C69> [cited August 2012].

15. Department of Homeland Security. *Cyber security procurement language for control systems* [available on the Internet]; August 2008. <http://www.us-cert.gov/control_systems/pdf/SCADA_Procurement_DHS_Final_to_Issue_08-19-08.pdf> [cited November 2012].

16. NIST.gov. *NIST framework and roadmap for Smart Grid interoperability standards, release 1.0* [available on the Internet]; January 2010. <http://www.nist.gov/public_affairs/releases/upload/smartgrid_interoperability_final.pdf> [cited August 2012].

17. Out-Law.com. *Zurich fined £2.3m by FSA over loss of back-up tape* [available on the Internet]; August 2010. <http://www.out-law.com/page-11333> [cited August 2012].

18. Homeland Security News Wire. *Government contractors now required to have cybersecurity plans* [available on the Internet]; January 2012. <http://www.homelandsecuritynewswire.com/srinfrastructure20120109-government-contractors-now-required-to-have-cybersecurity-plans> [cited August 2012].

19. CESG.gov.uk—*The National Technical Authority for Information Assurance. Supplier information assurance assessment framework and guidance* [available on the Internet]; January 2011. <http://www.cesg.gov.uk/publications/Documents/Fsupplier_ia_assessment_framework.pdf> [cited August 2012].

The Future of the Grid

INFORMATION IN THIS CHAPTER:

- The challenge of making predictions
- The value of personal data
- Cyber security considerations for the future
- The future of cyber security countermeasures

No one knows what the future will bring, but by looking at trends in malware activity, hacktivism, cyber espionage, and advanced persistent threats—as well as trends in regulations, industry activities, and cyber security technology—we can certainly speculate. This chapter takes a step away from fact and delves into the nebulous world of conjecture, supposition and hearsay: not everything here is as it seems!

DISCLAIMER

The views expressed hereafter belong entirely to the authors, and not to their employers, and are not based on any future product knowledge concerning their employers or other confidential information. The speculations, ideas, opinions, views, predictions, concerns etc., are entirely there own. Statements within this chapter should be treated as conjecture and not fact, and are intended primarily to spark discussion and debate.

The challenge of making predictions

Making predictions, in particular in the world of technology, is naturally fraught with numerous examples of those much cleverer than myself getting things frightfully wrong. Some of these examples include Thomas Watson, president of IBM, who in 1943 apparently said "I think there is a world market for maybe five computers," or "Television won't be able to hold on to any market it captures after the first six months. People will soon get tired of staring at a plywood box every night," according to Darryl Zanuck who was an executive at 20th Century Fox in 1946.

Now of course, the purpose of this chapter is not to present examples of the worst technology predictions,[1] regardless of how amusing they are. However, it is somewhat difficult to predict what the future of the Smart Grid, and in particular from a security perspective will be like. The Reason? Well because much of the content proposed in this book is something we HOPE will be included within the modern grid. Just to be clear, this is not necessarily something that we hope will be part of the Smart Grid for professional purposes, or with a view to achieve financial gain, but really as consumers. Therefore, the future of the grid and in particular the cyber security and privacy considerations must look to build assurance into the design of new implementations and regularly assess the threats to ensure that any new risks are adequately managed. This is what we have presented in this book, with a range of technical and process based controls that should be incorporated into the modern energy grid.

This of course makes this chapter somewhat redundant.

However what if? What if security and privacy controls are not incorporated into the Grid? What would our future look like? This of course is moving into the world of predictions and makes us somewhat doom merchants, which is not the intent. Moreover, we are then moving into the world of non-fiction, or are we?

An alternate world

I remember a joke I was once told, about a very simple process of ordering a pizza over the telephone. At the time, I simply discarded it in the mental bin of mildly amusing anecdotes but today it demonstrates the importance of privacy.

> Operator:"Thank you for calling Pizza House. May I have your..."
> Customer:"Hi, I'd like to order."
> Operator:"May I have your NIDN first, sir?"
> Customer:"My National ID Number, yeah, hold on, eh, it's 12324134-45-54610."
> Operator:"Thank you, Mr. Smith. I see you live at 1123 Cumberland Drive, and the phone number's 425-3242. Your office number over at Telenet Insurance is 234-2342 and your cell number's 266-2566. Which number are you calling from, sir?"
> Customer:"Huh? I'm at home. Where d'ya get all this information?"
> Operator:"We're wired into the system, sir."
> Customer:(Sighs) "Oh, well, I'd like to order a couple of your All-Meat Special pizzas..."
> Operator:"I don't think that's a good idea, sir."
> Customer:"Whaddya mean?"
> Operator:"Sir, your medical records indicate that you've got very high blood pressure and extremely high cholesterol. Your National Health Care provider won't allow such an unhealthy choice."
> Customer:"Damn. What do you recommend, then?"
> Operator:"You might try our low-fat Soybean Yogurt Pizza. I'm sure you'll like it"
> Customer:"What makes you think I'd like something like that?"
> Operator:"Well, you checked out 'Gourmet Soybean Recipes' from your local library last week, sir. That's why I made the suggestion."
> Customer:"All right, all right. Give me two family-sized ones, then. What's the damage?"

Operator:"That should be plenty for you, your wife and your four kids, sir. The 'damage,' as you put it, heh, heh, comes $49.99."
Customer:"Lemme give you my credit card number."
Operator:"I'm sorry sir, but I'm afraid you'll have to pay in cash Your credit card balance is over its limit."
Customer:"I'll run over to the ATM and get some cash before your driver gets here."
Operator:"That won't work either, sir. Your checking account's overdrawn"
Customer:"Never mind. Just send the pizzas. I'll have the cash ready. How long will it take?"
Operator:"We're running a little behind, sir. It'll be about 45 min, sir. If you're in a hurry you might want to pick 'em up while you're out getting the cash, but carrying pizzas on a motorcycle can be a little awkward."
Customer:"How the hell do you know I'm riding a bike?"
Operator:"It says here you're in arrears on your car payments, so your car got repo'ed. But your Harley's paid up, so I just assumed that you'd be using it."
Customer:"@#%/$@&?#!"
Operator:"I'd advise watching your language, sir. You've already got a July 2006 conviction for cussing out a cop."
Customer: (Speechless)
Operator: "Will there be anything else, sir?"
Customer: "No, nothing. Oh, yeah, don't forget the two free liters of Coke your ad says I get with the pizzas."
Operator: "I'm sorry sir, but our ad's exclusionary clause prevents us from offering free soda to diabetics." [2]

This is of course a joke. It is not intended by any stretch of the imagination to propose what our world will look like, however let us consider what will happen should security and privacy controls not be integrated into our daily lives, and the implication this can have on society.

Value of personal data

Ask yourself a simple question, who currently has personal information about me? Chances are that you can probably name 10, or maybe even 20 organizations, but deep down you probably know this is the tip of iceberg. As we move into a digital world, comprising of smart meters capturing how we consume energy, charging stations that also capture details, electric vehicles that capture details about every journey, there is no question that we will witness an explosion in the amount of personal data captured. Let us for a moment also consider that "Personal data are the new oil of the Internet and the new currency of the digital world" according to Meglena Kuneva, European Consumer Commissioner, March 2009,[3] in other words data have significant value (to third parties). Some people may take offense to the reference to the third party; however, we have to be realistic that many people today simply do NOT understand the true value of their data. We have seen many examples of this,

I personally witnessed a line 40 deep of people queuing to hand over data in exchange for chocolate. This disparity between the perceived value of personal data, compared with its true value, is probably at the widest it has ever been. This has allowed third party companies to utilize valuable information for the purposes of improving their bottom line through the offer tailored advertisements or other products/services to the public. The value proposition for the consumer at present is relatively weak, take loyalty cards as an example that in some cases offer less than one percent in return for detailed data about what subscribers purchase. So what does this mean in the world of energy? Well we briefly touched on examples in Chapter 4, whereby it would be possible to determine remarkable insights about what exactly individuals are doing in their own home simply from accessing information garnered from the smart meter. However, the vast majority of current and potential Smart Grid customers remain oblivious to such risks there are of course consumer groups that remain committed to opposing rollouts because of the potential privacy implications, for example:

- *Stop Smart Meters*[4]: A UK group who state "Smart Meters represent a globally-coordinated, locally-deployed Trojan Horse of our time. Health, privacy & safety at home now stand at a precipice. Now is the time to say 'NO!'."
- *No to Smart Meters*[5]: US group that warn consumers to "Just say NO to Big Brother's smart meters."

What is evident is that the majority of concern, in particular with regards to consumer groups opposed to smart metering relate to privacy concerns, and the view that third parties can gain unprecedented visibility into user activities. Of course this will be governed by Data Protection legislation, but the level of oversight provided by such legislation will be dependent on where the consumer actually lives. This is because Data Protection legislation is very country specific, with the exception of Europe that issues a Data Protection directive for member states. The Directive according to Article 288 "shall be binding, as to the result to be achieved, upon each Member State to which it is addressed, but shall leave to the national authorities the choice of form and methods." It is very unlikely that a common approach to data protection, and the preservation of privacy within the Smart Grid will be consistent globally, but there are some overarching principles we can take from the Data Protection legislations that focus on the protection of individuals with regard to the processing of personal data and on the free movement of such data. To preserve the privacy of consumers, there are principles that should act as recommended approaches for all operators. Adhering to such principles will begin to address some of the concerns raised by consumer groups (two of which were identified earlier).

Transparency

"Consumers have a right to easily understandable and accessible information about privacy and security practices."[6]

The consumer or data subject should be informed about when their data are being processed; moreover, the purpose of this collection should be done for a specified purpose.

What this means is that the personal data once collected, should only be for the purposes communicated and agreed with the consumer. Any other purposes should be prohibited unless consent from the consumer has been granted. In discussing the term agreement, from a legal perspective, this refers to the term consent and in particular the provision of explicit consent.

The objective to provide greater transparency is a critical component of a number of projects that fall under a broader consumer empowerment strategy. In the UK, the MiData project aims to "allow people to view, access, and use their personal and transaction data in a way that is portable and safe." The project had originally intended to be voluntary for businesses to provide such data to consumers; however following a lukewarm response, a recent consultation considered the introduction of legislation to mandate such a requirement. The consultation closed on September 10, 2012, to provide their response, and any new measures would likely be included in the Enterprise and Regulatory Reform Bill that could become law in 2013. The outcome of the initiative will result in consumers of utilities being provided with details of their transactions. At present of those organizations that have signed up to the voluntary program, there are six energy providers. This will allow at the very least allowing consumers to view their energy consumption details and download into a defined format for viewing after. Such data should enable the consumer the ability to compare more accurately other energy providers and determine if they are overpaying their bills. This level of transparency is important, it is however worthwhile noting that additional key questions regarding transparency will be asked by the consumer, such as "Who else has access to my data?" It is unclear if this will be included within the Midata initiative, however regardless as this initiative is only related to UK organizations, this key degree of transparency is or will be important to all consumers. In the world today, data are sold to third parties without that value being realized by the data subject. In the future, however, it is anticipated for the Personal Data Economy to actually be "Personal," in other words to include the wishes of the data subject. This economy puts the consumer in control and realizing the value of personal data for their own benefit. In other words, whereas today the value realized in allowing one's data to be used is to be given access to a service, the future should see that data potentially being financially rewarding. Therefore, if I as a consumer allow a consumer electronics company to review my transaction data with the energy provider, then perhaps I will receive discounts, or some money toward a device that will save me money. For example, the company can offer me a washing machine that will save me money over two years, because it is able to schedule times to operate, and I can schedule my washing to be done during off-peak hours. More importantly in this scenario, it is the explicit consent of the data subject that authorized the release of personal data, and this was based on the consideration of the value proposition by the third party that was seen as beneficial to the subject. Further, there are start-up companies that are proposing the development of a personal-RFP (Request for Proposal) (P-RFP). This P-RFP allows the consumer to "publish" information about what they are looking to buy, with appropriate historical information. Organizations could then offer their products to such individuals, where the consumer could select the most attractive offer to them. There are even suggestions that organizations would pay for such data; in some cases (for automobile suppliers), the amount of money can be quite significant as such information constitutes a very "hot" lead.

Proportionality

There have been many complaints by consumer groups about the amount of personal data that have been collected by organizations. According to the European Network Information Security Agency (ENISA) study on data collection and storage in the EU;

> *"According to the principle of minimal disclosure, when building a system that employs personal data, it should be taken into account that there is always a risk that the system may be breached, in order to minimise the possible damage arising from an eventual breach. Thus, data minimisation is presented as a design principle that minimises risk to data subjects, and which therefore improves the protection of their privacy."*[7]

There will be additional safeguards required for particularly sensitive data, for example information pertaining to medical conditions, religion, etc. However, it is unlikely that this type of data will be used within the energy grid.

Future cyber security considerations

In the preceding paragraph(s), we considered the future of personal data and the possible demands of consumers within the modern energy network. Well at least two of the key principles. One could argue that this is the easy part! In other words, how do you define a breach of privacy? A straightforward answer really is where there has been an unauthorized disclosure of personal data.

Equally we don't have to go particularly far to see how this works in practice with "Forty-six states, the District of Columbia, Guam, Puerto Rico and the Virgin Islands have enacted legislation requiring notification of security breaches involving personal information."[8]

When we talk about security incidents, it becomes slightly more difficult to quantify. For example, do we consider an incident something as simple as a port scan, or worst an unauthorized email being sent to a stakeholder? Other challenges when defining the rules for a security breach is what data about the incident really should be disclosed? For example, we cited transparency as critically important from a privacy standpoint, but in the security context does releasing information publicly potentially put the system at risk? This could lead to subsequent "copycat" attacks. Obviously, if the breach utilizes a previously unknown vulnerability, then other users that have the same systems would want to know, but even disclosing any vulnerabilities to a restricted group takes possibly critical information to third parties outside of the organization that may use that information for nefarious purposes. For example, on August 9, 2005, Microsoft released the MS05-039 patch to address vulnerability in the Windows 2000 Operating System. Four days later, the Zotob worm began to emerge on the Internet with reports of widespread disruption of infected computers around the world. It is common practice today for new exploits to be created by reverse engineering the patch that was released to close the vulnerability, and then introduced into security frameworks such as Metasploit.

Other questions that then will arise will be the concept of safe harbor, in the privacy perspective if we consider a simple example of how safe harbor is used would be the unauthorized disclosure of personal information. If the media that is used to store, the data were encrypted then the organization that lost the data may not need to report it. In the security context, defining the safe harbor rules will invariably be more difficult to define.

Of course, all of these questions are particularly relevant and become critical to the future cyber security considerations of the Smart Grid. New developments in legal/regulatory frameworks have initiated public consultations to consider the introduction of security breach notification. In Europe, the European Commission launched a public consultation that considered such a notification. This consultation was aimed at garnering views of recipients to provide their experiences to cyber incidents that would assist the Commission in the development of security breach notification legislation.

Notification is of course one important step toward improving cyber security, by identifying and learning from incidents. In the United States the approach also includes the development of a Computer Emergency Response Team focused on Industrial Control Systems (ICS-CERT), their responsibilities include:

"Industrial Control Systems Cyber Emergency Response Team

The Industrial Control Systems Cyber Emergency Response Team (ICS-CERT) provides a control system security focus in collaboration with US-CERT to:

- ICS-CERT Monthly Monitor Newsletters.
- Control Systems Advisories and Reports.
- Other Resources.
- Reporting.
- Notable Critical Infrastructure News Feed:

  - respond to and analyze control systems related incidents,
  - conduct vulnerability and malware analysis,
  - provide onsite support for incident response and forensic analysis,
  - provide situational awareness in the form of actionable intelligence,
  - coordinate the responsible disclosure of vulnerabilities/mitigations, and
  - share and coordinate vulnerability information and threat analysis through information products and alerts.

The ICS-CERT serves as a key component of the Strategy for Securing Control Systems, which outlines a long-term, common vision where effective risk management of control systems security can be realized through successful coordination efforts."[9]

The objectives of the ICS-CERT include to "coordinate the responsible disclosure of vulnerabilities/mitigations, and share and coordinate vulnerability information and threat analysis through information products and alert."[10] As systems become more connected, and more information becomes available, the attractiveness of targeting the energy grid will only increase. We have already seen this with the "NightDragon"[11] report, where attackers extracted Intellectual property through coordinated attacks against oil, energy, and petrochemical companies. Cyber-related attacks against this sector will be expected to increase, but in the future scenario, the amount of data held by operators will be enormous and will not only include Intellectual Property, but also include considerable volumes of personal data, transactional data, data critical to the security of operations, etc. Therefore, improving information sharing mechanisms is important in order to gain better intelligence about the threat landscape. While improving intelligence is important to build a proactive, however, there is a clear need to implement strong security controls to mitigate identified risks. This has been discussed in earlier chapters but one can expect that as the defense for a grid improves as will the effort to identify gaps or identify new and innovative ways to circumvent the security controls will be attempted. Many of the Advanced Persistent Threats (APTs) today look to leverage social engineering to coerce employees onto clicking onto links that redirect them to sites containing malware of malicious software. They also have shifted away from operating system weaknesses to vulnerabilities installed by often overlooked client-side applications like PDF readers, animation engines, etc. This of course remains one of the most common techniques, and while security awareness activities can reduce this likelihood, it can never truly eliminate it.

The future of cyber security countermeasures

Perhaps the most interesting and exciting area of speculation involves how "the good guys" will be able to fight back against increasingly dangerous and sophisticated cyber threats. The security countermeasures discussed herein—firewalls, IDS and IPS, anomaly detection, whitelisting, SIEM et al.—can be used very effectively, but even in a well planned, implemented and managed security plan there will be gaps. How will the countermeasures evolve to fill these gaps? Refining the tools we have, inventing new ones specific to the Smart Grid and investigating new levels of interoperability will extend security into a more cohesive defense. The challenge is a difficult one: to extend the capabilities and collaboration of security tools while at the same time simplifying them, pairing them down so that they can be widely distributed and embedded throughout the grid infrastructure.

Making the tools we have better

One trend that has already begun is the tailoring of these existing products to better protect the specialized use cases within the Smart Grid. Support for Smart Grid protocols such as DNP3, 61850, and others has already begun to appear in network inspection products from companies such as McAfee, Subnet, Tofino/Hirschmann, Wurldtech, and others. Improving the latency of inspection technologies (making them less disruptive when deployed inline) and minimizing the chances of false positives through finely tailored rule-sets has also been seen. But what will we see that's new?

The challenge seems clear: getting the security countermeasures further into the specialized devices and protocols used within the Smart Grid. This requires the reversal of a trend in enterprise cyber security, by minimizing technologies and miniaturizing software controls until they are small enough and lightweight enough to embed throughout the grid—from RTUs, reclosers, and relays all the way to transmission monitoring, transformers, and turbines. It also means focusing less on consumer computing and more on industrial computing—supporting Real Time Operating Systems (RTOSs) and inspecting real-time network communications. Again, there are companies doing this today, but it's a nascent market with significant room for innovation.

Another area is in hardware-assisted security. Intel has already begun this work by implementing key technologies into vPro capable chipsets such as firewalls, client VPNs, anti-spoofing technology, and advanced chip-level technologies such as Trusted Execution Technology (TXT), Supervisory Mode Execution Protection (SMEP), and the Intel/McAfee coloration called DeepSAFE[12] that protects the boot cycle in order to prevent persistent malware and rootkits.

New tools

What will the entirely new tools look like? There's no way to know for certain, but there are tools that we, the authors, would like to see. For example, the applicability of application whitelisting is undeniable and helps protect end devices against malware. Can the same paradigm be extending to whitelist network operation? There are companies that claim "process control whitelisting" through the use of 100% pattern-matching. This is as close to network whitelisting as is available today, but it is in effect nothing but a very restrictive blacklist—a highly refined control system IPS. Still, the promise of process whitelisting is intriguing as well. Is it possible to whitelist communication flows, including packet and protocol contents, so that rules may be defined as "only the following DNP3 functions are allowed between this source and this destination, and all others will be blocked" would greatly simplify network cyber security throughout the SmartGrid, reducing the overhead and footprint of a network IDS in the same way that application whitelisting reduced the overhead and footprint required by antivirus.

An interesting development with the concept of whitelisting is the Sophia project.[13] This is sponsored by the Department of Energy Office of Electricity Delivery and Energy Reliability (DOE-OE). As opposed to the concept of whitelisting within the endpoint as discussed previously, Sophia focuses on network traffic by extracting the source, destination, and ports between SCADA components and storing these conversations as a baseline list of "approved" interactions. This whitelist of conversations is then used by Sophia to monitor subsequent conversations and generate alerts any conversations outside of this list.

Just before publication of this book, Kaspersky announced a new secure OS is being developed for industrial control systems.[11] Will this negate the need for other, embedded controls? Will such an OS be successful and adopted within industry? Will something else emerge? Only time will tell.

Point security versus a secure framework

No discussion of futurism would be complete without a talk about frameworks. There have been many industry initiatives around building a secure communication framework for Smart Grids—perhaps the most well-known being the IEC standards around substation automation (IEC 62351). This is valuable work and will go a long way to improving the safety and reliability of the grid. However, as discussed in Chapters 2 and 3 ("Smart Grid Architecture," and "Hacking the Smart Grid"), we can see that securing the communications alone is not enough. The data must be protected (the data that are produced by a system as well as the data that are consumed by it), and the devices need to be protected. Is it possible to extend this concept to enable (and enforce) end-to-end security at the device, network (communication) and even data tiers? If such a framework is built—and the IEC is well on its way—is it possible to implement?

It is the opinion of the authors of this book that a framework approach will be the logical end-result of proper cyber security implementations and planning: as point products become deployed, the "3 × 3" security requirements will slowly become fulfilled until eventually an end-to-end protection profile has been achieved for key systems. In other words, frameworks are good, but they are by definition goals to be worked toward, and there is sometimes the need to stick a plug in the dyke versus re-architecting the whole dam. This more pragmatic approach can have the same end-result: as more and more assets and interconnections throughout the Grid are included, the cyber security posture will extend as well until, eventually encompassing all systems within the Smart Grid.

In other words, the goal of establishing a security framework across the Grid is a valuable, if somewhat lofty goal, but it is the ends rather than the means. A carefully assessed and implemented cyber security plan will eventually lead to a secure end-to-end framework within which the grid can operate, but an attempt to implement an over-arching framework as the first step of Smart Grid cyber security can delay the implementation of desperately needed security controls that are available and effective today (unless, of course, ubiquitous support can be obtained across all areas of industry and government—the challenge which the various standards bodies currently face).

We do need to mention the concept of continuous improvement, whereby the security posture of the Grid should be in a constant state of improvement. The attackers are constantly researching new ways to circumvent security controls; therefore, standing still is in fact going backwards.

SUMMARY

You've seen the movies: we're all going to have implants in our brains that rank us by serial number. We will be tracked by the Near Field Communication antennae in our smart phones, so that lights turn on and off as we enter and leave rooms, and so that the refrigerator can dispense the correct amount of beer or water depending upon our ambient temperature, stress level, and blood pressure. And as great as all of this will be, it will also be free for the world to see on a web portal or social media outlet.

But for right now, that's still all fiction. By securing the Smart Grid is it exists today, and speculating *only a little bit*, we'll be ready for the future when it comes.

References

1. PCWorld.com. *The 7 worst tech predictions of all time* [Available on the Internet]; December 31 2008. <http://www.pcworld.com/article/155984/worst_tech_predictions.html> [cited September 2012].
2. About.com. *Political jokes* [Available on the Internet]. <http://politicalhumor.about.com/library/jokes/bljokebigbrotherpizza.htm> [cited September 2012].
3. World Economic Forum. *Personal data: the emergence of a new asset class* [Available on the Internet]; January 2011. <http://www3.weforum.org/docs/WEF_ITTC_PersonalDataNewAsset_Report_2011.pdf> [cited September 2012].
4. *Stop smart meters UK* [Available on the Internet]. <http://stopsmartmeters.org.uk/> [cited September 2012].
5. *No to smart meters* [Available on the Internet]. <http://nosmartmeters.org/> [cited September 2012].
6. The White House. *Consumer data privacy in a networked world: a framework for protecting privacy and promoting innovation in the global digital economy* [Available on the Internet]; February 2012. <http://www.whitehouse.gov/sites/default/files/privacy-final.pdf> [cited September 2012].
7. European Network Information Security Agency. *Study on data collection and storage in the EU* [Available on the Internet]; August 2012. <http://www.enisa.europa.eu/library/deliverables/data-collection/Fat_download/fullReport> [cited October 2012].
8. *National conference of state legislatures. State security breach notification laws* [Available on the Internet]; August 2012. <http://www.ncsl.org/issues-research/telecom/security-breach-notification-laws.aspx> [cited October 2012].

9. US-CERT. United states computer emergency readiness team [Available on the Internet]. <http://www.us-cert.gov/control_systems/ics-cert/> [cited October 2012].

10. United States Computer Emergency Readiness Team. *Industrial control systems cyber emergency response team* [Available on the Internet]. <http://www.us-cert.gov/control_systems/ics-cert/> [cited November 2012].

11. McAfee.com. *Global energy cyber attacks: night dragon* [Available on the Internet]; February 2011. <http://www.mcafee.com/resources/white-papers/wp-global-energy-cyberattacks-night-dragon.pdf> [cited October 2012].

12. McAfee.com. *McAfee DeepSAFE* [Available on the Internet]. <http://www.mcafee.com/uk/solutions/mcafee-deepsafe.aspx> [cited November 2012].

13. SOPHIA fingerprinting tool [Available on the Internet]. <http://sophiahome.inl.gov/> [cited November 2012].

Reference Models and Architectures

INFORMATION IN THIS CHAPTER:

- Smart Grid cyber security reference model
- Smart Grid cyber security design template
- Generation cyber security reference model (detail)
- Generation cyber security design template (detail)
- NISTIR 7628 guidelines for Smart Grid cyber security
- IEEE 2030-2011 Smart Grid power system, communication technology, and information technology reference diagrams
- SGSC reference architecture for the Smart Grid
- Applying endpoint security controls
- Applying network security controls
- Applying data integrity and protection controls

Have ever tried to find that diagram you saw in a book and couldn't remember what it was titled or what chapter it was in? This appendix has been provided as a convenient way to quickly find reference diagrams from this book as well as from other sources, for that very reason.

Smart Grid cyber security reference model

A simplified representation of the Smart Grid, to show how different systems in different zones interconnect in order to determine where to implement different cyber security measures. Refer to Chapter 5, "Security Models for SCADA, ICS, and Smart Grid" (see Figure A.1).

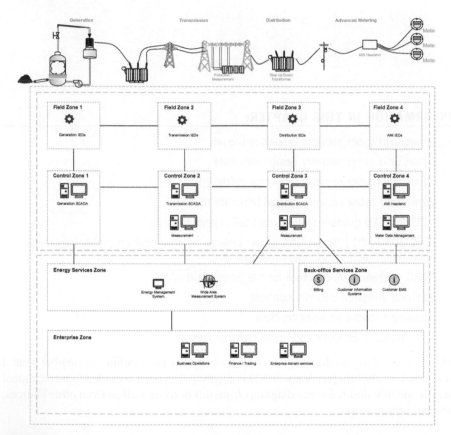

FIGURE A.1

A new Smart Grid cyber security reference model.

Smart Grid cyber security design template

Extrapolating the more generic security model above to a more accurate and detailed Smart Grid architecture. Refer to Chapter 6, "Protecting the Smart Grid" (see Figure A.2).

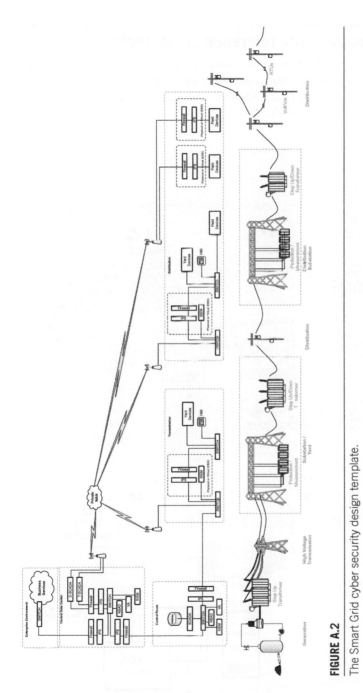

FIGURE A.2

The Smart Grid cyber security design template.

Generation cyber security reference model (detail)

A detailed model of a fossil fuel power generation system was designed to highlight the many dependent components that could be attacked or manipulated by a cyber threat. Refer to Chapter 2, "Smart Grid Network Architecture," and Chapter 6, "Protecting the Smart Grid" (see Figure A.3).

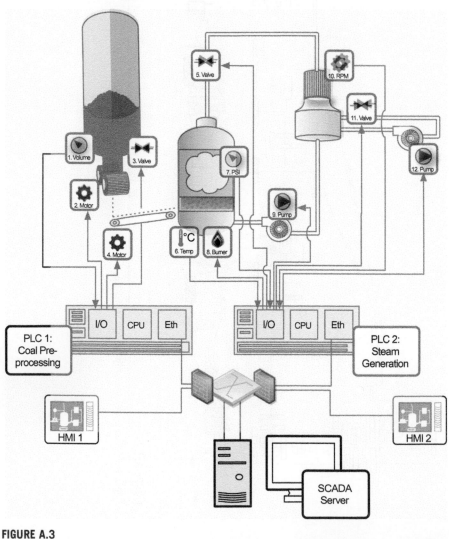

FIGURE A.3

Generation cyber security reference model (detail).

Generation cyber security design template (detail)

Common cyber security countermeasures applied to the above "Generation Cyber Security Reference Model." Refer to Chapter 6, "Protecting the Smart Grid" (see Figure A.4).

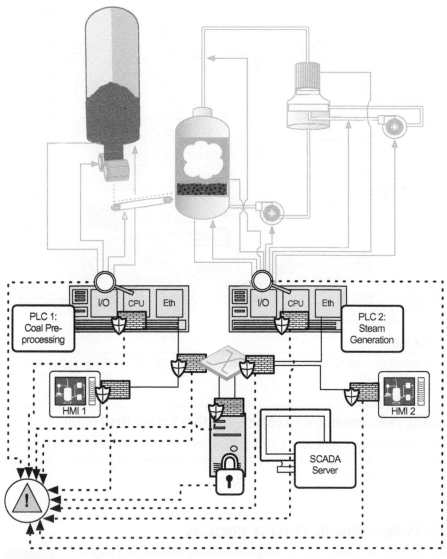

FIGURE A.4

Generation cyber security design template (detail).

NISTIR 7628 guidelines for Smart Grid cyber security

The NIST representation of the Smart Grid, and the interconnection of its many systems, grouped by actor (Transmission, Distribution, Bulk Generation, Operations, Marketing, Service Provider, and Customer). Refer to the NISTIR 7628 for more information (see Figure A.5).

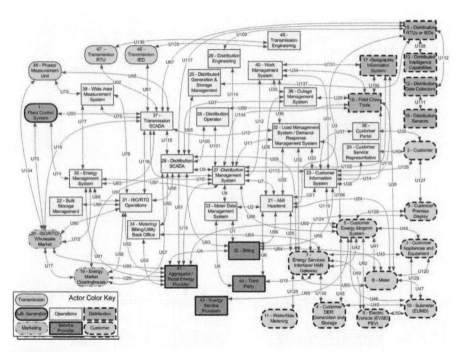

FIGURE A.5

NIST Smart Grid logical reference model (reprinted from NISTIR 7628 Figure 2.3 as public information).[1]

SGCG reference architecture for the Smart Grid

The Smart Grids Coordination Group Reference Architecture for the Smart Grid, highlighting the different domains, zones, and interoperability layers of the Smart Grid (see Figure A.6).

Applying endpoint security controls

Recommended applications of endpoint security (defined in Chapter 6, "Protecting the Smart Grid"), using the Smart Grid reference model (defined in Chapter 5, "Security Models for SCADA, ICS, and Smart Grid") (see Figure A.7).

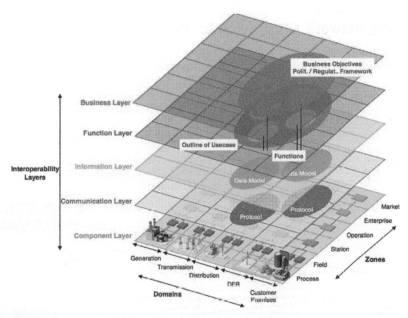

FIGURE A.6

The SGAM framework with interoperability layers (reprinted with permission from Figure 7 of the SGCG report on reference architecture for the Smart Grid).[2]

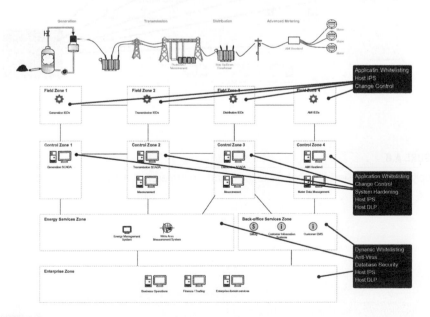

FIGURE A.7

Applying endpoint security controls to the Smart Grid reference model.

Applying network security controls

Recommended applications of network security (defined in Chapter 6, "Protecting the Smart Grid"), using the Smart Grid reference model (defined in Chapter 5, "Security Models for SCADA, ICS, and Smart Grid") (see Figure A.8).

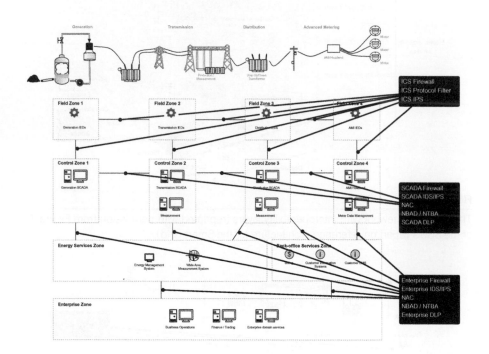

FIGURE A.8

Applying network security controls to the Smart Grid reference model.

Applying data integrity and protection controls

Recommended applications of data integrity and protection (defined in Chapter 6, "Protecting the Smart Grid"), using the Smart Grid reference model (defined in Chapter 5, "Security Models for SCADA, ICS, and Smart Grid") (see Figure A.9).

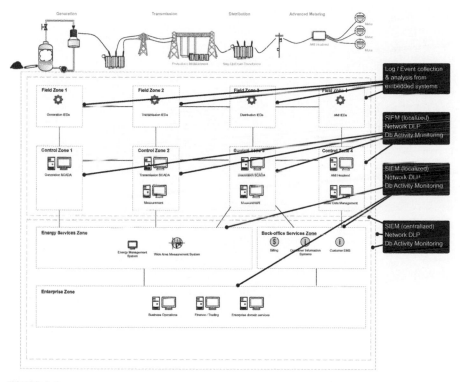

FIGURE A.9

Applying data integrity and protection controls to the Smart Grid reference model.

References

1. The Smart Grid Interoperability Panel – Cyber Security Working Group. *NISTIR 7628 guidelines for smart grid cyber security: Vol. 1, Smart Grid cyber security strategy, architecture, and high-level requirements*. US Department of Commerce, National Institute of Standards and Technologies; August 2010.
2. CEN, CENELEC and ETSI. *SGCG report on reference architecture for the Smart Grid external version V2.0*. SGSC Reference Architecture Working Group (RAWG); August 2012.

Continued Reading

There is a wealth of information available about the Smart Grid, although only a few references are available specific to the cyber security of the Smart Grid. The following are resources that the authors and editors of this book find particularly useful.

Smart Grid Security: An end-to-end view of security in the new electrical grid, by Gilbert N. Sorebo and Michael C. Echols

"The Smart Grid has the potential to revolutionize electricity delivery systems, and the security of its infrastructure is a vital concern not only for cyber-security practitioners, engineers, policy makers, and utility executives, but also for the media and consumers. Smart Grid Security: An End-to-End View of Security in the New Electrical Grid explores the important techniques, challenges, and forces that will shape how we achieve a secure 21st century electric grid."[1]

Industrial Network Security: Securing critical infrastructure networks for Smart Grid, SCADA, and other industrial control systems, by Eric D. Knapp

"Industrial Network Security examines the unique protocols and applications that are the foundation of industrial control systems and provides you with comprehensive guidelines for their protection. While covering compliance guidelines, attacks and vectors, and even evolving security tools, this book gives you a clear understanding of SCADA and control system protocols and how they operate.

Covers implementation guidelines for security measures of critical infrastructure; Applies the security measures for system-specific compliance; Discusses common pitfalls and mistakes and how to avoid them."[2]

Securing the Smart Grid: Next generation power grid security, by Tony Flick and Justin Morehouse

"Securing the Smart Grid takes a look at grid security today, how it is developing and being deployed into now over 10 million households in the US alone. Direct attacks to smart meters as well as attacks via the networks will be detailed along with suggestions for defense against them. A framework for how security should be implemented throughout this growing system will be included directing security consultants, and system and network architects on how to keep the grid strong against attackers big and small" [source: http://www.amazon.com/Securing-Smart-Grid-Generation-Security/dp/1597495700].

Smart Grid: Integrating renewable, distributed, and efficient energy, by Fereidoon P. Sioshansi

"This book covers Smart Grids from A to Z, providing a complete treatment of the topic, covering both policy and technology, explaining the most recent innovations supporting its development, and clarifying how the Smart Grid can support the integration of renewable energy resources.

Among the most important topics included are smart metering, renewable energy storage, plug-in hybrids, flexible demand response, strategies for offsetting intermittency issues, micro-grids for off-grid communities, and specific in-depth coverage of wind and solar power integration. The content draws lessons from an international panel of contributors, whose diverse experiences implementing Smart Grids will help to provide templates for success."[3]

Cybersecurity for Industrial Control Systems: SCADA, DCS, PLC, HMI, and SIS, by Tyson Macaulay and Bryan Singer

"Cybersecurity for Industrial Control Systems provides you with the tools to ensure network security without sacrificing the efficiency and functionality of ICS. Highlighting the key issues that need to be addressed, the book begins with a thorough introduction to ICS. It discusses business, cost, competitive, and regulatory drivers and the conflicting priorities of convergence. Next, it explains why security requirements differ from IT to ICS. It differentiates when standard IT security solutions can be used and where SCADA-specific practices are required.

The book examines the plethora of potential threats to ICS, including hi-jacking malware, botnets, spam engines, and porn dialers. It outlines the range of vulnerabilities inherent in the ICS quest for efficiency and functionality that necessitates risk behavior such as remote access and control of critical equipment. Reviewing risk assessment techniques and the evolving risk assessment process, the text concludes by examining what is on the horizon for ICS security, including IPv6, ICSv6 test lab designs, and IPv6 and ICS sensors."[4]

NISTIR 7628 guidelines for Smart Grid Cyber Security

Extensive guidelines for the cyber security of Smart Grids, available from NIST at http://csrc.nist.gov/publications/PubsNISTIRs.html.

SGCG report on reference architecture for the Smart Grid

An extremely comprehensive assessment and description of the Smart Grid and specific interoperability and cyber security issues, based upon the EU mandate M/490 on Smart Grid standardization. Available from CENELEC at http://www.cenelec.eu/aboutcenelec/whatwedo/technologysectors/smartgrids.html.

IEEE guide for Smart Grid interoperability of energy technology and information technology operation with the Electric Power System (EPS), end-use applications, and loads

The IEEE's perspective on Smart Grid interoperability, focusing on technology interoperability of the many interconnecting Smart Grid systems. Available from http://ieeexplore.ieee.org.

References

1. Sorebo Gilbert N, Echols Michael C. *Smart Grid Security: an end-to-end view of security in the new electrical grid.* 1st ed. CRC Press; December 5, 2011. 328 pages. <http://www.amazon.com/Smart-Grid-Security-End-End/dp/1439855870/ref=tmm_hrd_title_0>
2. Knapp Eric D. *Industrial Network Security: Securing critical infrastructure networks for smart grid, SCADA, and other industrial control systems.* 1st ed. Syngress; August 29, 2011. 360 pages. <http://www.amazon.com/Industrial-Network-Security-Securing-Infrastructure/dp/1597496456/>
3. Sioshansi Fereidoon P, editor. *Smart Grid: integrating renewable, distributed and efficient energy.* 1st ed. Academic Press; November 10, 2011. 568 pages. <http://www.amazon.com/Smart-Grid-Integrating-Renewable-Distributed/dp/0123864526/>
4. Macaulay Tyson, Singer Bryan L. *Cybersecurity for Industrial Control Systems: SCADA, DCS, PLC, HMI, and SIS.* 1st ed. Auerbach Publications; December 13, 2011. 203 pages. <http://www.amazon.com/Cybersecurity-Industrial-Control-Systems-SCADA/dp/1439801967/>

Glossary

3 x 3 Security Model A model developed to normalize the security challenges within critical infrastructure, using a 3-row, 3-column mapping of critical infrastructure environments addressing asset complexity and capability along with vendor dependency.

Advanced Metering Infrastructure A modern, digital measurement, and communications infrastructure designed to enable more frequent measurements and to provide those measurements to various parties in real or near-real time. The advanced metering infrastructure typically consists of an AMI headend that provides meter data management and communication aggregation to smart meters (see "Smart Meters").

Advanced Persistent Threat The advanced persistent threat (APT) refers to a class of sophisticated cyber threat designed to infiltrate a network and remains persistent through evasion and propagation techniques. APTs are typically used to establish and maintain an external command and control channel through which the attacker can continuously exfiltrate data.

AMI See Advanced Metering Infrastructure.

AMI Headend A concentration server responsible for managing AMI communications to a defined number of smart meters. The AMI headend typically aggregates messages from a group of deployed smart meters in a neighborhood or service area, to facilitate the communications of the metering infrastructure to inter-related back office systems such as demand-response, remote meter management, billing, etc.

Anti-virus Anti-virus (AV) systems inspect network and/or file content for indications of infection by malware. AV works by comparing file contents against a library of defined code signatures; if there is a match, the file is typically quarantined to prevent infection, at which point the option to clean the file maybe available.

Application Monitor/Application Data Monitor An application content monitoring system which functions much like an intrusion detection system, only performing deep inspection of a session rather than of a packet, so that application contents can be examined at all layers of the OSI model, from low-level protocols (layers 3–4) through application documents, attachments, etc. (layers 5–7). Application monitoring is useful for examining industrial network protocols for malicious content (malware).

Application Whitelisting Application whitelisting (AW) is a form of whitelisting intended to control which executable files (applications) are allowed to operate. AW systems typically work by first establishing the "whitelist" of allowed applications, after which point any attempt to execute code will compared against that list. If the application is not allowed, it will be prevented from executing. AW often operates at low levels within the kernel of the host operating system.

APT See Advanced Persistent Threat.

Asset An asset is any physical or logical object used within an industrial environment possessing either an actual or perceived value.

Attack Surface The attack surface of a system or asset refers to the collectively exposed portions of that system or asset. A large attack surface means that there are many exposed areas that an attack could target, while a small attack surface means that the target is relatively unexposed.

Attack Vector An attack vector is the direction(s) through which an attack occurs, often referring to specific vulnerabilities that are used by an attacker at any given stage of an attack.

Auditd Auditd is the auditing component of the Linux auditing system, responsible for writing audit events to disk.

AV See Anti-virus.

AWL See Application Whitelisting.

Blacklisting (see "Whitelisting") Blacklisting refers to the technique of defining known malicious behavior, content, code, etc. Blacklists are typically used for threat detection, comparing network traffic, files, users, or some other quantifiable metric against a relevant blacklist. For example, an intrusion prevention system (IPS) will compare the contents of network packets against blacklists of known malware, indicators of exploits, and other threats so that offending traffic (i.e. packets that match a signature within the blacklist) can be blocked.

CIP See Common Industrial Protocol and Critical Infrastructure Protection.

Common Industrial Protocol (CIP) An industrial protocol maintained by ODVA, Inc. CIP defines industrial messaging, command and control capabilities to supported devices. CIP can be transferred over TCP/IP using the EtherNet/IP. CIP is also used in DeviceNet, CompoNet, and ControlNet.

Communication Channel The logical or physical point-to-point or point-to-multi-point data flow between components in one zone to one or more components in another zone.

Compensating Controls The term "compensating controls" is typically used within regulatory standards or guidelines to indicate when an alternative method than those specifically addressed by the standard or guideline is used.

Conduit A logical grouping of communication assets that protect the security of the communication channels it contains is defined by the ISA-62443 standard. This can apply to not only network channels, but also, for example the connection of USB devices (an asset) connected to a USB port (a conduit) on a computer.

Control Center A control center typically refers to an operations center where a control system is managed. Control centers typically consist of SCADA and HMI systems that provide human interaction with industrial/automated processes.

Correlated Event A correlated event is a larger pattern match consisting of two or more regular logs or events, as detected by an event correlation system. For example, a combination of a network scan event (as reported by a firewall) followed by an injection attempt against an open port (as reported by an IPS) can be correlated together into a larger incident: in this example, an attempted reconnaissance and exploit. Correlated events may be very simple or very complex, and can be used to detect a wide variety of more sophisticated attack indicators.

Critical Infrastructure Protection (CIP) Referring to the protection of those networks and systems that maintain or operate critical functions within a society. The term CIP is most well known as one of the NERC reliability standards, NERC CIP, which mandates the cyber security of critical networks and systems as they relate to the reliability of the bulk electric systems (BES) within the power industry.

DAM See Database Activity Monitor.

Data Diode A data diode is a "one-way" data communication device, often consisting of a physical layer unidirectional limitation. Using only one half of a fiber optic "transmit/receive" pair would enforce unidirectional communication at the "physical" layer, while proper configuration of a network firewall could logically enforce unidirectional communication at the "network" layer.

Database Activity Monitor A database activity monitor (DAM) monitors database transactions, including SQL, DML, and other database commands and queries. A DAM may be network or host based. Network-based DAMs monitor database transactions by decoding and interpreting network traffic, while host-based DAMs provide system-level auditing directly from the database server. DAMs can be used for indications of malicious intent (e.g. SQL injection attacks), fraud (e.g. the manipulation of stored data), and/or as a means of logging data access for systems that do not or cannot produce auditable logs.

Database Monitor See Database Activity Monitor.

DB004D Database Monitor. See Database Activity Monitor.

DCS See Distributed Control System.

Deep Packet Inspection This is a process of inspecting a network packet all the way to layer 7 (application layer) of the OSI model. That is, past datalink, network or session headers to inspect into the payload of the packet. Deep packet inspection is used by most intrusion detection and prevention systems (IDS/IPS), newer firewalls, and other security devices within common IT networks, but due to the protocols involved, it is an emerging technology within the ICS networks.

Demand-Response System A system wherein the consumer of electricity is able to interact with the grid to control how and when electricity is distributed.

Distributed Control System An industrial control system deployed and controlled in a distributed manner, such that various distributed control systems or processes are controlled individually. Components within a DCS are typically connected via local area networks (LAN). See also: Process Control System, Supervisory Control and Data Acquisition and Industrial Control System.

Distributed Generation Distributed energy generation facilities that are used to feed power into the grid, to facilitate localized supply in remote areas or areas of high demand.

Distribution SCADA SCADA systems designed to control and supervise automation systems used in distribution networks. See Supervisory Control and Data Acquisition.

Distribution System The grid infrastructure responsible for delivering electricity to the end consumer, typically over lower voltages and shorter distances than the transmission system.

DPI See Deep Packet Inspection.

Electronic Security Perimeter An electronic security perimeter (ESP) refers to the demarcation point between a secured enclave, such as a control system, and a less trusted network, such as a business network. The ESP typically includes those devices that secure that demarcation point, including firewalls, IDS, IPS, industrial protocol filters, application monitors, and similar devices.

Enclave A logical grouping of assets, systems and/or services that defines and contains one (or more) functional groups. Enclaves represent network "zones" that can be used to isolate certain functions in order to more effectively secure them.

Energy Management System Systems responsible for analyzing energy quality and quantity on transmission or distribution lines in order to provide load management, prevent over- or undercurrent, swing, or other common line conditions.

EMS See Energy Management System.

Enumeration Enumeration is the process of identifying valid identities of devices and users in a network, typically as an initial step in a network attack process. Enumeration allows an attacker to identify valid systems and/or accounts that can then be targeted for exploitation or compromise.

ESP See Electronic Security Perimeter.

Ethernet/IP Ethernet/IP is a real-time Ethernet protocol supporting the common industrial protocol (CIP), for use in industrial control systems.

Ettercap Ettercap is a network sniffer designed for Man-in-the-Middle attacks.

Event An event is a generic term referring to any datapoint of interest, typically alerts that are generated by security devices, logs produced by systems and applications, alerts produced by network monitors, etc.

Fault A fault in electrical transmission and distribution typically refers to any abnormal flow of electrical current. Faults can occur due to any number of causes, including grounds, phase imbalance, overcurrent, undercurrent, swing, etc.

Fault Management System A computing system design to monitor and manage electrical faults, to facilitate the prediction of faults before they occur, and the location and remediation of faults that have occurred. Fault management systems may be standalone systems or part of a broader energy management system. Fault management systems typically interface with SCADA and field devices, as well as crew management and response systems.

Field Devices Field devices are those devices deployed "in the field" within the transmission, distribution, and metering infrastructures. Field devices consist of remote terminal units, programmable logic controllers and intelligent electronic devices, for example: reclosers, PMUs, Volt/VAR units, smart meters, etc.

Flame Flame, or flamer, is a common name for (and one of the modular components within) the Skywiper malware. See Skywiper.

Function Code Function codes refer to various numeric identifiers used within industrial network protocols for command and control purposes. For example, a function code may represent a request from a master device to a slave device(s), such as a request to read a register value, to write a register value, to restart the device.

Gauss Gauss is one of several recent examples of sophisticated, modular malware. While Gauss presents several similarities to Stuxnet, Gauss has primarily targeted financial and banking data.

GOOSE Generic object oriented substation events are messages defined within IEC 61850, typically transported as an Ethernet multi-cast between entities within a substation so that multiple devices can subscribe to published data, typically concerning device or relay status, measurements, etc.

HAN See Home Area Network.

HEMS See Home Energy Management System.

HIDS Host IDS. A host intrusion detection system detects intrusion attempts via a software agent running on a specific host. A HIDS detects intrusions by inspecting packets and matching the contents against defined patterns or "signatures" that indicate malicious content, and produce an alert.

HIPS Host IPS. A host intrusion prevention system detects and prevents intrusion attempts via a software agent running on a specific host. Like a HIDS, a HIPS detects intrusions by inspecting packets and matching the contents against defined patterns or "signatures" that indicate malicious content. Unlike a HIDS, a HIPS is able to perform active prevention by dropping the offending packet(s), resetting TCP/IP connections, or other actions in addition to passive alerting and logging actions.

HMI A human machine interface (HMI) is the user interface to the processes of an industrial control system. An HMI effectively translates the communications to and from PLCs, RTUs, and other industrial assets to a human-readable interface, which is used by control systems' operators to manage and monitor processes.

Home Area Network A network of energy management devices, digital consumer electronics, signal-controlled or enabled appliances, and applications within a home environment that is on the home side of the electric meter. It can also be considered as a home-based LAN, but it connects more than just computers. HAN specifications include Zigbee, HomePlug, Z-Wave, and Wireless *M*-Bus (a wireless variant of *M*-Bus).

Home Energy Management System A home energy management system (HEMS) provides a console or portal, typically web based, with which a home owner can monitor and manage their home energy consumption.

Host A host is a computer connected to a network, that is a cyber asset. The term differs from an asset in that hosts typically refer to computers connected to a routable network using the TCP/IP stack—i.e. most computers running a modern operating system and/or specialized network servers and equipment—where an asset refers to a broader range of not only the digitally connected physical devices, but also the logical data they possess.

IACS Industrial Automation Control System. See Industrial Control System.

IAM See Identity Access Management.

ICCP See Inter-control Center Communication Protocol.

ICS See Industrial Control System.

Identity Access Management Identity access management refers to the process of managing user identities and user accounts; related user access and authentication activities within a network; and a category of products designed to centralize and automate those functions.

IDS Intrusion detection system. Intrusion detection systems perform deep packet inspection and pattern matching to compare network packets against known "signatures" of malware or other malicious activity, in order to detect a possible network intrusion. IDS operates passively by monitoring networks either in-line or on a tap or span port, and providing security alerts or events to a network operator.

IEC See International Electrotechnical Commission.

IEC 61850 IEC 61850 is a standard for substation automation providing requirements for general functionality as well as system and project management, communication requirements for functions and device models, configuration language for communication in electrical substations related to IEDs, basic communication structure, specific communication service mappings, conformance testing.

IEC 62351 An International Electrotechnical Commission cyber security standard developed to ensure the secure communication and messaging of substation devices using 60870, 61850, etc.

IED See Intelligent Electronic Device.

IEEE C37.118 The IEEE standard for synchrophasors for power systems, which defines standard methods of time synchronization and messaging between multiple phasor measurement units.

IHD See In-home Device.

Industrial Automation and Control System See Industrial Control System.

In-home Device Any smart device in a home, typically communicating via a home area network (HAN) to a home energy management system (HEMS).

Industrial Control System An industrial control system (ICS) refers to the systems, devices, networks and controls used to operate and/or automate an industrial process. Two common forms of ICS include DCS and SCADA. See also: distributed control system and supervisory control and data acquisition.

Intelligent Electronic Device An intelligent electronic device (IED) is an electronic component—such as a regulator, circuit control—that has a microprocessor and is able to communicate, typically digitally using a fieldbus, real-time Ethernet, or other industrial protocols.

Inter-control Center Communication Protocol The Inter-control center communication protocol (ICCP) is a real-time industrial network protocol designed for wide area intercommunication between two or more control centers. ICCP is an internationally recognized standard published by the International Electrotechnical Commission (IEC) as IEC 60870-6. ICCP is also referred to as the Telecontrol Application Service Element 2 or TASE.2.

International Electrotechnical Commission The International Electrotechnical Commission (IEC) is an international standards organization that develops standards for the purposes of consensus and conformity.

International Organization for Standardization The International Organization for Standardization (ISO) is a network of standards organizations from over 160 countries, which develops and publishes standards covering a wide range of topics.

IPS Intrusion Prevention System. Intrusion protection systems perform the same detection functions of an IDS, with the added capability to block traffic. Traffic can typically be blocked by dropping the offending packet(s) or by forcing a reset of the offending TCP/IP session. IPS works in-line and therefore may introduce latency.

ISO See International Organization for Standardization.

Load A quantification, over time, of the amount of electric power delivered (supply) or required (demand).

Log A log is a file used to record activities or events, generated by a variety of devices including computer operating systems, applications, network switches and routers, and virtually any computing device. There is no standard for the common format or structure of a log.

Log Management Log management is the process of collecting and storing logs for purposes of log analysis and data forensics, and/or for purposes of regulatory compliance and accountability. Log management typically involves collection of logs, some degree of normalization or categorization, and both short-term storage (for analysis) and long-term storage (for compliance).

Log Management System A system or appliance designed to simplify and/or automate the process of log management. See also Log Management.

Master Station A master station is the controlling asset or host involved in an industrial protocol communication session. The master station, sometimes called a master terminal unit (MTU), is typically responsible for timing, synchronization, and command and control aspects of an industrial network protocol.

Metasploit Metasploit is a commercial package, used for penetration testing in exploiting specific system vulnerabilities.

Microgrids Self-sustained generation and distribution infrastructures often used by large campuses, industrial facilities, or government or military facilities where isolation and reliability are important, and where high voltage transmission from the bulk power system may be logistically impractical.

Modbus Originally developed in 1979 as a serial protocol by Modicon (now Schneider Electric), the Modbus protocol is used for intercommunication between industrial control assets. Modbus is a flexible master/slave command and control protocol available in several variants including Modbus ASCII, Modbus RTU, Modbus TCP/IP, Modbus over TCP/IP, and Modbus Plus.

Modbus ASCII A serial-based Modbus variant that uses ASCII characters rather than binary data representation.

Modbus Plus A Modbus extension that operates at higher speeds, which remains proprietary to Schneider Electric.

Modbus RTU A serial-based Modbus variant that uses binary data representation.

Modbus TCP/IP A Modbus variant that operates over TCP/IP by taking only the protocol data unit (PDU) and encapsulating this in an IP packet. The checksum is generated as part of the encapsulation process.

Modbus over TCP/IP A Modbus variant that operates over TCP/IP by taking the entire Modbus RTU application data unit (ADU) including checksum and encapsulating this as a payload in a IP packet.

NAC See Network Access Control.

NERC See North American Electric Reliability Corporation.

NERC CIP The North American Electric Reliability Corporation reliability standard for Critical Infrastructure Protection.

Network Access Control Network access control (NAC) provides measures of controlling access to the network, using technologies such as 802.1X (port network access control) to require authentication for a network port to be enabled, or other access control methods. NAC may also include additional security measures that include pre-connect health assessment and mitigation, and post-connect access flow control.

Network Layer Protocol Protocols for routing of messages through a complex network. Most modern industrial fieldbus protocols and SCADA protocols usually contain a network layer (e.g. IP address).

Network Whitelisting (see Whitelisting).

NIDS Network IDS. A network intrusion detection system detects intrusion attempts via a network interface card, which connects to the network either in-line or via a span or tap port.

NIPS Network IPS. A network prevention detection system detects and prevents intrusion attempts via a network-attached device using two or more network interface cards to support inbound and outbound network traffic, with optional bypass interfaces to preserve network reliability in the event of a NIPS failure.

NIST The National Institute of Standards and Technology. NIST is a non-regulatory federal agency within the United States Department of Commerce, whose mission is to promote innovation through the advancement of science, technology, and standards. NIST provides numerous research documents and recommendations (the "Special Publication 800 series") around information technology security.

Nmap Nmap or "Network Mapper" is a popular network scanner, enumeration and fingerprinting tool distributed under GNU General Public License GPL-2 by nmap.org.

North American Electric Reliability Corporation The North American Electric Reliability Corporation is an organization that develops and enforces reliability standards for and monitors the activities of the bulk electric system (BES) power grid in North America including the United States (excluding Alaska and Hawaii), Canada, and parts of Mexico.

NRC See Nuclear Regulatory Commission.

Nuclear Regulatory Commission The United States Nuclear Regulatory Commission (NRC) is a five-member presidentially appointed commission responsible for the safe use of radioactive materials including but not limited to nuclear energy, nuclear fuels, radioactive waste management, and the medical use of radioactive materials.

OSSIM OSSIM is an Open Source Security Information Management project, whose source code is distributed under GNU General Public License GPL-2 by AlienVault. See Security Information Management.

Outage Management System An outage management system is a computing system that utilizes transmission and distribution measurements to isolate the cause(s) and location(s) of outages, to help coordinate field crews and incident response teams.

PCS Process Control System. See Distributed Control System and Industrial Control System.

Pentest A Penetration Test. This is a method for determining the risk to a network by attempting to penetrate its defenses. Pentesting combines vulnerability assessment techniques with evasion techniques and other attack methods to simulate a "real attack" but attempted to exploit discovered vulnerabilities.

PDC See Phase Data Concentrator.

Phasor Data Concentrator A phasor data concentrator aggregates synchronized phasor measurements from multiple distributed phasor measurement units to enable analysis of over line quality and condition within transmission and distribution systems.

Phasor Measurement Unit A phasor measurement unit measures voltage and current of electricity throughout transmission and distribution systems. Synchronization of PMU measurements (i.e. "Synchrophasor Measurement") is used to obtain an accurate image of line condition throughout the grid at any given time.

Physical Layer Protocol Protocols for transmitting raw electrical signals over the communications channel. Deals with transmission physics such as cabling, modulation, and transmission rates (e.g. copper, fiber optic, VHF, GSM, satellite, WiMax).

PMU See Phasor Measurement Unit.

PLC See Programmable Logic Controller and Power Line Communications.

Process Control System See Distributed Control System and Industrial Control System.

Profibus Profibus is an industrial fieldbus protocol based on a serial-bus physical layer defined by IEC standard IEC-61158/IEC-61784-1. profibus supports two application layer protocols: distributed peripheral (DP) and process automation (PA).

Profinet Profinet is an implementation of Profibus designed to operate in real time over industrial Ethernet.

Programmable Logic Controller (PLC) A programmable logic controller (PLC) is an industrial device that uses a logical representation of input coils and output relays in combination with programmable logic in order to build a automated control logic. PLCs commonly use relay ladder logic (RLL) to read inputs, compare values against defined set points, perform logical operations (e.g. "and," "or," etc.) and (potentially) write to outputs.

Power Line Communications (PLC, alternate meaning) A communication mechanism using the power lines themselves to transmit digital communications relevant to Smart Grid systems.

Protection Protection refers to circuit breakers, fuses, reclosers, and other devices designed to trip a system to prevent a safety or reliability risk in the event of a fault.

Recloser A recloser is a device within the distribution system designed to automatically reopen a circuit that may have tripped due to a fault, to enable a degree of resiliency within the distribution system and minimize the need for the deployment of field crews to address momentary faults such as surges.

Remote Terminal Unit A remote terminal unit (RTU) is a device combining remote communication capabilities with programmable logic for the control of processes in remote locations. These devices are typically designed to support low communication bandwidth, high latency, and often lower power consumption requirements.

Resilience The ability of a system to accommodate significant changes in its environment by taking extraordinary actions to maintain acceptable system performance.

Risk Assessment The process of identifying and evaluating risks to the organization's operations (including mission, functions, image, or reputation), the organization's assets or individuals by determining the likelihood of occurrence, the resulting impact, and additional countermeasures that would mitigate this impact.

Risk Mitigation The actions used to reduce the likelihood and/or severity of an event.

Risk Tolerance The risk an organization is willing to accept.

RTU See Remote Terminal Unit.

SCADA See Supervisory Control and Data Acquisition.

SCADA-IDS SCADA aware intrusion detection System. An IDS system designed for use in SCADA and ICS networks. SCADA-IDS devices support pattern matching against the specific protocols and services used in control systems, such as Modbus, ICCP, DNP3, and others. SCADS-IDS are passive and are therefore suitable for deployment within a control system, as they do not introduce any risk to control system reliability.

SCADA-IPS SCADA aware intrusion prevention system. An IPS system designed for use in SCADA and ICS networks. SCADA-IPS devices support pattern matching against the specific protocols and services used in control systems, such as Modbus, ICCP, DNP3, and others. SCADA-IPS are active and can block or backlist traffic, making them most suitable for use at control system perimeters. SCADA-IPS are not typically deployed within a control system for fear of a false-positive disrupting normal control system operations.

Security Assessment A comprehensive process that not only looks for host and asset vulnerabilities, but also analyzes internal processes and procedures, system configuration, testing, usage, etc. that could potentially result in a "system" being compromised or attacked.

Security Audit A process that occurs on a recurring basis that evaluates the currently level of security provided by a system against a predetermined set of criteria, such as a compliance standard like NERC CIP.

Security Assurance Level The measure of confidence that computer systems and data are free from vulnerabilities, either intentionally designed computer components or accidently inserted at any time during its lifecycle and that the computer systems function in the intended manner.

Security Event Management See Security Information and Event Management.

Security Information Management See Security Information and Event Management.

Security Information and Event Management Security information and event management (SIEM) combines security information management (SIM or log management) with security event management (SEM) to provide a common centralized system for managing network threats and all associated information and context.

Security Testing See Security Assessment.

SEM See Security Information and Event Management.

Set Points Set points (SP) are defined values signifying a target metric against which automated control can operate. For example, a set point may define a high temperature range, or the optimum pressure of a container, etc. By comparing set points against sensory input also known as a process value (PV), automated controls can be established. For example, if the temperate in a furnace reaches the set point for the maximum temperature ceiling, reduce the flow of fuel to the burner.

SIEM See Security Information and Event Management.

SIM See Security Information and Event Management.

Situational Awareness Situational awareness is a term used by the National Institute of Standards and Technology (NIST) and others to indicate a desired state of awareness within a network in order to identify and respond to network based attacks. The term is derivative of the military command and control process of perceiving a threat, comprehending it, making a decision, and taking an action in order to maintain the security of the environment. Situational awareness in network security can be obtained through network and security monitoring (perception), alert notifications (comprehension), security threat analysis (decision making), and remediation (taking action).

Skywiper A complex cyber threat also known as flame or flamer.

Smart Grid An intelligent and automated evolution of energy generation, delivery and consumption designed to make energy more cost effective and efficient.

Smartlisting A term referring to the use of both blacklisting and whitelisting technologies in conjunction with a centralized intelligence system such as a SIEM in order to dynamically adapt common blacklists in response to observed security event activities. See also: whitelisting and blacklisting.

Smart Meter An intelligent meter that measures utility (electricity, water, or gas) consumption by the end user can communicate measurements and status back to supporting systems within the Smart Grid, such as demand response systems, distribution management, and home energy management systems (HEMS).

Step-down Transformer A step-down transformer converts high-voltage energy to low voltage energy, so that it is more suitable for distribution over shorter distances and to homes or businesses. See Transformer.

Step-up Transformer A step-up transformer converts low voltage energy to high voltage energy, so that it is more suitable for transmitting large amounts of energy over longer distances. See Transformer.

Stuxnet An advanced cyber attack against an industrial control system, consisting of multiple zero-day exploits used for the delivery of malware that then targeted and infected specific industrial controls for the purposes of sabotaging an automated manufacturing process.

St**t** A censored representation of "Stuxnet," is widely regarded as the first cyber attack to specifically target an industrial control system.

Substation A substation, or "yard," refers to a nexus point within or between generation, transmission, and distribution systems. A substation typically converges or diverges multiple lines while providing power conditioning and protection. Transmission substations refer to substations where high-voltage transmission lines aggregate, while distribution substations refer to substations where lower voltage distribution lines aggregate.

Substation Automation Substation automation refers to the communication within and between substation devices design to automatically perform load and line management in response to real-time grid measurements and conditions.

Supervisory Control and Data Acquisition Supervisory control and data acquisition (SCADA) refers to the systems and networks that communicate with industrial control systems to provide data to operators for supervisory purposes, as well as control capabilities for process management.

Swing Swing refers to oscillations in electrical conditions (active power, reactive power, voltage, phase, etc.), resulting in instabilities that typically predicate an impending fault and could cause a generation plant or transmission line to trip.

Synchrophasor A synchrophasor is a device designed to synchronize real-time electrical measurement throughout a distributed grid. Synchronization is typically performed using global positioning systems (GPS) according to the IEEE C37.118 synchrophasor protocol. See Phasor Measurement Unit and Phasor Data Concentrator.

Transformer A transformer is a device that transfers electrical energy from one circuit to another and converts it from one voltage to another, typically via the use of coils (inductive coupling conductors).

Transmission SCADA A supervisor control and data acquisition (SCADA) system tailored for use within energy transmission substations and lines.

Transmission System The system of high-voltage energy delivery is designed to move large amounts of data over long distances, such as between towns and regions. Transmission systems consist of transmission lines and transmission substations.

Unidirectional Gateway A network gateway device that only allows communication in one direction through specific use of physical layer technology, such as a data diode. See also Data Diode.

User Whitelisting The process of establishing a "whitelist" of known valid user identities and/or accounts, for the purpose of detecting and/or preventing rogue user activities. See also: Application Whitelisting.

VA See Vulnerability Assessment.

Volt/VAR A device designed to measure active (voltage) and reactive (voltage-ampere, or "VAR") within the grid.

Vulnerability A vulnerability refers to a weakness in a system that can be utilized by an attacker to damage the system, obtain unauthorized access, execute arbitrary code, or otherwise exploit the system.

Vulnerability Assessment The process of scanning networks to find hosts or assets, and probing those hosts to determine vulnerabilities. Vulnerability assessment can be automated using a vulnerability assessment scanner, which will typically examine a host to determine the version of the operating system and all running applications, which can then be compared against a repository of known software vulnerabilities to determine where patches should be applied.

Whitelists Whitelists refer defined lists of "known good" items: users, network addresses, applications, etc. typically for the purpose of exception-based security where any item not explicitly defined as "known good" results in a remediation action (e.g. alert, block). Whitelists contrast blacklists, which define "known bad" items.

Yard See Substation.

Zone A zone refers to a logical boundary or enclave containing assets of like function and/or criticality, or share a logical and/or physical relationship with one another (i.e. location), for the purposes of facilitating the security of common systems and services. Zone separation is one of the principal methodologies of the ISA-62443 security standard. See also: Enclave.

ZigBee A suite of specifications by the ZigBee Alliance, defining network and communication standards for building automation, smart energy, home automation, and other systems, many of which are relevant to the Smart Grid, smart metering, home area Networks, and home energy management systems (HEMS).

Index

Printed and bound by CPI Group (UK) Ltd, Croydon, CR0 4YY

03/10/2024

01040340-0010